With ex

course to ... good health, or career opportunities while gaining valuable insight into yourself and others. Offering a daily outlook for 18 full months, this fascinating guide shows you:

- The important dates in your life
- What to expect from an astrological reading
- How the stars can help you stay healthy and fit.
  And more!

Let this sound advice guide you through a year of heavenly possibilities—for today and for every day of 2012!

**SYDNEY OMARR'S® DAY-BY-DAY ASTROLOGICAL GUIDE FOR**

**ARIES**—March 21–April 19
**TAURUS**—April 20–May 20
**GEMINI**—May 21–June 20
**CANCER**—June 21–July 22
**LEO**—July 23–August 22
**VIRGO**—August 23–September 22
**LIBRA**—September 23–October 22
**SCORPIO**—October 23–November 21
**SAGITTARIUS**—November 22–December 21
**CAPRICORN**—December 22–January 19
**AQUARIUS**—January 20–February 18
**PISCES**—February 19–March 20

**IN 2012**

# Sydney Omarr's®

## Day-by-Day Astrological Guide for

# LIBRA

## September 23–October 22

# 2012

by Trish MacGregor
with Rob MacGregor

A SIGNET BOOK

SIGNET
Published by New American Library, a division of
Penguin Group (USA) Inc., 375 Hudson Street,
New York, New York 10014, USA
Penguin Group (Canada), 90 Eglinton Avenue East, Suite 700, Toronto,
Ontario M4P 2Y3, Canada (a division of Pearson Penguin Canada Inc.)
Penguin Books Ltd., 80 Strand, London WC2R 0RL, England
Penguin Ireland, 25 St. Stephen's Green, Dublin 2,
Ireland (a division of Penguin Books Ltd.)
Penguin Group (Australia), 250 Camberwell Road, Camberwell, Victoria 3124,
Australia (a division of Pearson Australia Group Pty. Ltd.)
Penguin Books India Pvt. Ltd., 11 Community Centre, Panchsheel Park,
New Delhi - 110 017, India
Penguin Group (NZ), 67 Apollo Drive, Rosedale, Auckland 0632,
New Zealand (a division of Pearson New Zealand Ltd.)
Penguin Books (South Africa) (Pty.) Ltd., 24 Sturdee Avenue,
Rosebank, Johannesburg 2196, South Africa

Penguin Books Ltd., Registered Offices:
80 Strand, London WC2R 0RL, England

First Printing, June 2011
10 9 8 7 6 5 4 3 2 1

First published by Signet, an imprint of New American Library,
a division of Penguin Group (USA) Inc.



Printed in the United States of America

# CONTENTS

## CHAPTER 1

# Paradigm Shift

There's more hype about December 21, 2012, than there was about the Y2K scare at the turn of the century. Depending on which Web site or book you read, the world will end on that day, the poles will shift, the aliens will land. In fact, there's been so much hype that in March 2007 *USA Today* ran an article titled "Does Maya Calendar Predict 2012 Apocalypse?"

"Maya civilization, known for advanced writing, mathematics and astronomy, flourished for centuries in Mesoamerica, especially between A.D. 300 and 900. Its Long Count calendar, which was discontinued under Spanish colonization, tracks more than 5,000 years, then resets at year zero," wrote G. Jeffrey MacDonald in the *USA Today* article.

It resets on December 21, 2012. It's the day that marks the winter solstice in the northern hemisphere. It's also the day that the sun will be aligned with the center of the Milky Way galaxy for the first time in nearly 26,000 years or, to be exact, in 25,625 years, what the Mayans considered to be a single galactic day. They divided that galactic day into five cycles of 5,125 years, and on December 21, that fifth cycle ends. So, what's that mean for us?

According to Mayan Indian elder Apolinario Chile Pixtum, it definitely doesn't mean the end of the world. He, in fact, says the doomsday theories spring from

Western, not Mayan ideas. "I came back from England last year and man, they had me fed up with this stuff."

Jose Huchin, a Yucatan Mayan archaeologist, says that if he went into Maya-speaking communities and asked people what was going to occur in 2012, they wouldn't have any idea. "That the world is going to end? They wouldn't believe you," he says.

A likely possibility for 2012 is a shift in paradigms. If 2011 was the year of transitions, then 2012 can be viewed as the year when people begin to embrace new ways of thinking about themselves, the society in which they live, and the world. With the meltdown in the financial and housing markets in 2008–2009, the election of the first African-American president, the bailouts of banks, rising foreclosures and unemployment, and the broken health-care system, a shift in belief systems seems inevitable.

As Daniel Pinchbeck wrote in *2012: The Return of Quetzalcoatl*: "If we were to conclude, after careful consideration, that our modern world is based upon fundamentally flawed conceptions of time and mind, that on these fatal defects we had erected a flawed civilization . . . then logic might indicate the necessity, as well as the inevitability, of change. Such a shift would not be 'the end of the world,' but the end of a world, and the opening of the next."

## How You Can Adapt to the Paradigm Shift

Our lives are marked by transitions. We make the *transition* from adolescence to adulthood, from dependent to independent, from being single to being married, from youth to middle age to old age, from life to death. These transitions are often marked by rituals—diplomas, ceremonies—that recognize our rites of passage.

In astrology, we have similar transitions, but they are triggered by the movement of the outer planets—Jupiter, Saturn, Uranus, Neptune, and Pluto. These planets are the slowest moving, so they exert the most impact on our lives. The lineup in 2011 pushed us toward the paradigm shift that will occur in 2012.

So now you're asking, *How's it going to affect me?* That depends on the angles these slower-moving planets make to your sun sign—and on your attitudes and deepest beliefs. After all, the planets only depict possible patterns that may occur. *We're* the scriptwriters. We have free will, the ability to make choices. Astrology simply provides information that makes those choices easier. To be informed is to be empowered.

The planet to watch in 2012 is Neptune, which enters Pisces on February 3 and remains there until the end of March 2025. Neptune was in Pisces briefly in 2011—from April 5 to August 5—then turned retrograde and slipped back into Aquarius for a final time. Since it takes this planet fourteen years to transit a single sign, it won't be back to Aquarius for another 168 years!

Now let's take a closer look at what Neptune's transit may mean for each of us.

## The Role of Neptune in 2012

Neptune is an elusive planet, so far away from the sun that it's one of two planets that can't be seen without a telescope. The temperature of its surface clouds is around -218 degrees Celsius. Its atmosphere is composed of hydrogen and helium, and its interior is mostly ice and rock.

When Voyager 2 flew past Neptune in 1989, it was discovered that Neptune had a dark area composed of gas that swirled violently with the force of a hurricane. They called it the Great Dark Spot and compared it to the Great Red Spot on Jupiter. In 1994, however, the Hubble telescope found that that spot had disappeared. So we know that Neptune, like Jupiter, has weather patterns.

To understand Neptune's influence in our lives and how it will impact us from 2012 to 2026, when it moves through Pisces, let's take a walk through a brief slice of history.

The planet was discovered in 1846—not because it was spotted through a telescope, but due to a disturbing characteristic in the orbit of Uranus. Astronomers suspected the erratic orbit was created by the gravitational pull of another planet. In a sense, then, the way in which Neptune was discovered is a metaphor for its elusive characteristics in astrology. It symbolizes imagination, spiritual and intuitive talents, psychic experiences, artistic inspiration. On the downside, it represents our illusions, our blind spots, and governs alcoholism, drug addiction, confusion, escapism of all kinds. Astrologer Steven Forrest calls Neptune "the planet of consciousness . . . the blank state."

Shortly after Neptune was discovered, the California gold rush began (illusions). The Romantic movement (inspiration) also started, a reaction against intellectualism, materialism, and the rigidity of social structures that protected the wealthy, the privileged. Then in 1848, just two years after Neptune's discovery, the Spiritualist movement was born in a small cottage in Hydesville, New York, where the Fox family lived.

John and Margaret Fox and two of their daughters, Margaret and Kate, had moved into the house in December 1847. The place was reputedly haunted and strange noises and rappings could be heard at night, which kept the family awake. On the night of March 31, about three nights after the family had moved into the house, young Kate heard the noises and responded by snapping her fingers and called out, "Mr. Splitfoot. Do as I do." She then clapped her hands several times.

The pattern of her clapping was instantly duplicated. Her sister then joined in and demanded that "Splitfoot" do what she did. Her four claps were immediately answered with four claps. Mrs. Fox asked the invisible guest to rap out the ages of all of her seven children, which it did, with a pause between each one to individualize them.

Mrs. Fox began to question the rapper. Was it a human being? There was no response. She then asked it to rap twice if it was a spirit. It rapped twice—and the spiritualist movement was born.

Twenty-nine years after Neptune's discovery, a medium named George Colby of Iowa was holding a séance at the home of a local resident, a fellow named Wadsworth. Nothing extraordinary had happened so far that night. Colby was already a successful medium, and he'd done the usual things that night—passed on messages from the dead to the living.

Then, suddenly, Colby received a message from his Indian guide, Seneca, instructing him to travel immediately to Eau Claire, Wisconsin, where he was to hook up with T. D. Giddings, a Spiritualist. Once he was in Wisconsin, Seneca said, further instructions would be given. Colby, being a product of a time when the Spiritualist movement was sweeping across the country, did the expected thing. The next morning he packed up and left for Wisconsin. He met up with Giddings, and at a séance shortly afterward Colby and Giddings were given instructions to leave Wisconsin and head to Florida.

Colby was only twenty-seven years old at the time, a single man ready for adventure. Giddings, however, had a family and took them along. Back then, steamboats and trains were the only route south, and this odd little entourage took both. They rode a train to Jacksonville, Florida, then traveled by steamboat down the St. John's River to a place called Blue Springs. This frontier town was supposedly in the general vicinity of their final destination.

Seneca had described the place they were going to settle as having hills and a chain of lakes. The only thing that lay beyond the borders of Blue Springs looked like dense, subtropical forest. But when Seneca made contact and told the two men to begin their trek into the woods and to follow his directions, they did so.

They made their way through dense growth and after several miles arrived at the spot where Seneca said the Spiritualist camp would be created. Everything—from the high bluffs to the lakes and the lay of the land—looked exactly as Seneca had described.

Colby built a house on the shores of Lake Colby, and Giddings and his family built a home nearby. Colby eventually obtained a government deed for seventy-four acres that adjoined the area where he and Giddings had settled. They were apparently the only people for miles around.

For eighteen years, Colby didn't do much of anything about establishing a Spiritualist community in the area. He adopted several orphans, however, and raised them. He also operated a dairy.

In 1893, a Spiritualist named Rowley showed up and decided to establish a Spiritualist center in either DeLeon Springs or Winter Park. He invited a number of prominent Spiritualists from the north to travel to Florida to check out the area. Two of these Spiritualists were women who were prominent in the Lily Dale Spiritualist camp in New York. They didn't particularly care for Rowley, but Colby won them over, and they decided to create a Spiritualist camp on his property.

In October 1894, twelve mediums signed the charter for the Southern Cassadaga Spiritualist Camp. According to the charter, the association was to be a nonprofit organization that would promote the Spiritualist beliefs in the soul's immortality, "the nearness of the Spirit World, the guardianship of Spirit friends, and the possibility of communion with them," as the charter reads.

Seneca, Colby's guide, apparently advised him to remain in the background during this time, so his name doesn't appear on the charter, and he didn't have much to do with the organization of the camp. However, in 1895, he deeded the association thirty-five acres of his land. The first meeting was held in late 1895 and lasted three days. A hundred people attended the event to meet and sit with the mediums who had been invited.

Within three years of that first meeting, eight cottages, a dancing pavilion, a lodging hall, and a library had been built on the association grounds. Wealthy mediums from the north were being enticed to move to Cassadaga on a more or less permanent basis. From the late 1800s to the early part of the twentieth century, not much is written about the town. The camp apparently flourished, however, because the Cassadaga Hotel was built in 1922 and so were most of the cottages that still stand today.

In the century plus since Cassadaga was established, the rest of central Florida has grown up around it. Just thirty minutes south of it on I-4 is a whole other kind of world—Disney World! But as soon as you turn off Interstate 4, memories of Dumbo and Epcot, Universal and MGM, give way to southern pine forests. A kind of presence infuses the still air. You can't help but feel that nothing is what it appears to be.

For years there wasn't even a sign for Cassadaga. It was almost as if the people who are supposed to find their way here did so in spite of the lack of directions. Even today Cassadaga is little more than a black dot on a map, a punctuation point in the vastness of the pine forest. Lake Helen is the nearest town.

But if you blink too fast, Lake Helen is already a memory. Just beyond the outer edge of the town, the road climbs and dips through a series of low hills and shallow valleys. The trees seem thicker and darker here, the Spanish moss sways in the breeze, and shapes eddy across the shadowed road. A hush lingers in the air. Stop your car, lower your windows, and you probably won't hear a sound.

About half a mile outside of Lake Helen, you'll see a sign announcing that you're now in Cassadaga. But it isn't until you come around the next sharp curve that you know you're there. A large two-story stucco building looms in front of you, the Cassadaga Hotel. Its Mediterranean architecture dates back to the 1920s, during the heyday of Spiritualism. Along the right side of the building stretches a wide porch filled with rocking chairs. At dusk some evenings, when the light plays tricks with perception, some of the empty chairs rock, creaking softly in the quiet.

Spirits enjoying the evening? One never knows for sure. But perhaps that's part of the lure and the mystique of Cassadaga.

Given the uncertainty of the times in which we live, it's not surprising that business in Cassadaga is flourishing. On any weekend, the hotel lot is jammed with cars, and everywhere you look, people are walking around in search of the right psychic. Both sides of the main street are lined with small buildings that have signs posted out front advertising the kind of reading available. Unlike the early days of Cassadaga, when it was mainly Spiritualists, today's psychic offerings are vast. You can find everything from astrologers, tarot readers, and Reiki healers. But the mediums are still the draw, the magnet. As one young woman explained to us during a recent trip, "Everything is changing so fast, life is moving at such a rapid clip, that people are turning more and more to spiritual and intuitive insights and guidance."

And that pretty much sums up a large part of what Neptune's transit through Pisces may bring for each of us.

## Neptune in Pisces

We had a brief taste of Neptune in Pisces, the sign it rules, between April 3, 2011, and August 4, 2011. Then Neptune turned retrograde and slipped back into Aquarius. But on February 3, 2012, it enters Pisces again. For clues about how this transit may manifest itself for you, look back to those four months in 2011. What was going on in your life then? Did you feel more creative? Did you take up a new artistic hobby? Did your spiritual beliefs undergo some sort of transformation? Were you more intuitive? Were you called upon to give selflessly in some respect? Did you feel your life was confusing, your goals muddled? Did you indulge more frequently in alcohol and drugs?

All of these areas fall under the governance of Neptune. So now let's look specifically at each sign for possible shifts under Neptune's fourteen-year transit through Pisces.

## Aries ♈

**Cardinal, fire**

You're the trailblazer of the zodiac, known for your fearlessness, impulsiveness, and well, yes, sometimes your recklessness. You enjoy anything that induces an adrenaline rush—from extreme sports to love affairs to high-wire creative projects. You think outside the box, aren't known as a team player, and would rather delegate than be delegated to. In love, your passions are often extreme, you can be jealous and possessive, but when you fall, you fall hard, with your entire heart.

You're like an action hero, always on the move, doing, figuring the angles. Even your strong intuition comes through action—mostly impulses and burning hunches on which you act quickly. Your spiritual beliefs probably aren't traditional, i.e., not associated with a particular religion or church. It's more likely that you've pieced together your own beliefs over the years and are still adding to them.

During Neptune's transit of Pisces and your solar twelfth house, your intuition and spirituality will deepen, the scope will broaden, and chances are it will all begin in the privacy of your interior world. Your dream life will be more vivid, and it should be easier to recall your dreams and work with them. You should have greater access to your own unconscious, so that it's easier to recall past lives and understand your own motives and psyche. In fact, the more you work consciously with your intuitive abilities and spiritual beliefs, the easier this paradigm shift will be for you.

Since the twelfth house represents institutions, it's possible that you may have more contact with hospitals, nursing homes, even prisons. You might be an employee or volunteer in one of these organizations. In some way, this experience enables you to reach for the greater good rather than for what is good only for you.

## Taurus ♉

**Fixed, earth**

Your stubbornness, patience, and resoluteness are legendary. You complete whatever you start and often end up completing what other people start as well. In other words, due to your resilience and endurance, you often win where others fail. Where Aries trailblazes, you cultivate—relationships, a beautiful home, a family, a career, a garden. You enjoy being surrounded by beauty but aren't necessarily an extravagant spender.

Some signs need drama to thrive, but you're not one of them. You're a romantic who enjoys a harmonious relationship in which creativity can flourish. You tend to keep things to yourself—not so much secretive as circumspect. You speak when you have something meaningful to say.

Once Neptune enters Pisces, the tide will turn more in your direction. Pisces is a water sign that's compatible with your earth-sign sun, and you'll find that it deepens your innate curiosity about the deeper mysteries in life—telepathy, precognition, psychokinesis, synchronicity, what makes the universe tick, communication with the dead, UFOs, crop circles. You may join groups that support these interests and get involved with charitable organizations that support ideals in which you believe.

The eleventh house symbolizes groups, friends, our wishes, hopes and dreams, the people you hang with, goals, your life plan. So during Neptune's transit through Pisces, groups will be a major theme for you. You may join online groups that support your ideals, interests, and goals. There may be a psychic or intuitive component to these groups. Perhaps you end up in England, investigating crop circles. Or you might join a ghost-hunting group, a writer's group, a theater group. You might teach yoga for meditation to groups. You get the idea. One way or another, through group participation, online or off, you learn to reach for the greater good, the higher inspiration, the greater spiritual ideal.

## Gemini ♊

**Mutable, air**

You're the communicator of the zodiac and can talk circles around anyone, anywhere, at any time, on virtually any subject. Your knowledge may not always be deep, but it's broad. When you don't know something, you research and ask questions incessantly, until your burning curiosity is sated.

Because you're ruled by Mercury, the planet of communication, you tend to use your rational, intellectual mind to explore your world. Your rational analysis of everything—from ideas to relationships—probably drives you nuts at times. But when this characteristic leads you into an exploration of psychic and spiritual realms, you're more grounded. With Neptune's transit through Pisces, you're going to have plenty of opportunities for this kind of exploration.

Neptune will be transiting the career section of your chart for fourteen years, suggesting that your professional life will be the focus of subtle but important change. In some way, psychic and spiritual exploration will become part of your professional endeavors. Opportunities will present themselves in these areas. Your creative ventures during this time will have a deeply psychic and spiritual texture to them. Your own intuition should deepen considerably, and as long as you act upon that inner knowledge, you won't be disappointed.

If you're not satisfied with your profession when this transit starts, then you may change career paths. Don't worry about how this will come about. You'll recognize the choices you should make and will have a strong inner sense about when to make them. During this transit, you'll learn to trust this inner sense and through your profession will learn to reach for inspired creativity and for what is best for the larger good, not just for what is good for you.

## Cancer ♋

**Cardinal, water**

You need roots, a place to call home, and it doesn't matter if that place is a camper, a palace, or a state of mind. Home is your harbor, your refuge, your retreat.

As a cardinal water sign, your intuition and perceptions are finely honed. Just about everything for you is filtered through a subjective lens, through your emotions and intuition. You may not always be able to explain to others why you make certain decisions, but you don't have an overpowering need to explain yourself. You do what you do because it feels right to you.

You're affectionate, passionate, and even possessive at times. Emotionally, you act and react the same way that a crab moves—sideways. It's how you avoid confrontation and revealing who you really are, deep within. You're often moody and changeable, but once you trust someone, you trust forever.

With Neptune in fellow water sign Pisces, transiting your solar ninth house, you'll be enjoying a prolonged period of psychic and spiritual development that your Cancer nature will love. Workshops and seminars on intuitive development are a possibility—you take them or teach them! Travel to foreign countries is likely, but it won't be strictly for pleasure. You could be on a spiritual quest of some kind, visiting sacred sites in different countries in search of answers, information, illumination.

In romance and love, any relationship that develops under this transit may have a deeply spiritual component to it. The person could be someone you have been with in past lives and now you're together again for this psychic exploration.

## Leo ♌

**Fixed, fire**

Life is your stage, Leo. Your flamboyance and flair for drama infuse you with great magnetic appeal toward which others gravitate. You seek to succeed in everything you do and undertake, want to make an impact in every situation and usually do. Your generosity and loyalty are legendary, but not without strings! You expect to be the sun around which others spin like planets. Nothing short of center stage suits you. Perhaps this is why so many Leos enter the dramatic and creative arts. It's an area where they excel.

Your leadership abilities, fun-loving nature, and genuine compassion are much appreciated by your friends and loved ones. You bring passion and commitment to everything you do, and it's these qualities that enable you to tackle challenges head on. In love and romance, you're passionate and loyal.

During Neptune's transit through Pisces and your solar eighth house, you may find the boundaries between you and others blurring. It's as if you're being asked to move off center stage for a while so that you can give freely of your time, money, energy, to others. The eighth house represents shared resources—usually with a spouse, but it can be anyone with whom you share expenses, time, energy, expertise. So it's possible that your spouse or partner's income may be muddled or confused during this transit.

Since the eighth house also represents inheritances, there could be some confusion concerning a will. But however this transit unfolds for you in terms of specific events, the point is to heighten your spiritual and intuitive awareness so that you reach first for the greater good.

## Virgo ♍

**Mutable, earth**

You're the perfectionist of the zodiac, something you probably consider both a blessing and curse. Your attention to detail is extraordinary—think Tony Shalhoub in *Monk*. The man walks into a room, and in a single sweeping glance the details leap out at him—the pencil aligned with due north, the faintest smudge of lipstick on a coffee mug, the rug slightly askew. Thanks to this attention to detail, you're able to penetrate deeply into any topic you study, any research you conduct. You dig and dig until you have all the information you need.

Like Gemini, you're ruled by Mercury, so your mind is lightning quick and you communicate your ideas with great authority. Duty and responsibility are important to you, and your focus is on doing your job, whatever it is, efficiently and well. There's no harder worker than you, Virgo.

Neptune's transit through Pisces and your solar seventh house means it will be opposed to your sun for fourteen years. Oppositions are like an itch you can't scratch; you just learn to live with it. During this period, your greatest lessons and challenges will come through business and personal partnerships. You may be called upon to place a partner's interests and well-being before your own. The best way to navigate this opposition is to develop your intuition and learn to rely on your inner guidance.

There may be some confusion around partnerships too. But if you continually strive to associate with upbeat, spiritual individuals, to seek out those of like minds and interests, you should do just fine. Any relationships in which you get involved are likely to have deep past-life connections.

## Libra ♎

**Cardinal, air**

You're the mediator, Libra, the one who sees both sides of an issue because you can step into the other guy's shoes, zip yourself up inside his skin, understand how and why he feels the way he does. You're all about finding harmony and balance, the very quality that often eludes you. But seek it you must, as if it's your prime directive. In love, you're a romantic who flourishes in a committed, enduring relationship. But regardless of how long the relationship lasts, you still need to be shown and told that you are loved.

You excel in any profession that requires a balanced intellect and sensitivities. Music and the arts suit you, but so does the law, teaching, research, investigation. During Neptune's transit through Pisces, your daily work will take a decided turn toward the spiritual and psychic. You may begin to take time each day to meditate, practice yoga, or engage in creative work that develops and enhances your intuition.

You may find that the individuals who enter your daily work life during this transit are people you have known in past lives, and you're coming together again for a specific purpose. Perhaps you're going to join forces for some large-scale project that makes a difference in the world. Or maybe you meet up again simply to support each other. One thing is for sure: it's going to be an intriguing fourteen years. The best way to navigate it, Libra, is to pay close attention to synchronicities. They're your guides.

## Scorpio ♏

**Fixed, water**

Intensely passionate, secretive, and downright psychic, you're one of the most strong-willed signs in the zodiac and certainly one of the most misunderstood. Like your fellow water signs Cancer and Pisces, you live in a world of feeling and intuition, filtering all your experiences through a subjective lens. But you're also vastly different from your brethren water signs. You're basically fearless, with a great capacity for endurance that rivals Taurus, and you don't know the meaning of the word "indifference." You live pretty much in a black and white world, where things are either right or wrong, without nuance.

You're the consummate investigator. Easy answers never suit you, so you dig deeper and deeper, connecting the dots the rest of us miss. You have a rich inner life, glean a lot of information through nontraditional means, i.e., psychically, and never apologize for it.

During Neptune's transit of Pisces and your solar fifth house, you're in for a treat, Scorpio. Your considerable intuition will deepen even more. You'll be so in tune with your muse that your creativity simply flows out of you. Since the fifth house also symbolizes love and romance, you can expect some intense relationships that are madly passionate and perhaps rooted in past lives. If you have a child during this transit, he or she will be intensely creative in some way, with some special talent. It will be up to you to help the child develop and nurture that talent.

Because Neptune blurs the boundaries between us and others, it's possible that you'll be called upon to give of yourself in a selfless way—to a lover, a child, a creative project. If you resist the urge to get lost in escapism—drugs, alcohol, sex—then this transit should prove beneficial in your evolution as a human being.

## Sagittarius ♐

**Mutable, fire**

You're blunt, witty, nomadic. You're the seeker of truth, express what you feel and believe, and don't care if anyone agrees with you. You're after the big picture, the broad canvas of any issue, belief, situation, relationship. Mundane details bore you. Intellectually, you're logical and rational, like Gemini, your polar opposite. But there are some important differences. Gemini is focused on the here and now; you've always got one eye on the future, on the larger family of humanity, the planet, the universe.

You love your freedom, the ability to just take off on a whim, with a pack and your ATM card, and chafe at any restrictions others try to put on you. Yet, in a relationship, you're passionate though rarely possessive; attentive to your partner and yet careful to maintain your freedom.

Once Neptune enters Pisces and your solar fourth house, you may find that your natural interest in mysticism, metaphysics, and things that go bump in the night takes on a whole new meaning. Suddenly, but subtly, your home and family life could become a hub of psychic activity and spiritual exploration. Your quest involves your family, your emotions toward them and vice versa, and you may discover layers of meaning in these relationships that you simply didn't see before.

There can be confusion during this transit too. If you move, there could be confusion about the neighborhood, the house, the contract. Depending on your age, one of your parents may need additional help and support or may move in with you. However this part of the equation unfolds, you may have to give more than you receive. But ultimately, your intuition becomes your compass, and through giving without expectation of compensation, you learn to extend yourself for the greater good.

## Capricorn ♑

**Cardinal, earth**

Any boss worth her job knows that if you give a task to a Capricorn, it gets done with a shocking efficiency, dedication, and understanding of the nuances involved. But it's not just work at which you excel, Capricorn. This is how you conduct everything in your life—you appraise the situation, event, or relationship, figure out a strategy, then set things in motion that are intended to reach the goal, whatever it may be.

You're industrious, disciplined, structured, and have so much common sense it sometimes works against you! When you need intuition, right-brain thinking, your left brain, your rational mind, hurls up blocks and urges you to rely solely on logic. But that's going to change under Neptune's transit through Pisces and your solar third house, Capricorn.

The third house governs communication, and during Neptune's fourteen-year transit through Pisces, your conscious mind becomes more intuitive, psychic, right-brain. It will be easier for you to grasp the larger picture of your goals, daily life, and relationships with siblings, friends, neighbors. Whereas before you might have been intent on a particular course, now you'll be urged to explore other options, to take interesting detours into unexplored realms.

You'll learn to rely more and more frequently on your gut feelings, your hunches, your initial sense about people, situations. Your intimate partnerships will have a richness and depth you haven't experienced before. The spiritual and psychic connections you feel in these relationships will be based on your genuine beliefs and not on something you've learned to believe from parents, peers, friends. You'll be operating on a whole different level and will learn to trust these feelings first and foremost.

## Aquarius ♒

**Fixed, air**

You value freedom and individuality above all else, and it's evident in the way you think, your belief system, your passions, and interests. Others may sometimes see you as eccentric, but in truth you're the visionary of the zodiac. You believe that whatever you can imagine, can become tangible.

You're a conundrum to the people who know you. You're a nonconformist who conforms when it suits you and a passionate advocate for your causes, but from an intellectual rather than an emotional basis. Once you commit in a relationship, you still demand your freedom and space, and this is true for all facets of your life. You work best in avant garde fields—film, electronics, the arts, television, broadcasting.

Neptune's transit through Pisces and your solar second house will impact your finances and your values. For instance, you may become more cognizant of how you spend your money. Do you, for instance, buy products from a company that promotes ideals that are contrary to your own? Do you use your power as a consumer to make statements about your ideals and beliefs? Are you generous toward charities and nonprofit organizations whose causes are in line with your ideals? Is your profession in line with them?

You may find that you begin to value different qualities in your romantic relationships. You may be looking for a deeper spiritual or psychic connection with a partner. You may decide that the area where you live no longer feels right for you. There are many possible ways this transit can unfold for you. But you will certainly discover that you now seek the greater good for the collective—family, friends, community, world.

## Pisces ♓

**Mutable, water**

Like Scorpio and Cancer, you live primarily through your emotions and intuition. You also have a fantastic imagination that takes you places denied to the rest of us. Your inner world is rich, textured, alive with archetypal material, past-life memories, and connections to the collective unconscious. Your empathic nature makes you something of a psychic sponge, so it's important that you associate with positive, upbeat people.

With Neptune in your sign for the next fourteen years, there will be many subtle changes in your life. You may decide to change careers, to pursue a line of work that is more spiritual or psychic in nature. You may find yourself growing away from certain people in your life whose interests and beliefs aren't aligned with your own. It's possible, too, that you take up meditation, yoga, or other mind/body practices that enable you to stay grounded and attuned.

In romance and love, your needs and desires will shift. You'll want a partner whose ideals match your own and will need to feel a deep spiritual connection with anyone with whom you get involved. There can be confusion with this transit—Neptune often fogs the brain!—but as long as you resist escapism, you should do fine.

CHAPTER 2

# Astrology 101

On the day you were born, what was the weather like? If you were born at night, had the moon already risen? Was it full or the shape of a Cheshire cat's grin? Was the delivery ward quiet or bustling with activity? Unless your mom or dad has a very good memory, you'll probably never know the full details. But there's one thing you can know for sure: on the day you were born, the sun was located in a particular zone of the zodiac, an imaginary 360-degree belt that circles the earth. The belt is divided into twelve 30-degree portions called signs.

If you were born between July 23 and August 22, then the sun was passing through the sign of Leo, so we say that your sun sign is Leo. Each of the twelve signs has distinct attributes and characteristics. Leos, for instance, love being the center of attention. They're warm, compassionate people with a flair for the dramatic. Virgos, born between August 23 and September 22, are perfectionists with discriminating intellects and a genius for details. Capricorns, born between December 22 and January 19, are the worker bees of the zodiac, serious-minded, ambitious, industrious.

# How Signs Are Classified

The twelve signs are categorized according to element and quality or modality. The first category, element, reads like a basic science lesson—fire, earth, air, and water—and describes the general physical characteristics of the signs.

Fire signs—Aries, Leo, Sagittarius—are warm, dynamic individuals who are always passionate about what they do.

Earth signs—Taurus, Virgo, Capricorn—are the builders of the zodiac, practical and efficient, grounded in everything they do.

Air signs—Gemini, Libra, Aquarius—are people who live mostly in the world of ideas. They are terrific communicators.

Water signs—Cancer, Scorpio, Pisces—live through their emotions, imaginations, and intuitions.

The second category describes how each sign operates in the physical world, how adaptable it is to circumstances:

Cardinal signs—Aries, Cancer, Libra, Capricorn—are initiators. These people are active, impatient, restless. They're great at starting things, but unless a project or a relationship holds their attention, they lose interest and may not finish what they start.

Fixed signs—Taurus, Leo, Scorpio, Aquarius—are deliberate, controlled, resolute. These individuals tend to move more slowly than cardinal signs, are often stubborn, and resist change. They seek roots and stability and are always in the game for the long haul. They aren't quitters.

Mutable signs—Gemini, Virgo, Sagittarius, Pisces—are adaptable. These people are flexible, changeable, communicative. They don't get locked into rigid patterns or belief systems.

## SUN SIGNS

| Sign | Date | Element | Quality |
|---|---|---|---|
| Aries ♈ | March 21–April 19 | Fire | Cardinal |
| Taurus ♉ | April 20–May 20 | Earth | Fixed |
| Gemini ♊ | May 21–June 21 | Air | Mutable |
| Cancer ♋ | June 22–July 22 | Water | Cardinal |
| Leo ♌ | July 23–August 22 | Fire | Fixed |
| Virgo ♍ | August 23–September 22 | Earth | Mutable |
| Libra ♎ | September 23–October 22 | Air | Cardinal |
| Scorpio ♏ | October 23–November 21 | Water | Fixed |
| Sagittarius ♐ | November 22–December 21 | Fire | Mutable |
| Capricorn ♑ | December 22–January 19 | Earth | Cardinal |
| Aquarius ♒ | January 20–February 18 | Air | Fixed |
| Pisces ♓ | February 19–March 20 | Water | Mutable |

# The Planets

The planets in astrology are the players who make things happen. They're the characters in the story of your life. This story always begins with the sun, the giver of life.

Your sun sign describes your self-expression, your primal energy, the essence of who you are. It's the archetypal pattern of your Self. When you know another person's sun sign, you already have a great deal of information about that person. Let's say you're a Taurus who has just started dating a Gemini. How compatible are you?

On the surface, it wouldn't seem that you have much in common. Taurus is a fixed earth sign; Gemini is a mutable air sign. Taurus is persistent, stubborn, practical, a cultivator as opposed to an initiator. Gemini is a chameleon, a communicator, social, with a mind as quick as lightning. Taurus is ruled by Venus, which governs the arts, money, beauty, love, and romance, and Gemini is ruled by Mercury, which governs communication and travel. There doesn't seem to be much common ground. But before we write off this combination, let's look a little deeper.

Suppose the Taurus has Mercury in Gemini and suppose the Gemini has Venus in Taurus? This would mean that the Taurus and Gemini each have their rulers in the other person's sign. They probably communicate well and enjoy travel and books (Mercury) and would see eye to eye on romance, art, and music (Venus). They might get along so well, in fact, that they collaborate on creative projects.

Each of us is also influenced by the other nine planets (the sun and moon are treated like planets in astrology) and the signs they were transiting when we were born. Suppose our Taurus and Gemini have the same moon sign? The moon rules our inner needs, emotions and intuition, and all that makes us feel secure within ourselves. Quite often, compatible moon signs can overcome even the most glaring difference in sun signs because the two people share similar emotions.

In the section on monthly predictions, your sun sign always takes center stage, and every prediction is based on the movement of the transiting planets in relation to your sun sign. Let's say you're a Sagittarius. Between January 7 and February 4 this year, Venus will be transiting your sign. What's this mean for you? Well, since Venus rules—among other things—romance, you can expect your love life to pick up significantly during these weeks. Other people will find you attractive and be more open to your ideas, and you'll radiate a certain charisma. Your creative endeavors will move full steam ahead.

The planets table provides an overview of the planets and the signs that they rule. Keep in mind that the moon is the swiftest-moving planet, changing signs about every two and a half days, and that Pluto is the snail of the zodiac, taking as long as thirty years to transit a single sign. Although the faster-moving planets—the moon,

Mercury, Venus, and Mars—have an impact on our lives, it's the slow pokes—Uranus, Neptune, and Pluto—that bring about the most profound influence and change. Jupiter and Saturn fall between the others in terms of speed. This year, Jupiter spends the first six months in Taurus, then enters Gemini on June 11 and doesn't leave that sign until late June 2013.

In the section on predictions, the most frequent references are to the transits of Mercury, Venus, and Mars. In the daily predictions for each sign, the predictions are based primarily on the transiting moon.

Now glance through the planets table. When a sign is in parentheses, it means the planet corules that sign. This assignation dates back to when we thought there were only seven planets in the solar system. But since there were still twelve signs, some of the planets had to do double duty!

## THE PLANETS

| Planet | Rules | Attributes of Planet |
|---|---|---|
| Sun ☉ | Leo | self-expression, primal energy, creative ability, ego, individuality |
| Moon ☽ | Cancer | emotions, intuition, mother or wife, security |
| Mercury ☿ | Gemini, Virgo | intellect, mental acuity, communication, logic, reasoning, travel, contracts |
| Venus ♀ | Taurus, Libra | love, romance, beauty, artistic instincts, the arts, music, material and financial resources |
| Mars ♂ | Aries (Scorpio) | physical and sexual energy, aggression, drive |

| Planet | Rules | Attributes of Planet |
|---|---|---|
| Jupiter ♃ | Sagittarius (Pisces) | luck, expansion, success, prosperity, growth, creativity, spiritual interests, higher education, law |
| Saturn ♄ | Capricorn (Aquarius) | laws of physical universe, discipline, responsibility, structure, karma, authority |
| Uranus ♅ | Aquarius | individuality, genius, eccentricity, originality, science, revolution |
| Neptune ♆ | Pisces | visionary self, illusions, what's hidden, psychic ability, dissolution of ego boundaries, spiritual insights, dreams |
| Pluto ♇ ♇ | Scorpio | the darker side, death, sex, regeneration, rebirth, profound and permanent change, transformation |

## Houses and Rising Signs

In the instant you drew your first breath, one of the signs of the zodiac was just passing over the eastern horizon. Astrologers refer to this as the rising sign or ascendant. It's what makes your horoscope unique. Think of your ascendant as the front door of your horoscope, the place where you enter into this life and begin your journey.

Your ascendant is based on the exact moment of your birth and the other signs follow counterclockwise. If you have Taurus rising, for example, that is the cusp of your first house. The cusp of the second would be Gemini, of the third Cancer, and so on around the horoscope circle in a counterclockwise direction. Each house governs a particular area of life, which is outlined below.

The best way to find out your rising sign is to have your horoscope drawn up by an astrologer. For those of you with access to the Internet, though, there are several sites that provide free birth horoscopes. www.astro.com and www.cafeastrology.com are two good ones.

In a horoscope, the ascendant (cusp of the first house), IC (cusp of the fourth house), descendant (cusp of the seventh house), and MC (cusp of the tenth house) are considered to be the most critical angles. Any planets that fall close to these angles are extremely important in the overall astrological picture of who you are. By the same token, planets that fall in the first, fourth, seventh, and tenth houses are also considered to be important.

Now here's a rundown on what the houses mean.

## Ascendant or Rising: The First of Four Important Critical Angles in a Horoscope

- How other people see you
- How you present yourself to the world
- Your physical appearance

### First House, Personality

- Early childhood
- Your ego
- Your body type and how you feel about your body
- General physical health
- Defense mechanisms
- Your creative thrust

## Second House, Personal Values

- How you earn and spend your money
- Your personal values
- Your material resources and assets
- Your attitudes and beliefs toward money
- Your possessions and your attitude toward those possessions
- Your self-worth
- Your attitudes about creativity

## Third House, Communication and Learning

- Personal expression
- Intellect and mental attitudes and perceptions
- Siblings, neighbors, and relatives
- How you learn
- School until college
- Reading, writing, teaching
- Short trips (the grocery store versus Europe in seven days)
- Earth-bound transportation
- Creativity as a communication device

## IC or Fourth House Cusp: The Second Critical Angle in a Horoscope

- Sign on IC describes the qualities and traits of your home during early childhood
- Describes roots of your creative abilities and talents

## Fourth House, Your Roots

- Personal environment
- Your home
- Your attitudes toward family

- Early childhood conditioning
- Real estate
- Your nurturing parent

Some astrologers say this house belongs to Mom or her equivalent in your life, others say it belongs to Dad or his equivalent. It makes sense to me that it's Mom because the fourth house is ruled by the moon, which rules mothers. But in this day and age, when parental roles are in flux, the only hard and fast rule is that the fourth belongs to the parent who nurtures you most of the time.

- The conditions at the end of your life
- Early childhood support of your creativity and interests

## Fifth House, Children and Creativity

- Kids, your firstborn in particular
- Love affairs, romance
- What you enjoy
- Creative ability
- Gambling and speculation
- Pets

Traditionally, pets belong in the sixth house. But that definition stems from the days when pets were chattel. These days, we don't even refer to them as pets. They are animal companions who bring us pleasure.

## Sixth House, Work and Responsibility

- Day-to-day working conditions and environment
- Competence and skills
- Your experience of employees and employers
- Duty to work, to employees
- Health and the daily maintenance of your health

## Descendant/Seventh House Cusp: The Third Critical Angle in a Horoscope

- The sign on the house cusp describes the qualities sought in intimate or business relationships
- Describes qualities of creative partnerships

## Seventh House, Partnerships and Marriage

- Marriage
- Marriage partner
- Significant others
- Business partnerships
- Close friends
- Open enemies
- Contracts

## Eighth House, Transformation

- Sexuality as transformation
- Secrets
- Death, taxes, inheritances, insurance, mortgages, and loans
- Resources shared with others
- Your partner's finances
- The occult (read: astrology, reincarnation, UFOs, everything weird and strange)
- Your hidden talents
- Psychology
- Life-threatening illnesses
- Your creative depths

## Ninth House, Worldview

- Philosophy and religion
- The law, courts, judicial system
- Publishing
- Foreign travels and cultures

- College, graduate school
- Spiritual beliefs
- Travel abroad

## MC or Cusp of Tenth House: The Fourth Critical Angle in a Horoscope

- Sign on cusp of MC describes qualities you seek in a profession
- Your public image
- Your creative and professional achievements

## Tenth House, Profession and Career

- Public image as opposed to a job that merely pays the bills (sixth house)
- Your status and position in the world
- The authoritarian parent and authority in general
- People who hold power over you
- Your public life
- Your career/profession

## Eleventh House, Ideals and Dreams

- Peer groups
- Social circles (your writers' group, your mother's bridge club)
- Your dreams and aspirations
- How you can realize your dreams

## Twelfth House, Personal Unconscious

- Power you have disowned that must be claimed again
- Institutions—hospitals, prisons, nursing homes—and what is hidden
- What you must confront this time around, your karma, issues brought in from other lives

- Psychic gifts and abilities
- Healing talents
- What you give unconditionally

In the section on predictions, you'll find references to transiting planets moving into certain houses. These houses are actually solar houses that are created by putting your sun sign on the ascendant. This technique is how most predictions are made for the general public rather than for specific individuals.

## Lunations

Every year there are twelve new moons and twelve full moons, with some years having thirteen full moons. The extra full moon is called the Blue Moon. New moons are typically when we should begin new projects, set new goals, seek new opportunities. They're times for beginnings. They usher in new opportunities according to house and sign.

Two weeks after each new moon, there's a full moon. This is the time of harvest, fruition, when we reap what we've sown.

Whenever a new moon falls in your sign, take time to brainstorm what you would like to achieve during the weeks and months until the full moon falls in your sign. These goals can be in any area of your life. Or, you can simply take the time on each new moon to set up goals and strategies for what you would like to achieve or manifest during the next two weeks—until the full moon—or until the next new moon.

Here's a list of all the new moons and full moons during 2012. The asterisk beside any new moon entry indicates a solar eclipse; the asterisk next to a full moon entry indicates a lunar eclipse.

### LUNATIONS OF 2012

| New Moons | Full Moons |
|---|---|
| January 23—Aquarius | January 9—Cancer |
| February 21—Pisces | February 7—Leo |
| March 22—Aries | March 8—Virgo |
| April 21—Taurus | April 6—Libra |
| *May 20—Gemini | May 5—Scorpio |
| June 19—Gemini | *June 4—Sagittarius |
| July 19—Cancer | July 3—Capricorn |
| August 17—Leo | August 1—Aquarius |
| September 15—Virgo | August 31—Pisces |
| October 15—Libra | September 29—Aries |
| *November 13—Scorpio | October 29—Taurus |
| December 13—Sagittarius | *November 28—Gemini |
| | December 28—Cancer |

Every year there are two lunar and two solar eclipses, separated from each other by about two weeks. Lunar eclipses tend to deal with emotional issues and our internal world and often bring an emotional issue to the surface related to the sign and house in which the eclipse falls. Solar eclipses deal with events and often enable us to see something that has eluded us. They also symbolize beginnings and endings.

Read more about eclipses in the Big Picture for your sign for 2012. I also recommend Celeste Teal's excellent book, *Eclipses.*

## Mercury Retrograde

Every year, Mercury—the planet that symbolizes communication and travel—turns retrograde three times. During these periods, our travel plans often go awry, communication breaks down, computers go berserk, cars or appliances develop problems. You get the idea. Things in our daily lives don't work as smoothly as we would like.

Here are some guidelines to follow for Mercury retrogrades:

- Try not to travel. But if you have to, be flexible and think of it as an adventure. If you're stuck overnight in an airport in Houston or Atlanta, though, the adventure part of this could be a stretch.
- Don't sign contracts—unless you don't mind revisiting them when Mercury is direct again.
- Communicate as succinctly and clearly as possible.
- Back up all computer files. Use an external hard drive and/or a flash drive. If you've had a computer crash, you already know how frustrating it can be to reconstruct your files.
- Don't buy expensive electronics. Expensive anything.
- Don't submit manuscripts or screenplays, pitch ideas, or launch new projects.
- Revise, rewrite, rethink, review.

In the Big Picture for each sign, check out the dates for this year's Mercury retrogrades and how these retrogrades are likely to impact you. Do the same for eclipses.

CHAPTER 3

# Matters of the Heart in 2012

When you're in the throes of a paradigm shift, every area of your life may feel more vulnerable. You may notice a distinct change in what you want and expect in a romantic partnership. You may find yourself attracted to people who are different from people to whom you've been attracted in the past. Whether you're in a new or long-term relationship or are just looking, it's important to keep the channels of communication wide open.

There are, however, some constants to keep in mind with romance and love—which sun signs are most compatible with your own.

## Astrology and Carl Jung

In 1950, Swiss psychologist Carl Jung undertook an astrological study about the compatibility of 180 married couples and used 50 aspects—or angles that planets make to each other. This was in the days before personal computers and astrology software that can erect a natal chart and compare several charts in just seconds. The study took several years, and the results were intriguing.

He found three aspects to be the best indicators for compatibility: a sun/moon conjunction, where one partner's sun sign is the same as the sign of the other person's moon; a moon/moon conjunction, where both individuals have their moons in the same sign; and a moon/ascendant conjunction, when one partner's moon is in the same sign as the other person's ascendant. In his book *Synchronicity, An Acausal Connecting Principle,* Jung noted that the first two aspects "have long been mentioned in the old literature as marriage characteristics, and they therefore represent the oldest tradition."

The sun/moon conjunction makes perfect sense astrologically. Your sun sign describes your overall personality; the sign of your moon describes your inner world, your emotions, what makes you feel secure. So if you're a Pisces involved with someone who has a Pisces moon, for example, then there's a beautiful give and take between you. You understand each other. If you have different sun signs, but your moons are in the same sign, then the emotional and intuitive connection is so strong you probably finish each other's sentences.

What about that third aspect, with the moon and ascendant in the same sign? This one also makes perfect sense. The ascendant is the doorway to your chart and describes, among other things, the persona you project to the outside world. So an individual with his or her moon in the same sign as your ascendant feels emotionally secure in your presence and sees the person behind the mask you wear.

Another compatibility aspect includes Venus, the planet that symbolizes love and romance. The most common I've seen are: Venus/sun, Venus/moon, Venus/ascendant; Venus/descendant cusp (cusp of the seventh house of partnerships); and Venus/Mars in the same sign. Another interesting connection I've noted is among couples who have "mirror" charts, where the sign of one partner's ascendant is the same as the other person's descendant. In other words, let's say you have Scorpio rising and your partner has Scorpio on the cusp of his or her seventh house. This aspect brings balance to the relationship.

But because one size doesn't fit all, you and your partner may have other aspects in your charts that make you compatible. For the purpose of this book, we're going to be looking only at sun-sign combinations for compatibility.

## Your Best Matches

### Aries

Your freedom and independence are paramount to your happiness, so you need a partner who understands and respects your space. But because you're a stranger to compromise, a vital part of any relationship, you may find intimate relationships challenging. Once you're involved, your passions are fierce and can easily topple into the dark extremes of jealousy, possessiveness, suspicion.

Your entrepreneurial and fearless spirit enjoys a partner who can compete with you on any level—on those long hikes into the wilderness, in the boardroom, in the classroom, in the garage out back where you're building your newest invention. You get the idea here, right, Aries? Boredom is your nemesis. So, which signs are good matches for you? Let's take a closer look at some of the possibilities.

*Sagittarius*. This fellow fire sign will give you all the freedom you crave—and then some. She'll match you joke for joke, drink for drink. If she's the physical type, and many of them are, she'll match you on those hikes. But for a Sadge, those hikes may be in some far-flung spot like Tibet. Like you, Sadge pushes herself, but she's more adaptable than you are. Sometimes she may come off like a know-it-all. But overall, this combination holds great promise.

*Gemini.* This air sign's wit, versatility, and ability to talk about virtually anything appeal to you. He's generally not possessive, either, a major plus when you're in one of your darker moods. His mind is sharp and lightning quick, and he probably has a vast, complicated network of friends and acquaintances. Also appealing. So what're the negatives? Gemini generally isn't as independent as you are and may spend more time with his friends than he does with you. But overall, this combination is lively, fun, and never boring.

*Leo.* Another fire sign. On the surface, it looks like a good match. Leo possesses an infinite capacity for enjoyment, which appeals to you. But she also loves having center stage—not just sometimes, but most of the time—and that can be a major turnoff for you.

*Libra, Aquarius.* Libra is your opposite sign. The match could be fantastic because you balance each other. Where you're the loner, she's the social butterfly. You're independent, she's a networker with more friends than a hive has bees. Whether this works or not depends on the signs of your natal moons, ascendants, and Venus. You and Aquarius could be a winning combination. His independence matches yours, he's as sharp as the proverbial tack, and he pulls no punches in expressing what he wants, when he wants it. Downside? He may not be as physical or competitive and lives much of his life in his head.

What about another *Aries*? Depends on the signs of your moons. Strictly on the basis of sun signs, you're both so independent the relationship may never get off the ground!

## Taurus

Stable, dependable, patient. You bring these qualities to any close relationship, and once you commit it's usually for keeps. You aren't into drama, artifice, flamboyance—not for yourself and not in a partner, either. But you enjoy a partner who is physically attractive or who has a particular artistic gift that you appreciate—music, art, a way with words, anything that appeals to your senses.

If you're a Taurus who is into sports and health, and many of them are, then a health-conscious partner is a major plus. But there's another side to you, too, an inner mystic, a quiet, observant Buddha who remains calm and centered, in tune with unseen forces. You would do well with a partner who possesses that quality as well.

*Leo, Sagittarius, Aries.* Unless you have a moon, rising, or Venus in one of those signs, the fire signs probably won't work for you. Too much drama, boisterous behavior, and anger to suit your tastes.

*Virgo, Capricorn.* Fellow earth signs. Virgo could be the ticket. She's as practical as you are and, in many instances, just as mystical. Capricorn is focused, as physical as you are, but may not be as mystically inclined.

*Scorpio.* Your opposite sign, so there may be a good balance. She's secretive and can be vengeful, but she's just as mystical as you are.

## Gemini

In a romantic relationship, conversation and discussion top your list. In fact, any potential partner must seduce your mind first—with ideas, information, books, theories that connect seemingly disparate bits of whatever it is that rushes through your head 24/7. You're up front about what you feel, but those feelings could change at a moment's notice, a dichotomy that can be confusing to a partner. And to everyone else around you, for that matter. No wonder your sign is represented by the twins.

For you, everything starts with a single burning question: *Why?* You then set about to find out why, and in the course of your quest you may be distracted by a million other pieces of information that are eventually integrated into your journey. This means, of course, that your journey toward the why of the original question may not end in *this* lifetime! So you need a partner whose curiosity matches your own.

*Sagittarius, Aries*. Sadge is your opposite sign. He matches you in curiosity, but may not be up to snuff in other areas. With Aries, there's never a dull moment. She's a match for your quickness and wit, but may not have the curiosity you do about other people.

*Libra and Aquarius.* Usually compatible in that both signs value information and communication.

*Water signs.* Oddly, Pisces might be a good match because it's the only other sign represented by two of something, and his imagination will appeal to you.

## Cancer

In romance, it's always about feelings first—not the mind, not even the body, but *emotions.* Your partner has to be as dedicated to her inner world as you are to yours, so that your inner worlds can, well, *merge.* That's the ideal. Yet, because you're a cardinal sign, like Aries, Libra, and Capricorn, there's a certain independence in you that demands emotional space. Contradictory, but not to you.

Despite your emotional depth, you tend to avoid confrontations. Like the crab that symbolizes your sign, you retreat into your shell at the first sign of trouble. Yet, how can you smooth out anything in a relationship if you can't discuss disagreements? It's as if you expect disagreements to be ironed out telepathically. So if that's true, then your best matches romantically are probably other water signs. Let's take a deeper look.

*Pisces, Scorpio.* Both signs are as psychic as you are, but in different ways. Pisces is the softer of the two signs, dreamier. Scorpio might overwhelm you, but gives you the emotional space you need.

*Taurus.* A good match. This earth sign helps you to ground yourself in the real world and gives you emotional space—maybe more than you need!

*Capricorn, Virgo.* Cappy is your opposite sign, so the possibility of balance is there. Virgo might be too picky for your tastes, but shows you how to communicate verbally.

Air signs? Fire signs? Not so good, unless you have a moon, ascendant, Venus, or Mars in one of those signs.

## Leo

You've got enough passion for all the other signs in the zodiac—and then some. That passion is often linked to the attention of others, which probably explains why so many actors and actresses have a Leo sun, moon, or ascendant. Your life is about drama, and the higher the drama, the deeper your passion. But it's that passion that busts through obstacles, that burns a path toward where you want to go in both life and love.

Your compassion extends to anyone in a tough situation—or to any creature that needs love and reassurance that we humans aren't heartless. So, let's be real here. Your partner, whoever he or she is, probably has to love animals the way you do. Even if there are twenty strays in your back yard, your partner must be amenable to the idea that you feed the multitudes. Not an easy request, says the universe. But there are some strong possibilities.

*Sagittarius, Aries,* fellow fire signs. Sadge, symbolized by a creature that is half human and half horse, usually has animal companions—not pets, but *companions.* There's a big difference. She's your match in the compassion area. She understands your need to connect to an audience. But she may not stick around to be a part of that audience. The energy match with Aries is great. But unless you've got the moon, ascendant, or Venus in Aries, she may not shower you—or your animal companions—with enough attention.

*Gemini, Libra.* These two air signs could be excellent matches for you, Leo. You'll enjoy Gemini's lively intellect and Libra's artistic sensibilities.

## Virgo

You're the absolute master of details. You collect massive amounts of information, sift through it all with an eye for what works and what doesn't, and toss out everything that is extraneous. Your quest for perfection is never compromised, and it's evident in the inner work you do, honing your own psyche, and in everything you take on in the external world. These qualities can make a romantic partnership somewhat challenging because your partner goes under the same microscope that everything else does.

You're a layered individual and benefit from a partner who understands that and knows how to peel away those layers without making you feel vulnerable or exposed. A partner who enjoys every single one of those layers. So who's your best match?

*Taurus and Capricorn.* Fellow earth signs. Taurus takes all the time the relationship needs to peel away the layers of your personality so she can find the gold at your core. She's patient, resolute, determined. Capricorn might consider the relationship as just one more challenge to be conquered, but could be a nice balance to your penchant for details.

*Cancer, Scorpio.* These two water signs complement you. Cancer grasps who you are emotionally, but may not be as willing as you are to discuss elements of the relationship. Since your sign is ruled by Mercury, the planet of communication, that could be a drawback. Scorpio's emotional intensity could be overwhelming, but he'll be delighted to peel away the layers of your personality!

*Gemini.* Even though air and earth aren't usually compatible, Gemini and Virgo share Mercury as a ruler. Communication in this combination is likely to be strong and fluid, with a constant exchange of ideas.

## Libra

There's a certain duality in your psychological makeup that isn't mentioned very often. It's not due to a penchant for secrecy or deviousness, but to a reluctance to hurt anyone's feelings. As a result, you often find yourself paralyzed by indecision. *Who do I really love? A or B?* Since you don't want to hurt either person, you maintain both relationships and make yourself and everyone around you absolutely nuts.

You have a need for harmony and balance in relationships. You dislike confrontation and dissension, so all too often you surrender to your partner's wants at your own expense. So which signs are good matches for you?

*Gemini, Aquarius.* Fellow air signs understand your psychological makeup. Gemini experiences some of the same duality that you do, but for different reasons. He isn't bothered by dichotomies, since his own life is predicated on them. He appeals to that part of you who needs to communicate honestly. Aquarius may be a bit too rigid for you, insisting that you bend to his desires, but the depth and breadth of his vision attract you at a visceral level.

*Sagittarius, Leo, Aries.* Any of the fire signs could be an excellent match. Sagittarius never bores you and enjoys you for *who you are*. Leo may want more attention than you're willing to give, but her warmth and compassion will delight you. You and Aries, your opposite sign, balance each other.

*Taurus, Virgo, Capricorn.* Of the three earth signs, Taurus is probably the best match because you share Venus as a ruler. That means you have similar tastes in music and art and probably share some of the same attitudes and beliefs about money.

## Scorpio

As the most emotionally intense sign of the zodiac and one of the most psychic, your powerful and magnetic personality can intimidate even heads of state. Your life patterns are about breaking taboos, digging deeper, looking for the absolute bottom line in whatever you do, in any relationship in which you become involved. You feel and intuit your way through life, and your partner must understand that.

All of this brooding and mulling takes place in the privacy of your own head. The side you show others is light and funny, with a dry wit that can charm, seduce, or spar with the best of them. Yet inside you're always asking, *What motivates him? What secrets does he have?* Given the complexities of your personality, which signs are most compatible with yours?

*Pisces, Cancer.* Of these two water signs, Pisces matches you in raw intuitive ability, but may be too indecisive to suit you long term. Cancer can be just as secretive as you, but unless you've got a moon or rising in Cancer, this sign could be too clingy.

*Taurus, Virgo, Capricorn.* The earth signs are compatible matches. Taurus, your opposite sign, brings sensuality to your sexuality and helps to dispel your suspicions about other people's motives. Her earthiness grounds your psychic ability. Virgo's discerning and gentle nature mitigates your emotional intensity. Capricorn's determination appeals to that same quality in you.

Fire signs? *Leos* and Scorpios are both fixed signs, and there seems to be something between them that is powerful. Look at Leo Bill Clinton and Scorpio Hillary.

## Sagittarius

You're so multifaceted, with so many different talents, that a relationship presents certain dilemmas—namely, commitment to another person. It's so much easier to commit to, well, your own interests! Also, there's that little ole thing called personal freedom, which you value every bit as much as Aries.

Like Libra, there's a curious duality in your makeup,

best explained, perhaps, by the symbol for your sign—the mythological centaur. Half-horse, half-human, this figure might be defined as the wild woman (or man) versus the conformist. A part of you operates from gut instinct and the other part of you is acculturated. Which signs are your best matches?

*Aries, Leo, Sagittarius.* As remarked under the Aries section, a relationship with this sign may not go anywhere because you're both so independent. Aries might want to be in charge all the time, and you get fed up and hit the open road. Leo could be a terrific choice, particularly if one of you has a moon in the other's sun sign. Another Sadge would be intriguing.

*Taurus, Virgo, Capricorn.* Of these three earth signs, Capricorn is the best match. Even if she lacks your intuitive gifts, her focus, direction, and resolute determination equal yours. Taurus, your opposite sign, could also be a good match. You share a fascination with the paranormal, and your energies would balance each other.

Air signs? Water signs? Probably not, unless you have a moon, rising, or some other prominent planet in those signs.

## Capricorn

You build relationships in the same careful way that you build everything else in your life—a brick at a time. A conversation here, a dinner there, a movie, a moonlit walk, an exchange of beliefs: you're methodical, consistent, disciplined. Pretty soon, the foundation is solid, the chemistry is exactly right, and you know exactly what you want.

A relationship, of course, involves the human heart—not mortar and bricks—and that's where it may get tricky. You could discover that your methodical approach doesn't work as well in a relationship as it does with your career. Your success will depend, to a certain extent, on your compatibility with your partner.

*Taurus, Virgo, Capricorn.* Taurus's solidity and dependability appeal to you, and he's as private as you are. But his still waters run deep, and he may not express his emotions as readily as you would like. Yet the match would be a good one. Virgo understands what drives you. Another Capricorn, i.e., type A personality, would wear you out!

*Scorpio, Pisces.* While either of these water signs is compatible with your earth-sign sun, Pisces may too ambivalent for you, too indecisive. Scorpio, though, is a strong match. All that intensity appeals to you at a visceral level, your sex lives would be fantastic, and you share a similar determination. *Cancer*, your opposite sign, might work if the Cancer has a moon or rising in your sign.

Fire signs? Air signs? Again, it depends on the distribution of fire- and air-sign planets in your natal chart.

## Aquarius

In love and romance, as in life, your mind is your haven, your sanctuary, your sacred place. It's where everything begins for you. From your visionary, cutting-edge ideas to your humanitarian causes and interests in esoterica, you're a wild card, not easily pigeonholed. It doesn't make any difference to you whether your partner shares these interests, as long as he or she recognizes your right to pursue them.

There's a rebel in you that pushes against the status quo, and that's something your partner has to understand too. Your connections to people and to the world aren't easily grasped by others. Too weird, they think. Too out there. But that's fine. You understand who and what you are, and in the end, that's all you need. So, which signs are your best matches?

*Gemini, Libra.* Your air sign *compadres* are excellent matches. Gemini suits your prodigious intellect, causes, and ideas. Good communication usually is a hallmark of this relationship, and Gemini is supportive of your causes. With Libra, the focus is on relationships—yours and Libra's connection to five million others. But the right mix exists for a strong partnership. A relationship with another *Aquarius* could be challenging since you'll both insist you're right. But if you can move past that, you'll do fine. Another Aquarius may be like looking in the mirror 24/7. Not for the faint-hearted.

*Aries, Leo, Sagittarius.* With these fire signs, you enjoy the freedom to be your own person. Life with Aries is never boring and the conversation and adventures are stimulating, but he may not share your humanitarian and esoteric interests. Sagittarius loves your mind and insights, your idealism and rebellion against the establishment. Great compatibility overall. Leo is your opposite sign, suggesting a good balance between your head and his heart.

Earth or water signs? Only if you have prominent planets in either of those elements.

## Pisces

It's true that your inner world is often more real and genuine to you than anything in the external world. The richness of your imagination, the breadth of your intuition . . . these qualities create a kind of seductive atmosphere that's tough to move beyond. But because you're a physical being, in a physical world, who has to eat and sleep, work and function, who loves and triumphs and yearns, you have to move beyond it. So you do.

But always there's an inner tension, a kind of bewilderment, a constant questioning. *Where am I going? What am I doing? Do I really want to do this or that?* Your head and your heart are forever at odds, so no wonder your sign is symbolized by two fish moving in opposite directions. In romance and love, this indecisiveness can be problematic. So which signs are most compatible for you?

*Scorpio, Cancer.* Scorpio's emotional intensity could overwhelm you, but he balances your indecisiveness with his unwavering commitment to a particular path. Intuitively, you're on the same page, a major plus. Cancer's innate gentleness appeals to you, and she appreciates you exactly as you are.

*Taurus, Capricorn.* These two earth signs appeal to you at a visceral level. Taurus's solid, grounded personality comforts that part of you that is so often torn between one direction and another. Her sensuality is also a major plus. Capricorn's singular vision and direction are a mystery to you, but there's much to learn from her. *Virgo*, your opposite sign, can bring balance.

Fire signs probably won't work for you unless you have a moon or rising in a fire sign. Of the air signs, *Gemini* is probably the most compatible for you. Since you're both symbolized by two of something—two fish, the twins—he understands your dichotomies.

## CHAPTER 4

# Your Career Choices in 2012

Despite how things may look in the job market, despite the grim statistics about the economy, the housing market, the banks, the plunging dollar, and all the rest of the depressing news that flows into our lives 24/7, many people flourish in economically difficult times. In fact, if you've been laid off from your job, the first thing you can do to turn things around is to look at it as an opportunity. The more positive and upbeat your attitude, the more frequently you view every challenge as an opportunity, the greater the chances that you'll turn things around.

Several years ago friends of ours, a married couple who are both writers, had pretty much hit rock bottom. The wife admitted that she was ready to start cleaning pools just to have a steady income. Then practically overnight everything turned around. Her husband sold a novel that became a popular cable TV show, a producer commissioned her to write a script, and suddenly their bank account fattened, they bought a second home, a new car and a boat, and the world opened up for them. It can open up for you, too.

We create our realities from the inside out. Everything you see around you is a manifestation of a belief that you hold. Some of our beliefs have been passed down to us by well-meaning family members, mentors, teachers, or friends, and we adopt those beliefs because we respect the people who handed them to us. But what do *you* believe about your abilities and talents and your ability to earn your living doing what you love? How do you handle stress? Change?

In 2012, when so much of the world seems to be shifting beneath our feet, we have a chance to delve into those beliefs and get rid of the ones we have adopted out of convenience. We can either go with the flow, change with the times, or we can offer up resistance. The more we resist, the more pain we experience. The more we go with the flow, the greater our capacity to discover where we should be. Which path will you take?

## Inventory

One way to prosper professionally during good *and* bad times is to know what you want. So let's take an inventory.

1. Describe your dream job/profession

______________________________________________

______________________________________________

______________________________________________

2. Lay out a strategy for finding/attaining this dream job/profession. Do you need more education, time, additional skills? If so, include those things, and set a goal for attaining them.

______________________________________________

______________________________________________

______________________________________________

3. Set realistic professional goals. Choose a time frame—a month, six months, a year—whatever feels right to you. Ask yourself what you would like to be doing a year from now. Describe it in detail. Make it real!

4. What kind of inner work can you do to make these goals a reality more quickly? Visualization? Take workshops or seminars? Develop your intuition? Describe in detail.

5. What are your greatest strengths? Describe them. Then focus on the strengths you have—not your weaknesses.

## Using Synchronicity in 2012

The Swiss psychologist Carl Jung coined the term. It means: the coming together of inner and outer events in a way that can't be explained by cause and effect and that is meaningful to the observer. Or, it's a meaningful coincidence. When it happens to you, don't dismiss it as a random curiosity. A synchronicity can be a navigational tool, a confirmation, warning, or guidance.

For Frank Morgan, an actor who played five different parts in *The Wizard of Oz*, a stunning synchronicity served as confirmation that he was on the right professional track by accepting parts in the movie.

One of the parts he played was the disreputable Professor Marvel. For that role, the director and wardrobe man wanted him dressed in a "nice-looking coat, but tattered," said Mary Mayer, a unit publicist on the film. So they traipsed down to a second-hand clothing store and purchased a rack of coats. Then Frank, the director, and the wardrobe guy all got together and selected one of the coats.

Imagine his surprise when he turned the pocket of the coat inside out and found a name sewn into the lining of the coat: L. Frank Baum, the author of *The Wizard of Oz*. The additional synchronicity here is that both men who wore the coat were named Frank.

In times of stress or major transitions—marriage, divorce, birth, a move, career change or change in employment and income—synchronicities may occur more frequently. Decipher the message if you can, and know that synchronicities indicate we're in the flow, exactly where we're supposed to be.

## Your Career Path in 2012

Regardless of what you do for a living, whether you love or detest it or merely tolcrate it, you can maximize your strengths and talents to enhance your professional opportunities.

### Aries

As a cardinal fire sign, your entire life is about movement, action, doing. You're the pioneer, the entrepreneur, the one who really does march to the beat of a different drummer. Your pioneering spirit is your most valuable asset for navigating any professional changes you encounter this year.

There is no such thing as a challenge for you. You simply rise to the occasion and banish the challenge. You also refuse to recognize defeat. What someone else might see as a setback, you view as an opportunity. In 2011, you learned to follow your passions, wherever they led, and in 2012 that faith starts paying off. Whenever a negative thought enters your mind, change it immediately to something upbeat and positive. Follow the methods that feel right to you.

## Taurus

Your senses are so finely tuned that you hear the music of the spheres, poetry flows through your dreams, you have the heart and soul of a mystic. You're the most enduring, taciturn, and physical of the twelve signs. You always finish what you start unless it's just unbearable! In 2011, you learned that your resolute determination is your greatest asset for navigating professional changes. In 2012, you learn to trust your intuition.

Until June 11 this year, Jupiter remains in your sign, a positive and lucky transit that you should take advantage of. Jupiter expands whatever it touches, and every twelve years it touches your sun. You're in the right place at the right time with this transit, so take full advantage of it. Don't shy away from new opportunities that broaden your life.

You already know your own value. In 2012, everyone around you learns it as well, and you keep moving forward and never look back.

## Gemini

You're the communicator, your mind buzzing constantly with information that you eagerly share with others.

Some people say you never shut up, that you talk just to fill the silence. Not true. Beneath your chatter lies an insatiable curiosity.

Your ability to multitask and your curiosity are your greatest assets for navigating any professional changes this year. In fact, in 2011 you learned to follow the impulses of your curiosity to see where they might lead, and they led some mighty strange places. But you were in the right place, at the right time. In 2012, your versatility and communication abilities enable you to navigate the paradigm shift that's underway.

## Cancer

You're completely attuned to emotions—yours and everyone else's. It's easy for you to slip into someone else's skin and feel what they feel. You hurt as they hurt. You weep as they weep. You laugh as they laugh. Like fellow water sign Pisces, you're a psychic sponge, an empath. Your extraordinary memory is intimately linked to your emotions, and your intuition is remarkable. All of these traits helped you to successfully navigate the transitions of 2011. During the first six months of 2012, when Jupiter is in compatible earth sign Taurus, your hard work last year really begins to pay off. You meet people who not only share your interests, but who are helpful in some way professionally. Your professional options expand. Perhaps you launch a business, write a novel, have a photography exhibit. One way or another, you begin to achieve your dreams, Taurus.

Embrace whatever change comes your way, and trust that the universe works for your highest good.

## Leo

You were born to express your creativity through performance. You love the applause, the recognition, the immediate gratification and feedback. Of course, not every

Leo is an actor or actress, but every Leo loves drama. So whether you're on the stage, in front of a classroom, or counseling a patient in therapy, your creative flair moves through you like a force of nature. In 2011, you learned how valuable this asset was in helping you to navigate any professional changes you experienced.

Now, in 2012, especially from June 11, 2012, to late June 2013, you're well positioned for seeing your dreams unfold. Jupiter will be in compatible air sign Gemini, and things should expand explosively for you. Join groups, engage your friends, and offer zero resistance to whatever comes your way.

## Virgo

Your gift is details. Whether it's your own life that you're honing, sculpting, and shining like some fine gem, or a particular project or relationship, you can see the finished product in a way that others can't. You also have a particular gift or ability that you're always willing to provide to others, without thought of compensation. These traits carried you through professional changes you may have experienced in 2011.

The first six months of 2012, when Jupiter is in fellow earth sign Taurus, should be fantastic for you, regardless of any doom and gloom around you. Your worldview expands, you may have a chance to travel overseas, perhaps even a publishing opportunity presents itself. It's all preparation for Jupiter's transit through Gemini and your career sector from June 11, 2012, to late June 2013. Now *that* period, Virgo, is going to blow your mind. So prepare yourself for a wild, wonderful career ride.

## Libra

You can work a room like a seasoned politician, spreading peace and harmony even among people who can't agree on anything. That's your magic. Yet the very qualities that you can instill in others often elude you. Not that any of us could tell by looking at you. Libra is a master of social camouflage. It seems that nothing ruffles you. But within, you're struggling to maintain harmony without compromising your principles. Your sphere is relationships. More than any other sign, you can see the many sides of an issue and understand that your truth may not be everyone's truth. But you can live with the paradox. It's your gift.

Any professional challenges you encountered in 2011 were undoubtedly overcome by your ability to connect with people. You're in for a real treat from June 11, 2012, to late June 2013, when expansive Jupiter transits fellow air sign Gemini. During this period, your professional opportunities should abound, taking you into new areas and new creative venues and bringing opportunities for foreign travel.

## Scorpio

You're the emotional vortex of the zodiac, a spinning whirlwind of contradictions. You aren't like the rest of us, and that's the way you prefer it. You dig deeply into everything you do, looking for the absolute bottom line, the most fundamental truth, and then you excavate everything at the discovery site just to make sure you've gotten it all.

Professional challenges that you encountered last year were met with the fortitude and resilience for which you're known. In 2012, your best bet is to team up with a professional or romantic partner and launch a business or some other endeavor you've always wanted to try. The best time for this is from January 1 to June 11, when expansive Jupiter is in Taurus, your solar seventh house. Your intuition will be spot on during this period. Listen to it.

## Sagittarius

You're the life of the party, just like your fellow fire sign Leo. But your approaches are different. Where Leo seeks recognition and applause, you're after the big picture, and it doesn't matter how far you have to travel to find it, how many people you have to talk to, how many books or blogs you must read. When your passion is seized, you're as doggedly relentless as Taurus. One part of you operates from raw instinct; the other part of you is acculturated, aware of how to work the system.

In 2011, the year of transition, you realized that you don't recognize professional challenges. You learned that any bump in a road simply means you take an alternate path to get to where you want to go. Between June 11, 2012, and late June 2013, expansive Jupiter will be in Gemini, in your solar seventh house. To maximize this beautiful transit—and to get the most out of it professionally—team up with a partner, romantic or professional, and try some entrepreneurial venture that suits your soul, Sadge.

## Capricorn

You're the achiever, the builder, the classic type A personality whose focus is so tight that everything and everyone becomes part of your journey toward . . . well, the top of the hill, the pinnacle of whatever you're attempting to reach. You can build anything, anywhere. A fictional world, a belief system, an invention, a concept, a family, a video world. Name it, and you can build it.

Any professional challenges you encountered in 2011 were undoubtedly tackled the same way that you have tackled any other challenge in your life—by finding a way around it. Or through it. As a cardinal earth sign, you value what is tangible, practical, efficient, and your journey through any obstacle reflects it. In 2011, you learned how not to fear, and that got you through every professional challenge you encountered. In 2012, particularly until June 11, when Jupiter is in fellow earth sign Taurus, your muse is so up close and personal that your creativity soars. Use it to navigate the shifting sands in your world.

## Aquarius

You're not easy to pigeonhole. Sometimes you seem to be the paragon of independence. Yet you enjoy the company of groups who share your passions. You're the one who thinks so far outside the box that people close to you may accuse you of communication with aliens, ghosts, goblins, elves. Even if it's true, you just laugh and continue on your journey into the strange, the unknown, on into the heart of the universe.

Any challenges you encountered professionally in 2011 were no major thing for you. You always managed to work your way around the challenge by continuing to explore what interests you. Between June 11, 2012, and late June 2013, Jupiter transits fellow air sign Gemini and your solar fifth house. This should be a huge bonus for you, Aquarius. Your creativity becomes your most valued asset for navigating the paradigm shift. And regardless of how out of the box your professional ideas are this year, you come through it all in great shape.

## Pisces

Dreamer, healer, mystic: all these adjectives fit you, Pisces. You live within a rich, inner world that is both a buffer and a conduit to deeper experiences. You don't need anyone else to tell you this. At some level you already know it, appreciate it, embrace it. While it's true that you're a sucker for a sob story, an attribute that can turn you from hero to martyr in the space of a single breath, there's no concrete evidence that you're more of a victim than any other sun sign.

Any professional challenges that came your way during 2011 were met with your powerful intuition, your prodigious imagination, and your unique way of dealing with adversity through faith in your role in the larger scheme of things. The tentacles of your psychic abilities were active 24/7, at your disposal, and awaited your instructions. In 2012, especially until June 11 when Jupiter transits compatible earth sign Taurus, your communication abilities shine. Everything that swirls through your head, in your imagination, can be expressed in ways that others understand. Professionally, this talent alone puts you well ahead of the pack.

CHAPTER 5

# Family Stuff

Our birth family is like a mini world. It's with them that we develop psychologically, emotionally, spiritually and intellectually. It's with them that we develop our defenses, needs, expectations, belief systems. They encourage certain behaviors and discourage others. We learn to rebel or conform or just fit in. Family, then, is where it all begins, which is probably why many books and movies deal with dysfunctional or eccentric families.

The paragon of dysfunctional families is probably the Corleones, in the *Godfather* movies. So much drama, violence, and emotion. The emotion is equally intense in *My Big Fat Greek Wedding*, where a young Greek woman falls in love with a non-Greek man. She tries to convince her family to accept him while she struggles to come to terms with her cultural identity. And it's all couched in comedy.

Jeanette Walls, in her memoir, *The Glass Castle,* recalls her bizarre childhood with an alcoholic father and a mother who abhorred domesticity. Jeanette and her siblings gradually made their way to New York. Their parents followed them but chose to be homeless.

*Brokeback Mountain,* based on a short story by Annie Proulx, is about a forbidden passion between two cowboys in the early sixties and how their love for each other impacts their families.

# Your Family

Take a look at your own family. What are the dynamics? Does everyone get along? Are there certain issues that surface time and again? If you have siblings, do they each seem to have different roles in the family? One might be the rebel, for instance, and the other might be the intellectual. What about your parents, partner, and your own kids? If you're an only child, what is your relationship with your parents like?

Families often have commonalities in their respective charts that illustrate the deep connections among them. The parents might have opposing signs, like Taurus/Scorpio, Gemini/Sagittarius, so there's a kind of balance. Then one child might have a moon in Sadge, and the other child has a Gemini sun. There's an infinite number of combinations, and some aren't as obvious as sun or moon signs. But for the purpose of this chapter, let's keep things simple.

# Your Style as a Parent

## Aries

Your parenting style isn't like anyone else's, that's for sure. Man or woman, you encourage independence in your children from a very young age. You're no control freak. Or, if you are, then it may be due to the sign of your moon. You may be one of those parents who keeps close tabs on your child's growth progress: *7 months, crawling; 9 months, utters first word; age 2, a puzzle prodigy!* Any rules you lay down are in the name of safety rather than an attempt to control your child's every move and decision.

Some Aries wing it as parents. They don't have a clue, really, about what they're doing, so they fine-tune their parenting style at every stage of their child's growth. But even for you, Aries, there are certain constants that probably won't change. In addition to the emphasis on independence, you have a finely honed sense of privacy and probably won't violate your child's unless you have a reasonable suspicion that you should. That's more likely to happen during the turbulent teen years. You give your child plenty of freedom to make his own choices. However, when you do offer guidance or advice, you may blurt it out, which could create some major tension if your child is an adult.

An *Aries mom* can be brash, funny, exciting, unpredictable. Kids enjoy her company because everything with her is an adventure. But she can be fiercely protective—that's the ram who symbolizes her sign—ready to defend her child's turf at the slightest provocation. She isn't nurturing in the traditional sense of the word, i.e., you won't find her slaving over a hot stove preparing the evening meals. She's more likely to have a pizza delivered. But when her child's in need, she's there in a flash.

When an *Aries dad* hangs out with the kids, there's an air of impatience, brashness, restlessness, a kind of *let's get this show on the road!* If he encourages his child to take risks—in sports, love, life—it's because he himself is so fearless. He's terrific at organizing activities, but they happen on the fly. *In ten minutes, we're going on a picnic,* he announces, and then everyone scrambles around grabbing stuff they need. He usually has great pride in and passion for his kids.

In 2012, with Uranus in your sign all year (until March 2019, actually), there may be sudden, unexpected events that impact your parenting style. If you've fallen into a personal rut (unlikely for an Aries, but it does happen now and then), then Uranus whips into your life, turns everything upside down, shakes out what is no longer needed or useful. Your temperament may be erratic, you may be more impatient than usual, your blood pressure could soar at the slightest provocation. Best advice? Sign up for yoga classes with your kids. Meditate with them. Hike with them. Engage them.

## Taurus

Your parenting style reflects your stability, determination, and patience. You enjoy your children immensely and strive to nurture their talents, strengths, and gifts. You try to create a beautiful home environment, a place in which everyone delights, where your kids feel comfortable bringing their friends. HOME. In caps.

You probably enjoy music, art, books, movies, and politics, and these interests are reflected in your environment—and are passed on to your kids through a kind of osmosis. So don't be surprised when your son or daughter cranks up the music so loudly it threatens to shatter crystal or when the weekly allowance is blown at the local bookstore!

Since you're the most stubborn sign in the zodiac, that stubbornness certainly surfaces in your parenting. Your child says *yes*. You shake your head *no.* The child keeps saying yes, yes, his voice growing louder and louder until your patience snaps, and the legendary bull's rush seizes you. *No,* you shout, and slam your door. End of story, end of argument, end of struggle.

Since Venus rules your sign, though, your bull's rush usually passes quickly and peace and tranquillity are restored. But you still refuse to change your mind!

A *Taurus mom* is loyal and dedicated to her role as a mother. It won't be her *only* role, but she's likely to consider it her most important role. She's in the line for school drop-offs in the morning, in that same line for pickup in the afternoon. In between she's in court, defending someone like you or me, or she's writing the great American novel, or teaching English to recalcitrant seventh-graders. Or she's selling real estate or jewelry or scooping the next big political story.

The *Taurus dad* works hard and patiently at whatever he does. He finishes everything he starts—and that includes the projects his kids begin for their science classes! He, like his female counterpart, is usually health conscious and watches his diet, exercises regularly, and takes good care of himself. Part of this could be vanity, but whatever it is, his kids pick up on it and sometimes take up the same sports in which dad indulges.

In 2012, Uranus in Aries is transiting your solar twelfth house, that place in your chart that is most hidden and secretive. With Uranus here until 2019, your inner world is shaken up, elements of your unconscious surface abruptly and inexplicably. It's as if you're confronted with psychological archetypes in yourself that you haven't seen before. This kind of turmoil certainly will affect your family and kids—*if* you let it. The bottom line here is that Taurus rarely shows anyone the face of that inner world. The best way to navigate whatever stuff is surfacing is to deal with it and move on.

## Gemini

Ideas and communication. That's what you're about, and it's evident in your parenting style. From the time your child is very young, you read to her, talk to her, encourage her to express herself verbally. You buy her puzzles, coloring books, picture books, anything that expands her knowledge and creativity. Your fascination with information and relationships is found in the way you encourage her to reach out to other people, to make friends, to invite them to her house. Don't be surprised, then, if by the time your child is a teen, she has several thousand friends on Facebook!

You're a voracious reader, and it's likely that your home has hundreds—if not thousands—of books. This love of reading is something you pass on to your child, and by the time she's preparing for college, her facility with language and ideas is a major plus. It's said that a typical Gemini is actually two people—the twins are the symbol for your sign—so you're comfortable with duality. This can be confusing to a young child, particularly if you vacillate about what's allowed and what isn't.

With Mercury ruling your sign, any connections between the Mercury in your chart and the sun, moon, rising, or Mercury in your child's chart portend strong communication.

A *Gemini mom* is the supreme multitasker. She can simultaneously pack school lunches, talk on the phone, and be writing a novel in her head. At times she may appear scattered to her kids, but then she suddenly comes out with a zinger of logic or insight that stops them in their tracks. Glances are exchanged, eyebrows shoot up. She's a fount of information and eagerly passes on what she knows to her kids—and their friends and the friends of their friends. If anything, when her kids are with their friends, she must learn to back off and give them space.

A *Gemini dad* is quick, witty, enigmatic. Just when his kids think they've got him figured out, he does or says something that makes him impossible to peg. His intellect is as finely honed as a Gemini woman's, but takes him in different directions. He might be an avid sports fan, for example, a master at chess, a general aviation pilot, or an animal lover. His interests and passions are passed on to his kids.

One thing is certain: a home with at least one Gemini parent in it is never boring!

In 2012, you have several fantastic things going for you astrologically that are sure to bolster your parenting style. First, Uranus in Aries is transiting your solar eleventh house, so you're going to be more involved with friends and groups that support your parenting style. These groups will be kid friendly, too, so it's not as if you have to find a sitter or drop the kids at someone else's place. These group associations may begin and end suddenly, but that's fine with you. They bring an excitement and unpredictability that suit you.

The second transit is fantastic—Jupiter moving

through your sign from June 11, 2012, to late June 2013. This transit enhances all the Gemini qualities of your parenting style—emphasis on communication, books, writing, travel. It will be a period your kids remember as pure fun and enjoyment.

## Cancer

You're the nurturer of the zodiac, the one who needs roots, a home, a place or state of mind and spirit that you can call your own. You're a gentle, kind person who takes everything to heart—and this is certainly reflected in your parenting style. Through your example, your kids learn to respect all forms of life, to never hurt others, to treat them as he would like to be treated.

You can be overprotective, for sure, and before your child hits his teens, you'll have to come to grips with how to handle those feelings. Emotionally, you rarely reveal yourself. Like the crab that represents your sign, you tend to move sideways, skirting unpleasant issues, anxious to avoid confrontation, reluctant to discuss the heart of the matter. Your exceptional intuition keeps you in tune with your children, alerting you when they're in danger or happy. You forgive easily, but rarely forget. So if one of your kids hurts your feelings, you'll remember it thirty years from now.

A *Cancer mom* is the prototypical nurturer—always there for her kids, supportive of their wishes and dreams. Yes, if she cooks, you'll find her whipping up delectable dishes that include everyone's favorite foods, whatever they are. Her home is her palace—but it could be the cabin of a boat, a tent in the wilderness, an RV. No matter where she is, she tends to the creature comforts of her family. As a parent, she has rules, but they're emotionally based, just like everything else in her life, so they won't change unless the emotions behind them change first.

A *Cancer dad,* like his female counterpart, is kind,

affectionate, and nurturing, but only to a point. When he feels his personal space is being violated in any way, he backs off, scurries into his crab's shell, and retreats quickly. For a child, he's hard to figure out. Sometimes he's the hero of the child's latest adventure story; other times he's the wet blanket at the party. If he's into metaphysics and alternative healing, then chances are he's in deep, and his kids will pick up on this interest and explore on their own.

In 2012, the period from the beginning of the year to June 11 should be wonderful for you and your kids. You get involved with new groups, your friends become more integral to your life, and in some way, shape, or form you begin to realize your dreams. Your children and family are part of the process. The other transit to watch is Neptune's through Pisces, which begins on February 3 and continues for the next fourteen years. This one brings an emphasis on spirituality and intuitive development that you pass on to your kids. You and your family may travel internationally, but it won't be strictly for pleasure. You'll be on a spiritual quest of some kind. Stonehenge? An ashram in India? Crop circles?

## Leo

You love being the center of attention, often surround yourself with admirers, and the world is your stage. But that's just the beginning of your story! You strive to succeed—to shine—at everything you do and to make an impact in every situation. Your personal magnetism draws admirers who are willing to help your cause, whatever it is. You prefer to hang with people whose beliefs are similar to your own, but can get along with just about everyone—as long as no one steals your thunder. Your kindness, generosity, and compassion are nearly legendary.

As a parent, you love unconditionally and fiercely. You tend to instill certain qualities into your children—optimism, loyalty, integrity, honor. When they're toddlers, you enjoy their company and watching them progress to each stage, from crib to crawling to kindergarten. Once they're off to school, particularly by the time they reach middle school and then high school, you may feel marginalized in some way. You really shouldn't. You've got enough interests and passions to fill your next five lives, and your ambitions keep propelling you forward. Generally, you delight in seeing your children fly off into the world, doing what they love.

The *Leo mom* is usually up front about everything—what she feels, why, and for how long. She's definitely disappointed when her kids aren't as forthright, but she gets over it! She likes being at the helm—at home, at work, while traveling—and can be a bit bossy at times. *You and you, do this and that.* Her kids quickly learn to either fall in line or stand up to her. Mom enjoys nice clothes and probably dresses with a flair and style all her own. She's clever at creating impressions and moods through the way she looks and acts (it's the actress in her), but her kids undoubtedly learn to see through it to the gem beneath.

The *Leo dad* is easy to get along with as long as you keep a couple of rules in mind. Never tell *him* what to do, and let him have center stage. If both of your parents are Leos, then the one thing you can count on in your household is plenty of drama! The Leo dad is fun, outgoing, and full of magic. He snaps his fingers and things happen. He has great leadership ability (and not just as a dad), and his energy and frankness endear him to children of any age.

In 2012, two transits will affect your parenting style. Uranus, the planet of sudden, unexpected change, is transiting fellow fire sign Aries, in your solar ninth house. This suggests that your belief system, your worldview, your spiritual beliefs are undergoing radical change. It will be an exciting, unpredictable time, and the whirlwind of events will sweep you and your kids and partner up into a vortex of unpredictable adventures.

The second transit, Jupiter's through Gemini, goes from June 11, 2012, to late June 2013, and emphasizes foreign travel, friends, mental stimulation. Suddenly everything in your life expands, you feel lucky, like you're in the right time and place, and this expansiveness is passed on to your kids.

## Virgo

Your mind is lightning quick, just like Gemini's, and you're so mentally dexterous and agile that the competition can't keep pace with you. Due to your attention to detail, to the discerning turn of your intellect, you tend to delve more deeply into subjects than Gemini, and when you gather information it usually has a purpose. You pass this ability on to your children, and it serves you well as a parent, i.e., not much escapes your notice. Your kids will never be able to put anything over on you! Since you're Mercury ruled, like Gemini, you need sufficient outlets for all your mental energy.

You're an attentive parent who does all the expected things—for school, health, your child's happiness—but who may not play by the book. In other words, you probably won't raise your children the way you were raised. If you were brought up in a religious household, for instance, your child won't be. If your parents stressed school over fun, you may do the opposite. If your parents were inordinately strict, you won't be. It's not that you have the heart of a rebel (although you might!) but that your finely honed intellect connects all the dots, and you grasp what's needed for your children to evolve and to achieve their full potential.

The *Virgo mom* is vibrant, upbeat, conscientious, loving. Even though she never *tries* to project a particular image, others sense something different about her, perhaps her softness, her caring. Deep down, she can be a worry wart, fretting about the smallest details, the inconsistencies in life, in her kids, her family. It's part of her insecurity. When she's in that mode, she can be critical—of her kids, her husband, herself. But she can be cajoled out of that mood by lively discussions about ideas, books, travel, any kind of information that seizes her passions. She's generous with her kids and strives to enrich their world through her own wisdom.

The *Virgo dad* is as intellectually curious as his female counterpart. He's a hard worker, detail oriented, with a biting humor that is rarely malicious. He may take his role as dad a bit too seriously at times, but his kids quickly learn how to loosen him up, how to make him laugh. He's an attentive father, the kind who reads to his kids at night, who listens to their dramas and woes as teens, who applauds loudly when they graduate from college. Always with him—and with the Virgo mom—there is tremendous pride in his children, as if he can't quite believe his extreme good fortune.

In 2012, the first six months of the year will be magnificent for you as a parent, for your kids, your family generally. Jupiter will be transiting fellow earth sign Taurus, your solar ninth house. This transit promises international traveling, dealings with publishers and educators, perhaps even living abroad for a while. The living abroad may last longer than the transit because for a year—from June 11, 2012, to late June 2013—Jupiter will be moving through Gemini and your career area. This transit suggests that one possible manifestation is working abroad, and you'll take your loved ones with you.

## Libra

You're one of the gentlest souls in the zodiac, usually soft spoken and treading lightly in all matters. You're also deeply romantic about your family and kids. They're your beacons. You love beauty in every shape and form, and when there's no obvious beauty, you find it in what you can imagine. You're an excellent strategist, a natural diplomat, and you often mitigate chaos and drama, dissension and disagreement. Sometimes you assume these roles to your own detriment, just to keep the peace.

As a parent, this tendency to keep the peace at your own expense could be thankless. So strive not to be a martyr, okay? Strive not to bend over backward to please . . . well, everyone. Once you can do that, your natural artistic tendencies take over in your parenting. You nurture your children's passions and interests, their gifts and talents as they emerge. You're tuned in to who they are on a soul level and understand how to help them bring that soul into their conscious awareness. Your love of art, music, literature, and every other creative talent is passed on to your kids. Your grasp of the complexities of relationships is translated into language they speak. Facebook, Myspace, and every other social networking group become their community. In short, you usher your children into the finer beauties of the twenty-first century.

The *Libra mom* creates a domestic environment in which her children flourish. But she also has her career, friends, passions, and interests that get mixed up in this collective soup called life and which, in turn, affect her kids. She brings in music, art, gardens, books, and people. Lots of interesting people. She creates moods and atmospheres and invites her children to participate. The lessons they learn, the insights they carry away from these encounters influence them for life. There's no pinning down the Libra mom. Just when you think you've got her figured out, she surprises you. Boring? Never. Not a chance.

The *Libra dad* loves having a team—wife, kids, friends of kids, neighbors, even stray animals, it doesn't matter. Everyone and everything is part of this team. Membership is open. He's an excellent organizer, supportive of his children's endeavors and dreams. But his high ideals can be problematic once his kids are adults, making choices that don't measure up—in his mind—to those ideals. Like the Libra mom, he rarely loses his temper.

Between June 11, 2012, and late June 2013, Jupiter will be transiting fellow air sign Gemini, in your solar ninth house. This transit will lead to an expansion in your educational opportunities, worldview, even in foreign travel. Until October, Saturn will be in your sign. The combination of these two transits should have positive benefits for you as a parent, your family, and kids. Even if you run into restrictions and delays in your personal life or experience sudden events related to your daily work, you come through this period with a stronger grasp of what it means to be a parent.

## Scorpio

You're intense, passionate, and strong willed. You often try to impose your will on others, a trait that may serve your children when they're young, but can prove to be problematic as they get older. Like Aries, you're fearless, but you possess an endurance that Aries lacks and can plow your way through virtually any obstacle, any challenge. This trait serves as an example to your children to never give up in their pursuit of what they want.

Your passions are such that you're never *indifferent*. You live in a world of either/or, approval or disapproval, agreement or disagreement, right or wrong. While this trait drives home the importance of values and purpose, it can be challenging for children whose lives are more nuanced. Your ability to dig deeply for the bottom-line answers indicates that you will usually know what's going on in your children's lives.

The *Scorpio mom* places a high value on honesty. It's the foundation of who she is. So it's no surprise that she expects honesty from her children. Even though she herself is secretive, she won't tolerate secrets from her child. She respects their privacy, certainly, but if she suspects something is going on that needs parental intervention, she investigates until she uncovers the truth. She is a loving, devoted mother who is very protective of her kids. At times she may be too protective and strive to shield them from the outside world.

The *Scorpio dad* is as intense as the Scorpio mom. Unless he has a moon or rising in an air or fire sign, he may be just as much of a control freak too. He often has a magnificent talent or interest that he pursues because he's passionate about it and not because he expects to make money at it. He's a nurturing parent, particularly when it comes to his children's talents and abilities and the educational training that helps them navigate life successfully.

In 2012, your role as a parent may shift in unexpected directions. Due to Uranus's transit through fire sign Aries, your work situation may be somewhat erratic at times—or, at the least, unpredictable. This may actually give you more time to spend with your kids, or you may decide to launch a home-based business or to enter a field that gives you more control over your time. With your ruler, Pluto, in compatible earth sign Capricorn until 2024, you're in the power seat when it comes to communication, Scorpio, so start talking to your kids about everything that interests you.

## Sagittarius

You're a wild card. There's a part of you who is always looking for the larger picture, the broader perspective, another part who believes you're always right, and yet another part who focuses on the future and the larger family of humanity. You can be very logical, but there's also a mystical element in your psyche that enables you to glimpse the future.

You dislike having your freedom restricted in any way, so you probably don't have a roll call of rules and regulations for your children. You're a loving parent, but expect your kids to find their own way, their own path.

Yet when they make mistakes, you may offer advice that makes you sound like a know-it-all. Your versatility and natural optimism are hallmarks of your parenting style.

The *Sagittarius mom* thinks big. When she suggests a family outing, it isn't just a trip to the next town for a picnic. It's a trip across country or to some far-flung corner of the world, and who cares if it's beyond the family budget? She wears many hats and excels in everything she does as long as she doesn't feel confined, limited, penned in. Her independent spirit radiates from her every pore, and her kids quickly learn to honor it. She offers her children broad guidelines and her own wisdom, but doesn't force her opinions on them.

The *Sagittarius dad* has a broad, sweeping vision about life, love, and the universe. He talks about it freely with his kids, never holding back. He is loving and devoted to his children, but because he expects big things from them may not be satisfied with what they achieve. He enjoys foreign travel and, given his financial situation, exposes his children to foreign places whenever he can. This man is always moving and has dozens of projects going on simultaneously, and his children learn early on that goals are attained through action.

In 2012, Uranus will be moving through Aries and the children area of your chart (which also governs creativity, romance, and enjoyment). This transit will bring about sudden, unexpected events—exciting, unpredictable events—concerning your kids. You'll have to think more outside the box to keep pace with them, but with your vivid imagination and ability to see the broader picture, it'll be a piece of cake for you.

## Capricorn

You're the worker bee of the zodiac, industrious, disciplined, efficient, focused. You dislike inertia in others, so it's likely that your children aren't couch potatoes! You probably get them involved in sports when they're young and nurture whatever athletic abilities they have. They learn their work ethic from you and develop common sense, a trait they witness constantly in you.

Even when you were a kid, you had a mature air about you, and as you get older, that maturity is a kind of calm presence, a rock-solid dependability that your children come to expect. Never mind that you're a worrier, that even when you've prepared long and hard and have all the bases covered, you're certain you've forgotten something. Your kids rarely see that side of you. You love them unconditionally—that's what they see.

The *Capricorn mom* always seems to know what she's doing, when, with whom, and what route she's going to take to get there. She appears to be self-confident, certain about who she is, tough as nails. But as her children come to know her as a person separate from her role as mother, they discover she's not tough at all. She simply runs her home and family life as though it's a business and she's the CEO. Even if she has a career—and many Capricorn women do—she's totally devoted to her kids. She might be a little rigid with rules and regulations, but if so, learns that such excessive control results in outright rebellion.

The *Capricorn dad* is as diligent a worker as the Capricorn mom. He's got work ethic written all over him. He prides himself on being well prepared for just about anything, including being a parent. He either has the answers or will find them—for himself, for his children, or their friends. He excels at problem-solving. He can be dictatorial and bossy, but if his kids call him on it, he backs off. For a while, anyway. He's as completely devoted to his kids as he is to his career goals. In fact, one mirrors the other.

In 2012, the period from January 1 to June 11 should be spectacular for you and your kids. Expansive Jupiter is transiting fellow earth sign Taurus then, and everything you and your kids engage in together turns to gold. The Midas touch, Capricorn. In addition, Uranus's transit through Aries and your solar fourth house brings surprising, unexpected events into your home life. A move, perhaps? The birth of another child? Once Jupiter enters Gemini on June 11, where it will be until late June 2013, your daily work schedule will expand and change, and it may be a bit tougher to accommodate your kids. Make time.

## Aquarius

You're such an original thinker, a visionary, that of course you apply these talents to parenting. Your household is really atypical. You might live on a boat, in a commune, in the suburbs, in an RV, or hey, maybe even on the space station. Your family structure isn't business as usual, either. But you aren't interested in typical. Everything you do is *different* from the status quo. You think in unique ways, way outside the box, and rarely if ever trust what authority tells you to believe. This ability to think and perceive in new ways is passed on to your children.

Your interests are vastly varied, and any causes in which you get involved are discussed with and communicated to your children. They learn early in life that mom or dad's interests and causes don't have to become theirs, but deserve respect. There probably aren't many rules in your family. Individuality is honored, encouraged, and thrives.

The *Aquarius mom* is a complete paradox. She's a peace-loving rebel who moves against the tide of the status quo, yet conforms when it suits her. She has the patience of a saint—until she doesn't—and can be more stubborn than Taurus unless it suits her purpose to bend with the wind. If her children are as eccentric as she is, then they have learned the value of individuality and probably share mom's love of freedom as well. Mom allows her kids the freedom to make their own decisions, revels in their achievements, and never lets them down.

The *Aquarius dad* considers his family—partner, kids, animals and orphans of all sizes and shapes—to be his sanctuary. Even if he seems undemonstrative and emotionally remote at times, his love for his kids runs deep. He takes every opportunity to expose them to everything that interests him, from ancient sites like Stonehenge and the Nazca lines to books on what the future may look like in a century. If he's a movie buff, his children are exposed to movies at a young age. If he's a traveler, his kids will be well traveled. He's terrific at sharing his knowledge, expertise, and curiosity.

From June 11 to late June 2013, you're in for a treat as a parent. You'll be watching your children's lives expand in unprecedented ways. Whether they're toddlers or adults, you'll delight in what they're learning about themselves and their world. With Uranus transiting compatible fire sign Aries, your communication skills will be sharp, and your conscious mind will be innovative.

## Pisces

Your wonderful imagination and remarkable intuition prove valuable in your parenting style. Your imagination enables you to enter the world of your children with ease and playful joy. Your intuition enables you to stay attuned to their emotions even if they don't discuss what they're feeling. Pisces individuals with highly developed gifts—psychics—may have to take a break now and then from parenting just to find their own centers. It's too easy for this type to be overwhelmed with what their kids are feeling.

At times you fluctuate between rigid left-brain logic and that softer intuitive certainty that you're doing the right thing. Try not to set down rules and restrictions when you're feeling like this. Moodiness and ambivalence can cause you to backtrack from your own rules. Guard against being a sucker for a sob story.

The *Pisces mom* often has a strong psychic connection to her children. If they have been together in past lives, chances are she has a grasp on which lives and how everyone's respective roles played out then. She's able to understand what they're feeling even when they're clueless. She is rarely dogmatic with her children, and any household rules she lays down are probably for the sake of safety—and her own peace of mind. Her love for her kids is bottomless. They're her greatest joy, and she just keeps on giving and giving.

The *Pisces dad* is a great listener. His self-containment, gentleness, quiet strength, and the full attention he gives his kids are enviable qualities that enable him to forge tight bonds with his offspring. He encourages and supports his children's artistic interests and may have artistic or musical talent himself. Like his female counterpart, he must learn to balance the demands of his inner life with his responsibilities in the outer world.

2012 should bring some surprises in how you parent and how you view your children. With Neptune in your sign from February 3 onward, your whole parenting approach may become more spiritual, creative, imaginative. Your own intuition is enhanced too during this fourteen-year transit, so you'll be in closer communication with your kids on an unspoken level, able to grasp their personal issues and concerns in a deeper way.

## Kids of the Zodiac

Now that we've looked at adults and their parenting styles, let's explore the kids of the zodiac.

### Aries

She's the kid who is off by herself, exploring fields and meadows for unusual bugs. Or she's the fearless teen who leaps into a rushing river to rescue a kitten stranded on a rock. Or on the family camping trip where the matches and lighter fluid have been left behind, she's the one who makes a fire by rubbing sticks together or using a magnifying glass to amplify the sunlight. Inventive, independent, entrepreneurial: welcome to the world of the Aries child. And whether she's a toddler or an adult, high drama and action swirl around her.

## Taurus

He's the loner. Or he has a small group of friends with whom he hangs out. But whether it's his friends or his family, no one really knows him. Like an iceberg, nine tenths of his personality is hidden. He only shows what he wants you to know. Yes, these still waters run deep. So much goes on inside his head as he figures out where he belongs in the scheme of things that he wouldn't have a clue where to begin verbalizing any of it. So he nurtures his creative gifts, enjoys the sensual pleasures of physical existence, and moves forward at his own pace, patient, certain that the answers will come to him, from somewhere, when he needs them.

## Gemini

If Taurus is the loner, she's the social butterfly, flitting from one person to another, one event to the next, and along the way she's passing on what she has learned, what she suspects, what she believes. She's impatient, quick, dexterous. Her life is propelled by a single burning question: *why?* Everything she does, every connection she makes, everyone she knows and loves serves to answer that question. Somehow. In some way. Forget trying to pigeonhole your Gemini child. It just won't happen. When she's young, provide her with an environment where she can learn and explore at her own pace. Nurture her self-confidence and her belief in herself. With those tools, she's well equipped for her journey out into the larger world.

## Cancer

She's a tough one to figure out. She feels her way through life, but you may never know about it. She'll talk if she's in the mood, but otherwise nothing and no one will prod her into an explanation about her feelings. As a parent, you sort of have to divine your way through this kid's childhood and beyond. She needs roots. She needs to feel she's an integral part of the family and is appreciated. Much of her life as an adult is based on her childhood memories—the smells and sights and emotions she was feeling at a particular time. If her childhood is happy and secure, then she grows into a happy, secure adult.

## Leo

The Leo child is like his own tribe. From the time he's very young, he has dozens of friends and they all hang out at his place. Even as he gets older, his friends are eager to spend time with him, and some of them are orphans and strays attracted by his innate generosity and compassion. Like fellow fire sign Aries, the Leo child is basically fearless. He accepts every dare and takes risks that would leave other kids gasping in awe. Most Leo kids enjoy the company of animals, and their homes tend to have a lot of pets.

## Virgo

She's impatient, wants everything yesterday, and is graced with abundant energy. She has questions about everything and is so eager to learn that in the right environment, she explores until she drops from exhaustion. Like Cancer, she can be moody, but these swings usually occur when she doesn't understand something. Her restless mind gnaws away at the puzzle, dissecting it, scrutinizing the details, the minutiae, until she gets it. She has enormous compassion, a quality that is evident at a very young age, and her ability to connect with people is as easy for her as connecting disparate bits of information is for a Gemini. Even when young, Virgo kids show discernment. They may be picky about what they eat, read, or watch on TV.

## Libra

The Libra child can be found listening to music in the comfort of his own room, connecting with friends on Facebook and MySpace, or hanging out with friends in some familiar and pretty spot. He isn't the type to play touch football (unless he's got a lot of fire or earth in his chart) or hunt for bugs under rocks or dissect frogs in the lab. As a youngster, the Libra child may have an imaginary playmate or one special friend in whom he confides. He's loyal to his friends, sometimes to a fault, so any friends he has as a youngster are probably going to be friends for life.

## Scorpio

She's distinctive in some way—physically, mentally, intuitively. She has fixed opinions even as a youngster, as if she came into life with a particular agenda or belief system. She feels deeply, of course, one of the trademarks of this sign, and the intensity of her emotions may lead to sudden outbursts if her feelings are hurt or she doesn't get what she wants. She flourishes in an environment that is varied and rich, where she can explore her creative abilities. She won't always be forthright about what's going on inside of her, but if you simply come out and ask her, her response may surprise you. She's wiser than her years.

## Sagittarius

This kid is Mr. Popularity, and it's evident from the time he's old enough to crawl and interact. He's vivacious and optimistic and makes other people feel good about themselves. It makes him a people magnet. He can be opinionated, though, and blunt. He doesn't think about what he's going to say before he says it. He just blurts it out, a tendency that can be disconcerting to people who aren't accustomed to it. But he needs the freedom to express himself and to know it's okay to defend what he believes. Rules and structure are a good idea as he's growing up. He probably has a fondness for animals, not surprising for a sign symbolized by a figure that is half human, half horse!

## Capricorn

From the time she utters her first word, she's as comfortable being and conversing with adults as she is with her peers. Sometimes she has a seriousness about her that is usually evident in her eyes, in the way she watches and appraises you, sizing you up for who knows what reason. Other times, she can be as wild and playful as any other child. Even then, though, her organizational skills are evident, and she can be bossy, no question about it. She is infinitely patient, intent on achieving her goal, whatever it might be.

## Aquarius

To this kid, all people truly are equal, so his friends span the racial and socio-economic spectrum. He's an extrovert, eager to know what makes other people tick, what motivates them, but he's also perfectly happy when he's by himself. His mind is as busy as a Gemini's, but in a much different way. Where a Gemini child collects trivia and information, the Aquarian child is immersed in the stuff of the universe. Although he enjoys people and gets involved in all sorts of groups, he's not a follower and will always defend not only his opinions, but his right to have those opinions.

## Pisces

She doesn't need many rules. She's so sensitive to her environment and to the people who inhabit it that a cross look from mom or dad keeps her in line. She's a dreamer, this one, whose imagination soars through time and space with the ease of a bird through sunlight. If her intuitive gifts are allowed to develop, this child can become a genuine medium, clairvoyant, mystic, healer. Her strong creative drive manifests itself early.

CHAPTER 6

# Your Finances in 2012

## Beliefs

Money and relationships are probably the trickiest areas for most of us to navigate successfully. But if we create our realities from the inside out, then in these two areas it's vitally important that we understand our beliefs.

Let's take a closer look. Here are some commonly held negative beliefs about money and relationships. Do you hold any of these?

- Money is the root of all evil
- My relationships never turn out
- Money is nonspiritual
- True love is rare
- The rich have major problems in their lives
- Marriage is a joke
- Money corrupts
- I'm not worthy of (fill in the blank)
- If you have too much money, you have to worry about losing it

You get the idea here. Many of these beliefs we've adopted from family and peers and have held on to them because they're comfortable, we believe they're true, or because we don't even realize we believe them!

So if you're not satisfied with what you're earning, start monitoring how you think about money. Any time you find yourself thinking a negative thought about money, turn the thought around by thinking something more positive. Also, read *Money and the Law of Attraction* by Esther and Jerry Hicks and *You Can Heal Your Life* by Louise Hay.

Now let's take a look at how you can maximize your earning potential in 2012.

## Jupiter

From chapter 2, we know that Jupiter represents luck, expansion, success, prosperity, growth, creativity, spiritual interests, higher education, and the law. It also governs publishing, overseas travel, and foreign countries and any of our dealings with them. But for the purpose of this chapter, we're going to focus on Jupiter's impact on our money for 2012.

This year, Jupiter transits two signs. From January 1 to June 11, it's moving through earth sign Taurus. From June 11, 2012, to June 25, 2013, it's moving through air sign Gemini. It will be retrograde in Gemini between October 14, 2012, and January 30, 2013. A Jupiter retrograde simply means that planet isn't functioning at full capacity.

Let's see how these two Jupiter transits this year impact your sun sign.

# Jupiter in 2012 and Its Impact on Your Sun Sign

## Aries

Jupiter's transit of Taurus, through your solar second house, began in early June 2011, and initially you may have been spending more money than usual. But as the transit stabilized, your income is likely to have expanded in some way. That trend will continue this year, until June 11.

Your second house doesn't just govern your income, but also your values, personal debt, giving and receiving, jewelry, possessions (particularly those that are valuable), reverses in finances, your earning and spending capacity. And with Jupiter in this house, in stable, dependable Taurus, you may be looking for long-term stable investments that will increase your profit and minimize your risk.

If you dislike your job, i.e., the way you earn your daily bread, then Jupiter should bring plenty of new options and opportunities for expansion. You may decide to return to school to update your skills and knowledge, may decide to go to college or graduate school, or may expand your earning possibilities to overseas markets. Since Jupiter governs publishing, law, and higher education, any of these areas are possibilities for increasing your earning capacity.

Once Jupiter enters Gemini for a year-long transit, you'll feel more comfortable because Gemini is compatible with your fire-sign sun. In fact, this transit should be terrific for you, expanding all the areas governed by the third house and Gemini: communication, your conscious mind, daily activities, siblings, short-distance travel. You may write that book you've had in your head for years, build a Web site, start a blog. More frequent travel could be part of your daily activities—car pools, a longer commute. However this transit manifests for you, Jupiter brings luck and expansion, and you, ever innovative, turn it into a potential cash cow.

## Taurus

In early June of 2011, Jupiter entered your sign, Taurus, and suddenly life took on a whole new dimension. The trend of expansion and luck that started with that transit continues until June 11 of this year. Whenever Jupiter transits your sign, the ramifications are big—you're in the right place at the right time, luck is your new best friend, your options and opportunities broaden.

Sometimes when Jupiter initially enters your sign, it seems that more money is going out than is coming in. But eventually your net worth rises, you land the dream job, your investments begin to pay off. You tend to be conservative with money, but if there's something you really want, don't hesitate to buy it if you can pay cash for it. You want to avoid credit-card debt during this transit and the one coming up between June 11, 2011, and June 25, 2013. Conserve your resources, but don't be stingy and don't do it out of fear.

When Jupiter enters Gemini on June 11, you're in for another treat. It will be transiting your solar second house of money, so it's likely that your earning capacity will rise, your values will broaden, your opportunities for self-improvement will increase. Jupiter's transits are nearly always fortunate, but there's a risk with excess in some area. When you see a sharp increase in your income, follow your parents' advice—sock some of it away. But again, don't do it out of fear. Any action taken from a basis of fear is likely to attract circumstances that will cause real fear.

## Gemini

During Jupiter's transit of Taurus between January 1 and June 11, your unconscious is easier for you to delve into. Dream work, meditation, yoga, or some other kind of mind/body activity benefits you. In fact, you may discover that your dreams hold important information that will help you with issues or concerns that you have. Ideas come to you through dreams and meditations. Consider a past-life regression with a qualified therapist. Everything you learn during this transit is creative fodder, Gemini, and is preparing the way for Jupiter's transit through your sign between June 11, 2012, and June 25, 2013.

Jupiter transits your sign just once every twelve years. So look back to 2000 for hints about what sorts of experiences you may have during this year-long transit. What were your finances like that year? Did you land a new job that paid more? Did you move into a better neighborhood, a larger house? Did you take unnecessary financial risks? All of these areas are possibilities this year.

One thing you definitely want to avoid during this transit is gambling or speculating with your money. Because Jupiter can be excessive, you may feel cocky, as if you can do no wrong. It's smarter to save and to invest in things that further your education, skills, and future.

## Cancer

Since last June, Jupiter has been moving through Taurus and your solar eleventh house, a transit that continues until June 11 of this year. This brings an expansion to your social contacts, your wishes and dreams, and opportunities to promote and publicize your work or product or that of your company. Since this transit forms a beautiful angle to your sun sign, other areas of your life will benefit as well, and one of them is your finances.

You might decide, for example, to join an investment group that shares ideas about which stocks or bonds to buy. Or you and a group of friends may invest in rental property or even buy a place together, fix it up, and then sell it for a handsome profit. Any dealing with real estate and homes is a nonbrainer for you, Cancer. It's what you enjoy doing.

Between June 11, 2012, and June 25, 2013, Jupiter will transit Gemini, through your solar twelfth house. It makes it easier for you to delve into your own unconscious, to recall your dreams. If you don't meditate yet, then this transit presents the opportunity to do so. You may discover moneymaking ideas through meditations and dream recall. You may start a blog or build a Web site and find an innovative technique for making money in this way. Use this transit to find out who you are, Cancer. Self-knowledge can lead to a greater understanding about how the universe works, and such knowledge can lead to greater financial stability and more money.

## Leo

Jupiter entered Taurus and your career area in June 2011 and won't leave it until June 11, 2012. That gives you six months this year to enjoy the professional expansion—and thus, the financial expansion—of this transit. The last time Jupiter touched this area of your chart was twelve years ago, so look back to 2000 for clues about how the last six months of this transit may unfold for you.

If you would like to change jobs or careers, then it could happen during this transit. Equally possible? Your responsibilities, job description, and salary increase substantially, you launch your own business, sell a book, work overseas. Regardless of the specifics, you will have plenty of opportunities to do what you do best, Leo—shine!

Between June 11, 2012, and June 25, 2013, Jupiter transits compatible air sign Gemini and your solar eleventh house. This transit not only stimulates your social life, but brings you into a whole new sphere of individuals who help you to attain your dreams, whatever they may be. Any groups you join may also prove to be helpful financially.

With Jupiter in Gemini, your communication skills—which aren't too shabby to begin with!—really sharpen. Your mind becomes a steel trap, and you're able to snap out facts, figures, statistics that astound even you. You learn to make money using your ability to communicate and connect with others.

## Virgo

When Jupiter entered fellow earth sign Taurus last June, your income probably increased, and that trend will continue until June 11 of this year. It's possible that your work or a quest of some sort takes you overseas, and whatever you learn and experience changes your fundamental beliefs about money. You may suddenly realize, for example, that you're worthy of being rich. Or that your book is just as good as anything on the market and will find the right publisher. In other words, your inner world is shifting, becoming more certain, stronger. As that happens, your life in the outer world will change accordingly.

If you're a writer, this transit expands your publishing opportunities, could bring about significant foreign sales, and makes it easier, generally, to sell what you write. Regardless of what profession you're in, your business could expand to overseas markets. Other possibilities: you head off to college or graduate school, go to law school, or even move overseas.

Once Jupiter enters Gemini and the career area of your chart, you're in for an exciting time. The specifics of this transit vary for each of us, but here are some possibilities: you switch jobs/careers and land something with a larger salary; you work overseas; you sell your novel or screenplay. One way or another, the professional and financial payoff for you is excellent.

## Libra

With Jupiter in Taurus until June 11, you and/or your partner may be accruing items like art and jewelry for investments, could delve more deeply into esoteric subjects like ghosts, past lives, communication with the dead, or may combine your resources in some way. Whatever it is, it pays off financially. Let's say that you and your partner have separate homes, then during this transit you may decide to sell one place and move in together. This transit should bring breaks with mortgages, loans, taxes, and insurance.

When Jupiter transits fellow air sign Gemini between June 11, 2012, and June 25, 2013, you have a wonderful opportunity to explore your worldview and spiritual beliefs and to divest yourself of any that are holding you back from achieving your financial goals. The exploration may come through opportunities for foreign travel, to write a book on whatever seizes your passions, or to even go to graduate school to further your skills.

## Scorpio

With Jupiter transiting Taurus, your opposite sign, for six months this year, you and your partner may launch a business together, or you may find a business partner for a venture you've had in mind. By combining talents and resources, your income increases, your self-confidence benefits, and you discover that in order to live the way you want, it's important to do what you love.

Air signs aren't compatible with your water-sign sun. However, there's much to learn from this transit—namely, never hesitate to communicate what you believe and why. Don't hide your wisdom; share it with others. On a mundane level, this transit may increase your partner's income, and the two of you may find investments with large payoffs. Your joint finances benefit tremendously.

The trick with this transit is to share—not just money, but resources, time, energy. If you do that, if you go with Jupiter's flow, you'll benefit greatly from everything this planet has to offer.

## Sagittarius

Since Jupiter started transiting Taurus in June 2011, your daily work schedule has been exploding like crazy. So much to do, so little time, but yes, you're having fun! Expect that trend to continue until June 11 of this year. If you work out of your home, then it's possible you add a room onto the house or expand your home to accommodate your office. If you work a regular job, then your schedule keeps growing by leaps and bounds until you feel as if you're all over the place. But it suits you. If you own your own business, then you may add more employees or expand your product/services to overseas markets.

Between June 11, 2012, and June 25, 2013, Jupiter transits Gemini, your opposite sign. This transit augurs well for any joint business venture—with your romantic partner or a business partner or both! By pooling talents and resources, anything done in partnership can pay off handsomely. If you're reading this and thinking that you don't have a partner—either romantic or business—don't fret about it. Chances are good that before this transit ends, you'll have both!

## Capricorn

Since June 2011, you've been enjoying Jupiter's transit through fellow earth sign Taurus, in your solar fifth house. It is expanding all your creative ventures, your muse is undoubtedly in attendance 24/7, and some days the ideas flow so fast you forget them before you can find a pen or get to your computer to write them down. This trend continues until June 11. So enjoy it while it lasts, and have faith that your creativity is going to increase your bank account!

Jupiter's transit through Gemini and your solar sixth house lasts from June 11, 2012, to June 25, 2013. Buckle up for the wild ride, Capricorn. This transit should expand your daily work routine and schedule to the point where it's bursting at the proverbial seams. You'll have to be more organized than usual during this transit, but the potential benefits in terms of income can be great. With greater responsibility comes a salary boost. With a salary boost comes greater security for you. Even more important, though, is that with this expansion you can build stronger professional goals.

## Aquarius

Jupiter has been transiting Taurus and your solar fourth house since June of 2011 and will be there until June 11 of this year. This transit should expand everything to do with your home, family, and the fundamentals of your life. A birth is a possibility. Or you may move into a larger home or expand the home where you currently live. One of your parents may move in with you. Since the fourth house also governs real estate, it's possible that you buy property as an investment.

Between June 11, 2012, and June 25, 2013, Jupiter transits fellow air sign Gemini in the creativity sector of your chart. It's your ticket, Aquarius. The more creative you are, the greater your earning capacity. You may get involved in a creative venture with one of your kids or a new romantic interest, and because it's done from a basis of pure joy, it has a positive effect on your finances.

## Pisces

Since June 2011, Jupiter in Taurus, an earth sign compatible with your water-sign sun, has been transiting your solar third house, and it continues this year until June 11. During this period, your communication skills sharpen your conscious mind expands. You suddenly understand how to make money from, well, talking and writing. A blog, your Web site, magazine articles, a book: any of these venues is possible. The Taurus part of the equation helps to ground your imagination, to bring your ideas into the practical daily world.

From June 11, 2012, to June 25, 2013, Jupiter transits your solar fourth house and Gemini. This transit brings luck and expansion to your home life. In terms of finances, you may start working out of your home, doing something you love, and the money follows. Or perhaps you move to a different city or area where your opportunities for employment are better, where your family is happier, where conditions are more conducive to an increase in your income. Since Jupiter is coruler of your sun sign, its transits are nearly always significant for you in some way.

CHAPTER 7

# The Structures in Our Lives

Saturn takes two and a half years to go through a sign, so its effects tend to unfold more slowly than those of the moon, which changes signs about every two and a half days. This planet governs the rules and parameters of physical life and represents responsibility, structure, discipline, limitations and delays, obedience, authority, the building of foundations. So by its transit we are confronted, challenged, or helped by Saturn, depending on the angle it makes to our sun signs.

With Saturn occupying two signs this year, the end of Libra and the beginning of Scorpio (which lasts until December 2014), we're all called upon this year to meet our obligations and responsibilities in two different areas. So let's take a closer look at how Saturn's transits in 2012 impact your sun sign.

## Aries

Saturn has been opposite your sun sign since October 2009 and finally leaves Libra on October 5 of this year. During this transit, you're learning to structure your personal and professional partnerships and are deepening your understanding of team work and cooperative living. This last part may not be an easy lesson for a spirit as independent as yours, but learn you will. Chances are that your partner—business or romantic—may have met with some restrictions or delays during this transit that have in turn impacted you in some way.

The Saturn opposition to your sun can be a discouraging time—if you let it. You may feel drained physically, so it's important to have a regular exercise routine. It's also important to maintain contact with friends, family, and other people you love. Try not to resist things that are happening to you. Learn to go with the flow.

Once Saturn enters Scorpio, you feel a distinct relief. A weight has been lifted. During this transit, which lasts until December 2014, you'll learn how to accept other people's values, even when those values aren't in line with your own. It may be more difficult to obtain mortgages and loans during this transit, or sources of income you have depended on may dry up. So it's important that you become as self-sufficient as possible before this transit begins.

## Taurus

During Saturn's transit through Libra and your solar sixth house, your daily work responsibility has undoubtedly increased. You may be working longer hours, too, but if you're doing something you love and are getting paid more for your efforts, then it certainly isn't a burden. Due to other demands on your time, you're probably learning how to maximize the time you have and are becoming more organized about your daily work schedule. If you're self-employed, then organization and good time use are vital tools.

Once Saturn enters Scorpio and your solar seventh house, you may be dealing with some of the same issues that Aries dealt with during Saturn's transit through Libra. If you allow this transit—an opposition to your sun—to discourage you, if you resist change, then the transit becomes much more difficult. The important lessons with this transit are about learning to cooperate with partners—business and romantic—and to allow relationships that no longer work to fall out of your experience.

## Gemini

Saturn's transit through fellow air sign Libra should be quite productive for you, Gemini. Saturn is now forming a harmonious angle with your sun, strengthening your assets, enabling you to find the proper structures for your creative projects, relationships, your life! This transit may bring professional recognition of some kind and a solid boost in your career and creative output. During this transit, it's smart to establish and/or maintain an exercise routine. Although your health should be fine during this transit, you're building up stamina for times when you may have more stress in your life—like during the Saturn opposition to your sun. This transit also helps you to build solid relationships with your children and to find grounded venues of enjoyment.

Once Saturn enters Scorpio and your solar sixth house, your daily work schedule may have to be revamped. More responsibility will bring a greater need for organization and efficient use of your time. If you're self-employed, Saturn in Scorpio will prompt you to always look at the absolute bottom line—costs in terms of money, time, energy, and resources. Be sure to tend to your health during this transit too. Keep exercising and eating responsibly, and stay away from fad diets.

## Cancer

As Saturn transits Libra and your solar fourth house, you're learning to balance responsibilities of home and career. This requires you to be more organized and use your time more efficiently. You may have to cubbyhole your life, with an emphasis on family on certain days and an emphasis on career/work on other days. You tend to go with the flow more than other signs, so it's important that you keep doing that. Any time you feel yourself resisting something that's happening, try to understand why and correct it. If you don't know why you feel resistance, then simply reach for a better thought and feeling.

Once Saturn enters fellow water sign Scorpio and forms a beneficial angle to your sun, you're a much happier camper. This transit helps you to solidify all creative projects. Instead of just writing screenplays, for instance, you begin selling what you write. You discover great depth in your own creativity, your relationship with your children, in romance, and in what you do for fun and enjoyment. Maintain an exercise program during this transit, so that when Saturn enters Sagittarius in late December 2014, your physical strength is at a peak.

## Leo

Saturn in Libra forms a beneficial angle to your sun, so you're benefiting from this transit. Your communication skills find a proper venue for expression. A book? Blog? Web site? Radio or TV? Whatever it is, you dazzle with your language skills and win accolades from friends, family, peers. If you move during this transit, the place has to be exactly right for you—and your family. Preferably, it should be in the thick of things—theater, restaurants, bookstores. During this transit, you're enormously productive too and enjoy the work.

Once Saturn enters Scorpio and your fourth house, Saturn is opposed to your career area. This transit indicates that you'll have to learn how to reasonably balance your home and work responsibilities. You'll be aware of the absolute bottom line too, in just about everything—with your family, kids, parents, your family's budget. Your intuition should deepen appreciably, and it will be wise to follow any hunches you have.

## Virgo

During Saturn's transit through Libra and your solar second house, your financial earnings may be restricted in some way. Or you find the proper structure for your finances through investments, for example, or a pension plan. You may feel that your values are somehow holding you back, preventing you from doing something or going somewhere. The truth is that you're the only one holding you back. During this transit, you're supposed to learn how to conserve your financial resources and to live within a budget.

When Saturn enters compatible water sign Scorpio on October 5, your relief will be palpable. During this transit, with Saturn forming a beneficial angle to your sun, you'll be in a very good position to bolster your communication skills, find a neighborhood that fits your specific criteria, return to school to enhance your skills. Your conscious mind will be able to take abstract ideas and turn them into practical tools. This transit lasts until December 2014.

## Libra

Whenever Saturn conjuncts or opposes your sun sign, it's considered to be a major transit—challenging, but filled with potential. During this transit, you divest yourself of relationships and situations that no longer work or which aren't in your best interest. You may change jobs, get divorced or married, or have to provide support for one of your parents. There can be delays, or your freedom is restricted in some way, but the purpose is to slow down your life so that you tend to what is personal and immediate.

Sometimes Saturn conjunct your sun brings about external events that turn your life in a different direction. The more resistance you offer, the more difficult it is. So it's important to learn to go with the flow.

With Saturn's transit through Scorpio and your solar second house from October 5, 2012, to late December 2014, you learn how to conserve your financial resources, how to budget, how to save. If there's a decrease in your earnings during this transit, try not to fret about it. Your intuition should increase. It's the small voice whispering in the back of your mind to go here, do that, try this. Follow its guidance.

## Scorpio

During Saturn's transit through Libra and your solar twelfth house, you're being asked to funnel your discoveries about your own psyche and unconscious into some sort of structure. This transit would be a great time to go through therapy, to take up yoga or some other mind/body discipline, and to start meditating, if you don't already. The twelfth house governs not only the personal unconscious, but past lives, institutions, and everything that is hidden. So with Saturn here, you may run into people you have known in previous lives, will have greater access to your dreams and information that comes to you through meditation, and may have contact with institutions like hospitals and nursing homes, even prisons. This doesn't mean *you* will be institutionalized, but that someone you know may be.

Once Saturn enters your sign, you may feel that your freedom of movement is restricted in some way. It could be due to increased responsibility in some area of your life—career, family, work, no telling. The last time Saturn conjuncted your sun was about twenty-nine to thirty years ago. If you're old enough, look back to that time and remember what was going on in your life. Big changes? How? In what areas? One thing you'll have to do is divest yourself of relationships and situations that aren't in your best interest. You may change jobs, move, get married or divorced. Regardless of the specifics, offer no resistance to events. Go with the flow.

## Sagittarius

Saturn's transit through Libra forms a beneficial angle to your sun. It brings structure and solidity to your friendships and wishes and dreams. It actually should be easier to attain your dreams during this transit, particularly if you have laid the groundwork and met your obligations and responsibilities to others. If you don't attain your dreams during this transit, then before it ends you'll have a clearer grasp of what you need to clear out of your life to make room for the attainment of these dreams. Saturn's transit through Scorpio and your solar twelfth house should give you the opportunity to do that.

Saturn transits Scorpio from October 5, 2012, to late December 2014. During this period, you benefit from therapy, meditation, yoga, or any other mind/body discipline. Your dreams can be a source of information and insights. Since the twelfth house represents institutions—prisons, hospitals, nursing homes—it's possible that you have more contact than usual with these places. Basically, this transit enables you to clear your life of what no longer works—relationships, situations, belief systems.

## Capricorn

Saturn's transit through Libra and your career area is a major transit that could solidify your professional life and bring recognition from peers and bosses. You may assume more responsibility during this period and work longer hours, and there could be some delays or restrictions on your freedom to come and go as you please. Hard work has never bothered you, especially if you're compensated fairly for it. If you're self-employed, then this transit enables you to solidify your business, client base and income.

During Saturn's transit through compatible water sign

Scorpio and your solar eleventh house, you'll be more in your element. Your friendships and any groups to which you belong will be helpful in achieving your dreams and goals. It's important that you learn how to work with groups and to grasp what group dynamics are in a work situation.

## Aquarius

During Saturn's transit through fellow air sign Libra and your solar ninth house, you benefit in a major way. This transit solidifies your worldview and spiritual beliefs and enables you to find the right structure for expressing these beliefs. The ninth house also governs higher education, overseas travel, and foreign cultures, countries, and people, so any foreign travel you do will be structured in some way to fit your goals or needs. If you're in a business that sells products overseas, this transit helps to create a good foundation in overseas markets.

Saturn's transit through Scorpio and your solar tenth house brings increased responsibility in your career, longer hours, perhaps recognition by peers and bosses. It could bring about a promotion, or you may decide to launch your own business. If it's the latter, you're going to love the freedom even if it means a lot of hard work and long hours.

## Pisces

During Saturn's transit through Libra and your solar eighth house, your access to funds that have been available previously may be restricted or denied you. If you apply for a mortgage or loan, for example, it may be difficult obtaining it. Your partner's income may take a hit. With Saturn here, you're urged to conserve your resources—money, time, energy. This transit helps you to channel your enormous imagination and intuitive ability.

During Saturn's transit through fellow water sign Scorpio and your solar ninth house, you'll benefit from a positive angle that Saturn makes to your sun. This transit should enable you to explore your worldview and spiritual beliefs in a structured way. You may, for instance, travel overseas to various sacred sites on some sort of spiritual quest. Or you may take courses or workshops in metaphysical areas to explore your intuition or alternative healing methods. This transit lasts from October 5, 2012, to late December 2014.

## Saturn in Your Birth Chart

Wherever Saturn appears in your birth chart indicates an area where you will learn lessons in this lifetime. It also indicates life issues you may have brought in from previous lives. Saturn's lessons can be harsh, but it teaches us through experience what we need in order to grow and evolve and what our souls intend to accomplish in this life. It shows us our limitations, teaches us the rules of the game. Without it, our lives would be chaos. Individuals with well-aspected Saturns in their birth charts—the angles other planets make to it—have a practical outlook. With a poorly aspect Saturn, growth may be restricted or limited in some way, and the person's outlook could be rigid.

The sign that Saturn occupies shows how we handle obstacles in our lives, deal with authority, and cope with serious issues. The house placement in your natal chart indicates the area of your life that's affected. If you have Saturn in your tenth house, for example, then your career ambition is one of the driving forces in your life, and you'll work tirelessly to succeed. If your Saturn is in Leo, you may need to learn that it isn't all about just *you* and your career.

Every twenty-eight to thirty years, we experience a Saturn return, when transiting Saturn returns to the place it occupied at our birth. The first return, around the age of twenty-nine, brings major life transitions—we get married or divorced, start a family, move, begin a career. The second return, between the ages of fifty-eight and sixty, is considered to be the harvest. We experience major events—retirement, our kids have left home, we downsize, move, inherit money.

Whenever a Saturn transit hits a natal planet, that period should be navigated carefully, with understanding of what's required of you. Saturn takes about twenty-nine years to circle the zodiac. It entered Libra in late October 2009, retrograded from January 13 to May 29, 2010, then entered Libra again on July 22, 2010, and will be there until October 5, 2012. Then it enters Scorpio for a run of about two and a half years.

## Natal Saturn in Aries

Your impetuosity and rashness need to be tempered somewhat, so that you think before you act. You consistently encounter circumstances that force you to develop patience and initiative. If you push against these circumstances, then setbacks occur. With Saturn, you can't take shortcuts. This position of Saturn urges you to develop resourcefulness and discipline and to complete what you start. Once you learn these lessons, you're capable of innovative and unique creations.

The downside with this placement is that you're prone to defensiveness and a kind of self-centered attitude that puts people off. Tact and diplomacy will take you farther and, in the end, may be one of the lessons you're here to learn.

## Natal Saturn in Taurus

One of your lessons in this lifetime is to develop persistence and resoluteness, an unshakeable belief in yourself and your talents. This belief helps you to win material security and comfort through hard work, discipline, and perseverance. You may not be the fastest-moving person in the world, but you hang in there long after the competition has bitten the dust.

It behooves you to learn how to handle money and your finances. You tend to be frugal even when you don't have to be, but this frugality may become one of your hobbies. You might, for example, hit garage sales, flea markets, any spot where secondhand goods are sold, and could develop a business around it. On the other hand, if this frugality turns to miserliness, you may want to rethink your attitudes and beliefs about money. The downside is a preoccupation with materialism.

## Natal Saturn in Gemini

Since Saturn corules air sign Aquarius and is exalted in air sign Libra, it's pretty comfortable in air sign Gemini. It brings discipline and structure to your mental process and suggests that part of what you're here to learn is how to think through problems logically, working them out in detail so that your solutions are practical. Saturn here may restrict a free flowing expression of ideas, but once you've learned to channel your ideas in a pragmatic way, perhaps through writing or some sort of group activity, you reap the benefits. In other words, it's not enough to have a great idea. How can the idea be put into practice to benefit not only you, but others?

Communication is important to you, but it has to be organized, structured in some way, honest, and dependable. That may be one of the lessons you're here to learn. Downside? If you don't do the grunt work this placement demands, your obstacles multiply.

## Natal Saturn in Cancer

This placement may restrict your intuitive gifts and your emotions. Or it could provide the proper structure for expressing both. It depends on how you use your conscious desires and intent to create your life. It depends, too, on your deepest beliefs. Do you believe we have free will or that life is somehow scripted, destined? Are events random, or do they rise from some hidden quantum order? While your crablike tenacity helps you to navigate successfully through obstacles, Saturn here urges you to confront obstacles head on, to reveal what's in your heart, and to channel your intuitive talents in a practical, focused way.

Your home and family are important to you. But strive not to impose so many restrictions in this area that the people who are closest to you—and you yourself—feel suffocated.

## Natal Saturn in Leo

This placement is all about power and recognition. The desire for both, however, takes many forms. At one extreme, it results in a need to control your environment and everyone inside of it and a hungry ambition that blinds you to everything else. At the other extreme, this placement results in structures that help you to channel your ambition in a constructive, directed way. This placement also suggests that your ego and need for recognition can be your worst enemies, so be aware of that tendency and do whatever you can to mitigate it.

For Boomers born with this configuration, there can be multiple setbacks that prompt you to work harder, put in longer hours, meet all your obligations—and then some. Eventually, though, if you learn patience and resilience, you succeed. You achieve your goals. Cooperative endeavors are beneficial with this placement, i.e., anything in the professional arena in which you have partners, where you're a team player, where your voice is just one among many.

## Natal Saturn in Virgo

The tendency with this placement is that you're such a perfectionist you get bogged down in details. You walk into someone else's house, for example, and immediately notice streaks on the cabinets that scream for a dose of Pledge. Or you enter your son's apartment and are overwhelmed by the disorder and chaos. But if you can direct this tendency toward your work and career, you can handle anything, manifest anything, and perform a service that helps many people understand their roles in this lifetime. It's simply a matter of separating the essential from the inconsequential.

Your intuition is highly developed, just waiting for you to pay attention, to connect all the dots. Find humor in everything you do. Take breaks from work. Treat yourself to a trip to Paris or some other far-flung corner of the globe. Learn to revel in your experiences.

## Natal Saturn in Libra

Your lesson this time around is to learn the value of cooperation. The success of any partnership, personal or business, involves the ability to compromise. What can you live with to keep the peace? How much can you surrender without giving away your personal power? Your values? Karma is part and parcel of your most intimate relationships, and the sooner you recognize that, the better off you are. The question, though, is how do you recognize which relationships are karmic and which ones are just the luck (or misfortune) of the draw? Well, bottom line, it's about what you feel when in the presence of another person. It comes down to resonance.

The dark side of this placement is a tendency to surrender too much in the hope that you can keep the peace. The real key here is the ability to forgive and forget and move on.

## Natal Saturn in Scorpio

In your work, you're as much of a perfectionist as Saturn in Virgo. But in everything else, you're pure Scorpio—after the bottom line, the absolute truth, the real deal. You're secretive in the way you handle stress and difficulties of any kind and must learn how to deal with this stuff in a calm, centered manner. Allow your intuition to guide you. It's an infallible tool. Your persistence, resilience, and determination are among your greatest assets.

That said, there's a proclivity here for incredible discipline in achieving your goals, but you may need help, and help won't be forthcoming unless you ask for it. *Can* you ask for it? Is a request for help even in your lexicon? Check out the sign of your moon. If it's in a water or earth sign, chances are good that you realize you are part of a collective of like-minded individuals. Start there. You won't be disappointed.

## Natal Saturn in Sagittarius

Your pursuit of philosophy and/or religious and spiritual beliefs is one of the primary driving forces in your life. You may have a desire to be recognized as an authority in one of the above areas or in higher education, publishing, politics, or the law. You probably have a strict moral code that guides you, but which could stifle creative thinking. Any kind of rigid approach to problem-solving complicates your challenges and problems. It's best to loosen up, to allow yourself the freedom to explore your ideals free of political or religious restraints.

You're happiest if you can structure your life by incorporating your ideals into your daily life in a practical way. Your professional reputation is vitally important to you, but try not to obsess about every little detail, every little word. You're after the big picture. The darker side of this placement is self-righteousness.

## Natal Saturn in Capricorn

Saturn rules this sign, so it's very happy here and functions at optimum capacity. Your ambitions are powerful, and from the time you're old enough to understand what a career is, you are pursuing your own. Your talents are varied, and you may be able to integrate all of them in some unique way to achieve what you desire. Your goals are specific; your discipline is astounding.

The usual description about this placement is that the person may appear cold, detached, remote. But I've found this isn't necessarily true. My daughter and her friends, all of them born in 1989 when Saturn was in the early degrees of Capricorn, are among the most joyful group of people I've ever known. But they're also incredibly focused in their pursuit of educational goals, which certainly fits this placement.

## Natal Saturn in Aquarius

Saturn, as the coruler of Aquarius, is pretty comfortable here. Your visionary qualities are channeled and expressed in practical ways that benefit others. Your intellect is organized, focused, objective, and capable of innovative discoveries and solutions. With this placement, there's usually mathematical and scientific ability and the ability to conceptualize. The challenge is to integrate your abilities into your daily life and to ground them. You benefit from regular physical exercise that serves to remind you there's more to life than the mind! Yoga, tai chi, or any other mind/body discipline would be a good place to start.

The downside of this placement can be a lack of feeling, intellectual pride, and impersonal relationships.

## Natal Saturn in Pisces

The consensus about this placement is that it's difficult. But any challenges can be overcome by channeling your intuitive ability through a structure that Saturn provides. Instead of letting your memories of the past trap you, use memories of past triumphs as a springboard to achieve what you desire. Your psychic ability is the doorway to spiritual and creative development and to higher spiritual truths.

There can be an inordinate amount of worrying that accompanies this placement, so be sure you always allow yourself solitude, a refuge where you can kick back and relax. It helps to practice yoga, meditate, nurture yourself first.

CHAPTER 8

# Health and Fitness Tips for the Paradigm Shift

When paradigms shift, it's not just belief systems that are impacted. Our minds, spirits, and physical bodies are also affected. The slowest-moving outer planets exert the most influence over our lives, so let's take a look at the areas of the body these planets rule for hints about how we can take better care of ourselves in 2012.

## Saturn

This planet rules bones, teeth, joints, knees, and spine. So during Saturn transits, these are the areas in your body that are most likely to be affected. With Saturn in Libra until October 5, 2011, your lower back, kidneys, ovaries, and sugar levels—all governed by Libra—could be impacted too. Between October 5 and late December, Saturn transits Scorpio, which rules the endocrine system, menstruation, sex organs, and blood, so these areas could be affected too.

## Uranus

This planet rules ankles, nervous ailments, miscarriages, reflexes, and sprains. With Uranus in Aries all year, other areas that could be affected are: adrenals, head, insomnia, retinas, scalp.

## Neptune

With Neptune in Pisces, the sign that it rules, from February 3, 2012, for the next fourteen years, areas of the body that can be affected are: feet, glandular swellings, eyes, addictions, parathyroid, pituitary, hard to diagnose diseases.

## Pluto

Pluto will be in Capricorn until 2024. Possible trouble areas include: enzyme levels, reproductive organs, hemorrhoids. Capricorn rules pretty much the same areas that Saturn does: bones, joints, knees and kneecaps, gout, rheumatism, sprains.

So when you know that one of these outer planets will be forming an angle to one of your natal planets—your sun, moon, and rising in particular—then you can take extra care with the parts of your body that may be more vulnerable. If Saturn is forming a difficult angle to your sun sign, for example, then it would be smart to take yoga regularly to keep your spine and joints flexible.

## Your General Health

If you were an alien watching the evening news and the drug commercials that sponsor it, you might get the impression that Americans are a sickly lot in search of the quickest fix. While drugs certainly have their place, more and more Americans are seeking alternative treatments for whatever ails them. From acupuncture to yoga and homeopathy, from vitamin regimens to nutritional programs, we're seeking control over our own health and bodies.

Health and fitness is more than just eating right and getting sufficient exercise. It's also about our emotions, our inner worlds, our belief systems. How happy are you in your job? Your closest partnerships? Your friendships? Are you generally happy with the money you earn? What would you change about your life? Do you believe you have free will or that everything is destined? Is your mood generally upbeat? Do you feel you have choices? Do you feel empowered? By asking yourself these kinds of questions, you can glean a sense of your emotional state at any given time. The state of your emotions may tell you a great deal about the state of your health.

Louise Hay, author of *You Can Heal Your Life* and founder of Hay House Publishing, is a living testament to the impact of emotions on health. As a young woman, she was diagnosed with vaginal cancer. The doctors wanted to operate, but Hay bought herself time—three months—by telling them she didn't have the money. She then took control of her treatment.

As a battered child who had been raped at the age of five, it wasn't surprising to her that the cancer had shown up where it had. She knew that cancer was "a disease of deep resentment that has been held for a long period of time until it literally eats away at the body." She felt that if she could change the mental pattern that had created the cancer, if she could release the patterns of resentment, then she could cure herself.

She set out a program for her treatment—and forgiveness was at the top of her list. She also knew she had to "love and approve" of herself more. In addition, she found a good therapist, a nutritionist, a foot reflexologist, had colonics three times a week, exercised. Her treatment is spelled out in her book. The end result? Within six months, the doctors pronounced her free of cancer.

In her book, there's an invaluable list: next to every ailment and disease is the probable emotional cause and the new thought pattern that will lead to healing. Her techniques may not be for everyone, but when dealing with health and fitness issues, remember that medical science doesn't have all the answers, and you, in fact, may be your own best healer.

## The Physical You

These descriptions fit both sun and rising signs. For a more complete look at the physical you, of course, your entire natal chart should be taken into account, with a particularly close look at the sign of your moon—the root of your emotions, the cradle of your inner world.

## Aries

**Rules: head and face**

***What You Look Like***

Physically these people tend to have ruddy complexions, narrow chins, and arched eyebrows. Sometimes they have a scar or mole on the head or face. Aries men often have profuse body hair, and in both men and women the hair is sometimes tinged with red.

### *Health and Fitness Tips*

Aries rules the head and face, so these areas are often the most vulnerable physically. Headaches, dizziness, and skin eruptions can be common. If you're an athletic Aries, then do more of whatever it is that you enjoy. Competitive sports? Great, go for it. Long-distance runner? Run farther. Gym? Double your time and your workout. Yoga once a week? Do it three times a week. One way or another, you need to burn off your excessive energy, so that it doesn't turn inward and short-circuit your body!

As a cardinal fire sign, you're an active person who gravitates toward daring, risky sports—mountain climbing, rappelling, bungee jumping, trekking through high mountainous regions, leaping out of airplanes. It's probably a great idea to have good health insurance or to have a Louise Hay attitude toward your health—*I'm attracting only magnificent experiences into my life.*

For maximum benefit, you probably should try to eliminate red meat from your diet. Chicken and fish are fine, but a vegan diet would be best. Herbs like mustard, eyebright, and bay are beneficial for you. Any antioxidant is helpful—particularly vitamins C, E, A or Lutein for your eyes, zinc, Co-Q10, Black Cohosh if you're a female in menopause, or Saw Palmetto if you're a man older than fifty. If you pull a muscle or throw your back out of whack, look for a good acupuncturist and avoid painkillers.

## Taurus

**Rules: neck, throat, cervical vertebrae**

### *What You Look Like*

In a Taurus, the neck is usually thick and sturdy and rises from broad, often muscular shoulders that seem to bear the weight of the world. They tend to be attractive individuals with broad foreheads and expressive faces. Yet their faces can be as inscrutable as fortune cookies when they are hiding something or feel threatened in some way. They usually look more youthful than other people their age, the result of good genes and a daily regimen of exercise.

### *Health and Fitness Tips*

Thanks to the sensuality of your sign, you may be a gourmet cook and enjoy rich foods. But because your metabolism may be somewhat slow, you benefit from daily exercise and moderation in your diet. In fact, moderation in all things is probably a good rule to follow.

As a fixed earth sign, you benefit from any outdoor activity, and the more physical it is, the better it is for you. Hiking, skiing, windsurfing, biking are all excellent pursuits. You also benefit from any mind/body discipline like tai chi or yoga. The latter is especially good since it keeps you flexible, and that flexibility spills over into your attitudes and beliefs and the way you deal with situations and people. You probably enjoy puttering in a garden, but because you have such an artistic side, you don't just putter. You remake the garden into a work of art—fountains, bold colors, mysterious paths that twist through greenery and flowers. Once you add wind chimes and bird feeders, nature's music adds the finishing touches.

If your job entails long hours of sitting in front of a computer, your neck and shoulders may be more tense than usual. You would benefit through regular massage and hot tub soaks.

If you're the silent type of Taurus, then chances are you don't discuss your emotions. This tendency can cause health challenges if you keep anger or resentment bottled up inside you. Best to have an outlet—through exercise, for example, or through some sort of creative endeavor. Art, music, photography, writing: any of those would help. Better yet, learn to open up to at least one or two people!

## Gemini

**Rules: hands, arms, lungs, nervous system**

### *What You Look Like*

Geminis generally radiate a lot of nervous energy. It keeps them slender and wiry, and they're always on the move—if not physically, then mentally. They often have twinkling eyes, clear-cut features, a nose that turns up slightly at the end. Some of them have thick hair. They talk and move fast, many are ambidextrous and usually have excellent coordination.

### *Health and Fitness Tips*

You benefit from periodic breaks in your established routine. Whether it's a trip to some exotic port or a trip to the grocery, it's a breath of fresh air, a way to hit the pause button on your busy mind. Regular physical exercise helps to bleed off some of your energy and keeps your already youthful body supple and in shape.

As a mutable air sign, you need intellectual stimulation and a constant array of experiences and information to keep your curiosity piqued. Otherwise it's too easy for all that nervous energy to turn inward and affect your health. The kind of work you do is important in the overall scheme of your health. You do best in nonroutine kind of work with flexible hours or, preferably, in a profession where you make your own hours! Any job in communication, travel, public relations, would suit you. When you're passionate about what you do, you're happier. If you're happy, your immune system remains healthy.

With your natural dexterity and coordination, you

would do well at yoga. If you don't take classes yet, sign up for some. Not only will it keep you flexible, but you'll benefit mentally. Meditation would also be an excellent practice for you. Anything to calm your busy head!

Since your respiratory and nervous systems are your most vulnerable areas, your diet should include plenty of fish, fresh fruits, and vegetables. If you live in a place where you can garden, then plant some of these items for optimum freshness. Vitamin C, zinc, the B vitamins, and vitamins E and A are also beneficial for you. With your energy always in fast-forward, it's smart to get at least seven and preferably eight hours of sleep a night. If you're the type of Gemini with a high metabolism, then you benefit from eating several small meals throughout the day rather than just the usual three.

## Cancer

### Rules: breasts, stomach, digestive system

### *What You Look Like*

Cancers are recognizable because of their round faces. Their bodies are sometimes round, too, though not necessarily overweight. Those who don't have roundness as part of their physical appearance may have some other distinguishing trait—liquid, soulful eyes, a lovely-shaped mouth, generally expressive features. They're moody individuals, and their moods are often reflected on their faces and in the way they walk and carry themselves.

### *Health and Fitness Tips*

As a cardinal water sign, you benefit from proximity to water. If you can live or work close to a body of water, you'll notice a marked difference in your energy and intuition and how you feel and think. Even a vacation close to the water is healing. This seems to hold true not only for Cancer sun signs, but for moon and rising signs in Cancer too. The body of water can be anything—a lake, river, ocean, salt marsh, even a pond!

Not surprisingly, you benefit from any kind of water sport, even a day at the beach or a picnic by the river. The point is that water speaks to you. It feels like your natural element. You might want to read *The Secret of Water* or any of the other books by Masaru Emoto. You will never think of water in the same way again and will be more conscious of how human emotions affect water—and thus our bodies, since we consist of nearly 70 percent water.

Emotionally, you may cling to past injuries and hurts more than other signs or may still be dragging around issues from childhood or even from a past life. Unresolved emotional stuff can lodge in your body and create problems. So it's important that you rid yourself of past resentments and anger. Use hypnosis to dislodge these feelings. Forgive and forget. Have a past-life regression. Read Louise Hay's book *You Can Heal Your Life.*

If you have a moon, rising, or another planet in an earth sign, then consider regular workouts at a gym.

## Leo

### Rules: heart, back, spinal cord

#### *What You Look Like*

From Jacqueline Kennedy to Madonna to Presidents Obama and Clinton, the typical Leo looks regal. Hair that is thick or in some way distinguished, compelling eyes, a smile that can light up the dark side of the moon: these are the Leo hallmarks. Male or female, they project dignity and intelligence and move with a certain elegance. In a crowded room, the Leo is usually the one surrounded by people!

### *Health and Fitness Tips*

Leo rules the heart. So you benefit from a low-fat diet, exercise, work that you love, and relationships in which you are recognized as the unique person that you are. Yes, those last two things count in the overall picture of your health!

Let's talk about your work. Acting, of course, is what you're known for. And performance. And politics. And, well, anything where you can show off your abundant talents. So if right now you're locked into a humdrum job, are the low person on the bureaucratic totem pole, and don't receive the attention you feel you deserve, then your pride and ambition are suffering. That, in turn, creates resentment that could be eating you alive. Turn the situation around by finding a career or an outlet where your talents shine and you're appreciated and recognized. You're a natural leader whose flamboyant style and magnetism attract the supporters who can help you.

You have a temper, but once you blow, that's it. Unlike Cancer, you don't hold on to grudges or harbor resentments or anger from childhood. You tend to be forward looking in your outlook, and your natural optimism is healthy for your heart and immune system. Anything you can do to maintain your cheerful disposition is a plus. When you feel yourself getting down, rent comedies, find books that make you laugh out loud, blog about your feelings.

## Virgo

**Rules: intestines, abdomen, female reproductive system**

### *What You Look Like*

Their physiques are usually slender and distinctive in some way—beautifully sculpted fingers and hands, for instance, nice legs, gorgeous teeth. They're physically attractive as a rule, which they enhance through their fastidious attention to detail. Their eyes may be unusual in some way, and their features tend to be sharp, clearly defined. They're fastidious about personal hygiene.

### *Health and Fitness Tips*

If you're the type of Virgo who worries and frets a lot, then the first place it's likely to show up is in your digestive tract. You might have colic as an infant, stomach upsets as a teenager, ulcers as an adult. The best way to mitigate this tendency, of course, is to learn how NOT to worry and to simply go with the flow.

You do best on a diet that includes plenty of fresh fruits and vegetables, fish, and chicken. Try to stay away from fried or heavily spiced foods. Red meat might be difficult to digest. If you live in a place where fresh fruits and vegetables are difficult to find during the winter, then supplement your diet with the appropriate vitamins and minerals. If you're a fussy eater—and some Virgos are—then the vitamin and mineral supplements are even more important.

You benefit from hot baths, massages, anything that allows you to relax into the moment. Yoga, running, swimming, gym workouts, any of these exercise regimens benefit you. Some Virgos, particularly double Virgos—with a moon or rising in that sign—have an acute sense of smell. If you're one of those, then be sure to treat yourself to scented soaps and lotions, fragrant candles and incense, and any other scent that soothes your soul.

Virgo is typically associated with service, and you may find that whenever you do a good deed for someone, when you volunteer your time or expertise, you feel better about yourself and life in general. The more you can do to trigger these feelings, the healthier you'll be. You have a tendency toward self-criticism that's part and parcel of your need for perfection, and whenever you find yourself shifting into that critical frame of mind, stop it in its tracks. Reach for a more uplifting thought. This will help you to maintain your health.

## Libra

### Rules: lower back, kidney, diaphragm

### *What You Look Like*

Even in a crowd of beautiful people, they stand out in some way. As a Venus-ruled sign, they have distinctive features—beautiful eyes, gorgeous skin, well-formed bodies, expressive mouths. They're often slender, good-looking. They enjoy beauty—in their partners, their surroundings, their aesthetic tastes. So it isn't surprising that they often dress beautifully and have homes that are boldly colored and uniquely decorated.

### *Health and Fitness Tips*

If your love life is terrific, then your health probably is too. You're happiest when you're in a relationship, preferably a committed, lifetime relationship. When things between you and your partner are on an even keel, your energy is greater, your immune system works without a hitch, you sleep more soundly, and you're more apt to have a healthier lifestyle.

You prefer working in an environment that's aesthetically pleasing, where there's a minimum of drama with congenial people. If your work situation doesn't fit that description, then it could affect your health—and for the same reasons as a love life that is lacking. Emotions. Your lower back, kidneys, and diaphragm are vulnerable areas for you, and unvented emotions could manifest in those areas first. If it isn't possible to change jobs or careers right now, then find an artistic outlet for your creative expression. Music, photography, art, writing, dance, any area that allows you to flex your creativity.

You benefit from yoga, walking, swimming, and any kind of exercise that strengthens your lower back muscles. Meditation is also beneficial, particularly when it's combined with an awareness of breathing.

The healthiest diet for you should consist of foods with varied tastes, plenty of fresh fruits and vegetables, organic if possible, and a minimum of meats. Anything that benefits your kidneys is good. Drink at least eight glasses of water a day, so that your kidneys are continually flushed out.

## Scorpio

### Rules: sexual organs, elimination

### *What You Look Like*

The body types vary, but the eyes . . . well, the eyes are nearly always compelling, intense, piercing. They rarely reveal what they're feeling and are masters at disguising their expressions. Their masks are carefully honed through years of hiding their emotions. Many Scorpios have thick eyebrows, sharp noses, seductive mouths. Their voices are often husky and low.

### *Health and Fitness Tips*

As a fixed water sign, you probably benefit by a proximity to water every bit as much as Cancer does. Lake, ocean, river, pond, salt marsh: take your pick. If none of these is available, then put a fountain in your backyard or somewhere in your house and create a meditation area. It's important that you have a quiet center where you can decompress at the end of the day, particularly if you have a busy family life and a lot of demands on your time.

You tend to keep a lot of emotion locked inside, and if the emotions are negative—resentment, anger—they fester and affect your health. So try to find someone you can talk to freely about your emotions—a partner, friend, family member. Or pour these feelings into a creative outlet. One way or another, get them out.

Scorpio rules the sexual and elimination organs, so these areas could be where ill health hits first. Be sure that you eat plenty of roughage in your diet and enjoy what you eat while you're eating it. Stay away from the usual culprits—fried or heavily processed foods. You do best with plenty of fresh food, but may want to consider eliminating red meats. Consider colonics treatments for cleaning out the bowels.

For your overall health, it's important to enjoy sex with a partner whom you trust. Avoid using sex as a leverage for power in a relationship.

## Sagittarius

### Rules: hips, thighs, liver

### *What You Look Like*

They tend to come in two types—tall and broad through the shoulders or shorter and heavier. The second description comes in part from Jupiter, which rules the sign and causes them to indulge their appetites. They look athletic and have high foreheads that get higher in men as they age and their hair recedes. They move quickly, but not necessarily gracefully.

### *Health and Fitness Tips*

As a mutable fire sign, you can't tolerate any kind of restriction or limitation on your freedom. You must be able to get up and go whenever you want. If you work in a job that demands you punch a time clock, where your hours are strictly regulated, or are in a relationship where you feel constricted, then you probably aren't happy. For a naturally buoyant and happy person like you, that could spell health challenges. Sadge rules the hips, the sacral region of the spine, the coccygeal vertebrae, the femur, the ileum, the iliac arteries, and the sciatic nerves, so any of these areas could be impacted health-wise.

You benefit from any kind of athletic activity. From competitive sports to an exercise regimen you create, your body craves regular activity. You also benefit from yoga, which keeps your spine and hips flexible.

If you're prone to putting on weight—and even if you're not!—strive to minimize sweets and carbs in your diet. The usual recommendations—abundant fresh vegetables and fruits—also apply. If you're the type who eats on the run, then you may be eating fast or heavily processed foods and should try to keep that at a minimum or eliminate it altogether. Even though your digestive system is hardy enough to tolerate just about anything, the fast foods and processed foods add carbs and calories.

Antioxidants are beneficial, of course, and these include vitamins C, A, and E. Minerals like zinc should be included in your diet and also a glucosamine supplement for joints.

## Capricorn

**Rules: knees, skin, bones**

### *What You Look Like*

As a cardinal earth sign, these individuals understand the benefits of exercise, and their bodies show it. While they generally aren't muscular—some are, but not as a rule—they look to be in shape. Their bodies are often angular and slender, and their faces, regardless of their age, have a maturity about them.

### *Health and Fitness Tips*

Since you seem to have been born with an innate sense of where you're going—or want to go—it's likely that you take care of yourself. You know the routine as well as anyone—eat right, stay fit, exercise, get enough rest. But there are other components to living long and prospering (to paraphrase Spock!), and that's your emotions.

You, like Scorpio, are secretive, although your motives are different. For you, it's a privacy factor more than anything else. You keep your emotions to yourself and may not express what you feel when you feel it. This can create blockages in your body, notably in your joints or knees. It's vital that you learn to vent your emotions, to rid yourself of anger before it has a chance to move inward.

You're focused, ambitious, and patient in the attainment of your goals. But your work—and your satisfaction with it—is a primary component in your health. If you feel you've reached a dead end in your career, if you're frustrated more often than you're happy with what you do, then it's time to revamp and get out of Dodge. By taking clear, definite steps toward something else, you feel you're more in control of your destiny and mitigate the possibility of health challenges.

Since your knees are vulnerable, running is probably not the best form of exercise for you, unless you do it only once or twice a week and engage in some other form of exercise the rest of the time. For a cardio workout that isn't as tough on your knees, try a rowing machine. For general flexibility, there's nothing like yoga!

## Aquarius

### Rules: ankles, shins, circulatory system

### *What You Look Like*

Tall and slender or short and round, their body types are as different and varied as they are. But many have deeply set eyes and classic profiles. Many of them move as quickly as Geminis; others move like molasses. Most aren't particularly coordinated, but some are. So, bottom line, it's tough to spot these individuals in a crowd. But as soon as you listen to them for five minutes, they're easier to peg. They talk eloquently about their ideas and ideals, and you'll recognize them by their discussions of alternative foods, alternative fuels, alternative lifestyles, alternative everything.

### *Health and Fitness Tips*

Let's start with the effect of Uranus ruling your sign. It sometimes can set your nerves on edge—too many sounds, too much chaos around you, loud noises deep into the night, the backfiring of cars, the incessant drone of traffic, even a crowd at the local mall. You're sensitive to all of that. It's part of what makes it important for you to have a private space to which you can withdraw—a quiet back yard filled with plants, a room inside your house with an altar for your Wiccan practice filled with scents from candles or incense that soothe your frazzled nerves. Or perhaps a book on tape can shut it all out. But shut it out you must to protect your health.

Because you live so much inside your own head, exercise is definitely beneficial for you. It doesn't have to be anything complicated—yoga done in the privacy of your own home, long walks, regular bike rides. But do *something* to ground your body, to get your blood moving, to silence the buzz inside your head. It will all benefit your health.

Nutrition? Well, for an Aquarian, this can go any number of different ways. You enjoy different types of food, so that's a place to start—with what you *enjoy*. The foods are likely to be unusual—organically grown, for instance, prepared in unusual ways, or purchased from a local co-op. If you live in the city, then perhaps you purchase food from a grocery store you've been frequenting for years. The idea here is that *you* know what's best for your body, what you can tolerate, what you need. Even though Aquarians aren't generally as in touch with their bodies as earth signs, they have an intuitive sense about what works for them. In the end, that's all that matters.

## Pisces

### Rules: the feet, is associated with the lymphatic system

#### *What You Look Like*

Common wisdom in astrology says there are two types of Pisces—the whale and the dolphin. And this goes for the sun, moon, or rising in Pisces. The whale is, well, large, but also tuned into everything and everyone on the planet. The dolphin type is slender, sleek, quick, joyful, graceful. But both body types usually have extraordinary eyes that are not only soulful, but seem to be able to peer through time.

#### *Health and Fitness Tips*

Let's start with emotions. Let's start with the fact that you're a psychic sponge, able to absorb other people's moods and thoughts with the ease of magnet attracting every other piece of metal around it. Yes, let's start there. It's why you should associate only with optimistic, upbeat people. The negative types steal your energy, wreck your immune system, and leave you in a tearful mess at the end of the rainbow with nothing to show for your journey.

Like your fellow water signs Cancer and Scorpio, you probably benefit from proximity to water. Whether you live near water, work near it, vacation near it, water refreshes your soul, spirit, intuition, and your immune system. Read Masaru Emoto's books on how water responds to emotions and intent. You'll never think about water in the same way again. You'll never think about your sun sign in the same way again, either.

You benefit from any kind of exercise, but try something that speaks to your soul. Swimming. Rowing, but in an actual boat, on an actual river instead of in a gym. Even a hot tub where you kick your legs is beneficial. Pay attention to the water you drink. Is your tap water filled with fluorides? Then avoid it and look for distilled water. Drink at least eight glasses a day. Indulge yourself in massages, foot reflexology, periodic dips in the ocean. Any ocean.

Meditate. Find the calm center of your storm.

## CHAPTER 9

# Aspects

Throughout this material, we've talked about beneficial or challenging angles that a transiting planet makes to your sun sign or that transiting planets make to each other. These angles are called *aspects.* Think of them as a symbolic network of arteries and veins that transport the blood of astrology. In a natal chart, these angles connect our inner and outer worlds, accentuate certain traits and play down others. Each aspect represents a certain type of energy, so there really aren't any good or bad aspects because energy is neutral. It's what we do with the energy that counts. It comes back to free will. When transiting planets make angles to each other, energy is also exchanged.

For instance, every year there is at least one very lucky day when the transiting sun and transiting Jupiter form a beneficial angle to each other—a conjunction (same sign and degree), a sextile (60 degrees apart), or a trine (120 degrees apart). The lucky day in 2012 falls on May 13, when the sun and Jupiter are exactly conjunct. This means that the sun's life energy and Jupiter's expansive energy combine and create, well, some magic for all of us! It's especially good for Taurus and other earth signs, but since we all have Taurus somewhere in our charts, everyone benefits.

If you look back to the presidential election in November 2008, Saturn in Virgo and Uranus in Pisces formed an exact opposition to each other. They were 180 degrees apart, an aspect that is like a tug-of-war. In this case, the tug-of-war was between the candidate that represented the old paradigm, the established order—Saturn—and the candidate who symbolized sweeping change—Uranus.

Aspects are most powerful as they are approaching exactness. So even though a conjunction, for example, is 00 degrees of separation or a square is technically 90 degrees of separation, many astrologers use *orbs* that can be as wide as five or ten degrees. Some astrologers use small orbs, but others assign larger orbs for the sun and moon and smaller orbs for other planets. The closer the orb, the more powerful the combination. If you're sensitive to transits, then, you may be feeling lucky for several days before May 13!

In terms of a natal chart, any transiting planet that is approaching an aspect with one of your natal planets is also most powerful on its approach. The traditional aspects have been used since the second century A.D. They are the conjunction, sextile, square, trine, and opposition. These aspects are considered to be the major or hard angles and are also the most powerful. There are other minor aspects that astrologers use, but for the purpose of this chapter, we'll only talk about the traditional aspects.

At the end of this chapter is a natal chart. We'll be referring to it as we go through the aspects.

### *Conjunction, major hard aspect, 0 degrees*

This aspect is easy to identify—clusters of planets within a few degrees of each other, usually but not always in the same sign and house. But it's a complex aspect because energies combine, fuse, merge. Think of it as power, intensity. So if you have conjunctions in your natal chart, the astrologer who reads for you should address what it means and how you can use it to maximize your potential.

Let's look at the young woman's chart. With her Saturn—♄—and Neptune—♆—conjunct in her tenth house of career, there's already a tension and power in her chart. Saturn builds structures and boundaries and seeks to hold back, restrict. It's about rules and responsibilities. Neptune urges us to allow boundaries to dissolve, to release the ego, to reach for higher ideals. So this woman will confront these dualities in her career—her tenth house.

With Uranus—♅—thrown into the mix, these experiences and dualities will come at her out of the blue, suddenly and without warning. Her career will be unusual, strange, filled with idiosyncratic people and defined by strange experiences—the Uranus influence. Uranus shakes up the status quo and when it's conjunct Saturn—even widely, by 7 degrees in this case—she will feel conflicted at times about which path to follow, which choices to make.

In this same chart, notice the close conjunction between the moon—☽—and Mars—♂—in the sixth house. One degree of separation. One possible repercussion is that her emotions are especially intense, even volatile at times, when it comes to her daily work routine and the maintenance of her health. Her health stuff may occur in fits and starts—one week she'll run two miles a day, the next week she's a couch potato, and the next week she meditates and practices yoga. It's the same way with her work. Erratic, moved by the spirit and passion of the moment. But because Mars is in Virgo, she's diligent, a hard worker at whatever she takes on.

Since Mars is within a degree of the seventh-house cusp, this passion she has spills over into her personal and business partnerships.

### *Sextile, major soft aspect, 60 degrees*

Again, look at the young woman's chart. An example of a sextile occurs between her sun—☉—at 8 degrees Virgo in her sixth house and her Jupiter—♃—at 5 degrees Cancer in her fourth house . The orb, according to the aspect grid, is 2 degrees and 41 minutes. Close enough to have significant impact.

A sextile is a point of ease. It represents a free-flowing energy between the planets involved. No tension. The sextile is a kind of buffer, a shield against turmoil, indecision, instability. But if there are too many sextiles, then the person may be too passive!

In the young woman's chart, her Pluto in Scorpio in the eighth house—12♇♏49—is closely sextile her Neptune in the tenth, within 5 degrees of her Saturn in the tenth, within a 6-degree orb of her Virgo Mars in the sixth, and within 5 degrees of her Virgo moon in the sixth. That's a whole lot of energy stacked in her favor and suggests that whatever she does on a daily basis with her work somehow feeds into the larger picture of her career. During her college years, she was able to manifest jobs out of thin air while in school and during the summers.

When she was in high school, for instance, she and her parents vacationed in windsurfing spots in the Caribbean and South America because her dad is a windsurfer. So she learned to windsurf and became so proficient at it that she was able to teach windsurfing at her college, through the sailing club, to any students who were interested. The college paid her ten bucks an hour. Gas money! Food money!

From the time she was old enough to walk, she enjoyed horseback riding and loved working with horses, being around them. She lived near an equestrian community, so becoming a barn rat was not a tough thing to do. During the summer of her freshman year, with her parents breathing down her back about getting a job, she manifested a job teaching riding at an equestrian summer camp.

These examples are precisely the kinds of experiences that accompany the sextiles in her chart. That Pluto in Scorpio, a sign that planet rules, gives her enormous power and ability to hone in on what she needs and wants and make it happen.

### *Square, major hard aspect, 90 degrees*

Friction, angst, *oh my God, the sky is falling*: that's how squares feel in a natal chart. The sky, of course, is never falling, but the friction and angst are quite real and act as triggers for action, forward thrust. They force us to develop, evolve, and reach aggressively for our desires.

How's this play out in real life? Look at the young woman's chart. She has three squares to her natal Mercury in Libra, in her seventh house of partnerships, all of them from that cluster of planets in her tenth house of career. Her natal Mercury—05☿♎33—is square to those tenth house planets from between 2 to 4 degrees. Ouch. The need to achieve something professionally is very strong. But it's not just about achieving. She wants to make her mark on the world, to leave something behind, some sort of legacy, something unique that bears *her stamp*. Because Mercury rules communication and this young woman enjoys writing and is good at it, that could be one of her signatures.

Mercury is also square her Jupiter in Cancer in the fourth house, suggesting that she may try to take on too much—in her writing, her life, her partnerships. Hit the pause button, breathe, ask for guidance through imagination, visualization, your family (fourth house), and dreams.

Squares spur us to action.

### *Trines, major soft aspect, 120 degrees*

This aspect works like a sextile, linking energies in a harmonious way. It's associated with general ease and good fortune. Again, though, if there are too many in the chart, passivity may result.

Look at the chart again. The young woman's 8-degree Virgo sun in her sixth house is closely trine to both Neptune and Saturn in Capricorn. The Saturn/Sun trine enables the young woman to set realistic goals and to attain them. The Neptune/Sun trine gives her deep compassion, psychic and artistic ability. She's able to attract the right opportunities for her career. The trine to Uranus is a bit wider—7 degrees—but is still significant. It suggests that her profession is or will be unusual and that her freedom is important to her. It's doubtful this young woman will be found in an office, confined to a 9 to 5 job. Whatever she does is likely to be unique.

### *Opposition, major hard aspect, 180 degrees*

This aspect feels like a persistent itch that you can't reach and usually involves polarities—Taurus/Scorpio, for example, or Aries/Libra. It brings about change through conflict and sometimes represents traits we project onto others because we haven't fully integrated them into ourselves.

In the woman's chart, her natal Jupiter in Cancer is opposed to all three planets in her tenth house. Jupiter expands everything it touches, so with Saturn, the woman's professional success comes about through persistence and dedication and by working with her beliefs in a constructive, positive way. With her Jupiter opposed to Uranus, the freedom to call her own shots, make her own schedule, to do her own thing, is paramount. In a chart that lacks direction and focus, this aspect can lead to involvement with revolutionary groups or religious cults. In a strong chart like this one, however, the Uranus/Jupiter opposition can indicate involvement in humanitarian efforts. The Neptune/Jupiter opposition can indicate utopian ideals, getting suckered by a sob story or trusting smooth talkers with a devious agenda. But it can also lead to great spiritual awareness and enhanced psychic ability.

Some other minor aspects that astrologers use are:

- the semi-square, 45 degrees. It creates irritation and friction between the planets involved.
- the septile, 51 degrees. Indicative of harmony and union in a nontraditional way. Can suggest spiritual power.
- the quincunx or inconjunct, 150 degrees separation. Indicates a need for adjustment in attitude and beliefs.

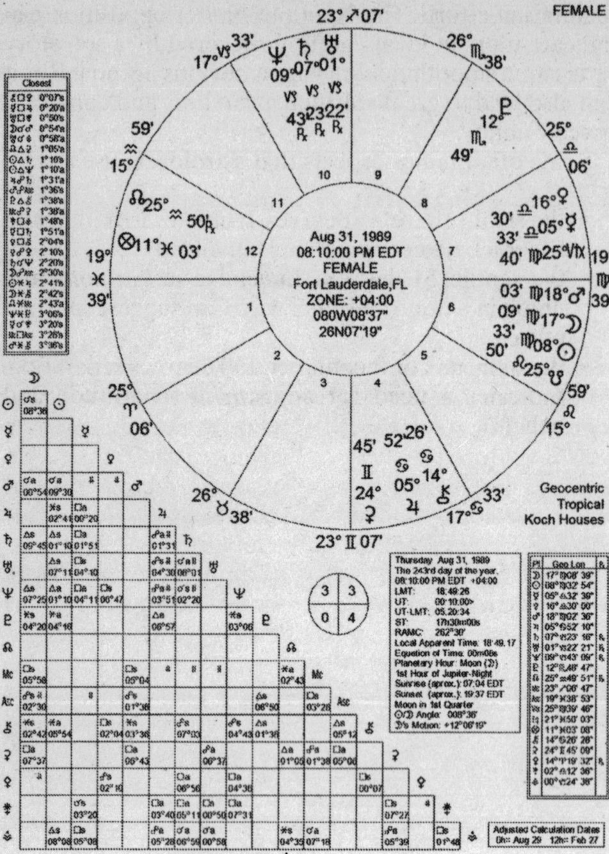
FEMALE
Aug 31, 1989
08:10:00 PM EDT
FEMALE
Fort Lauderdale,FL
ZONE: +04:00
080W08'37"
26N07'19"
Geocentric
Tropical
Koch Houses
Thursday Aug 31, 1989
The 243rd day of the year.
08:10:00 PM EDT +04:00
LMT: 18:49:26
UT: 00:10:00>
UT-LMT: 05:20:34
ST: 17h30m00s
RAMC: 262°30'
Local Apparent Time: 18:49:17
Equation of Time: 00m08s
Planetary Hour: Moon
1st Hour of Jupiter-Night
Sunrise (aprox.): 07:04 EDT
Sunset (aprox.): 19:37 EDT
Moon in 1st Quarter
Angle: 008°36'
Motion: +12°08'19"
Closest
Geo Lon
Adjusted Calculation Dates
0h:: Aug 29 12h:: Feb 27

CHAPTER 10

# The Astrological Neighborhood

Whether you're just learning astrology or are a seasoned pro or somewhere in between, the Internet is a wonderful tool for studying astrology. You can Google anything—a planet, an aspect, some obscure detail about astrology—and some Web site or blog undoubtedly has the information you're looking for.

Astrology sites offer a vast spectrum of services, from free natal charts, daily transits, and monthly horoscopes to political and world predictions—it's all at your fingertips. Here are some of the best sites:

**www.astro.com**: Enter your birth data and obtain a free natal chart. This site is also chocked full of information about astrology. Great for the beginner, the intermediary, and the advanced astrologer. Something for everyone here. There are also some terrific articles by well-known astrologers.

**www.astrologyzone.com**: Susan Miller's site is a favorite for neophytes and pros alike. Every month she writes around three thousand words per sign about what you can expect in the upcoming month. Her predictions are eerily accurate!

**www.moonvalleyastrologer.com**: Celeste Teal is *the* expert on eclipses, a specialized area of astrology that few have researched the way she has. Her two books on eclipses are seminal works.

**www.astrocollege.com**: Lois Rodden's site is extraordinary. This woman spent most of her life collecting birth data and then created a piece of software that is invaluable in research. This site also rates and sells astrology software. Lois has passed on, but her work survives.

**http://astrofuturetrends.com**: Author and astrologer Anthony Louis does just what the site says. He predicts future trends, covers political stuff, and provides an overall view of astrology.

**www.starlightnews.com**: Click on Nancy's blog. Here you'll find the latest predictions and insights about world affairs. Nancy's predictions about politics have been right on. Before the 2004 election, she made some predictions about tight senatorial races that were totally accurate. She also called the presidential race in 2008. We've been following her closely ever since.

**www.astro-yoga.com:** This site combines astrology and yoga. We created it and this system of yoga.

**www.tjmacgregor.com**: Here you'll find monthly astrological predictions for writers.

**www.ofscarabs.blogspot.com**: About synchronicities—what they are, how they show up in our lives, what they might mean, and hundreds of stories.

## Software

Computers have transformed everything about astrology. In the days before, you had to figure all this stuff by hand, through complicated mathematical formulas that left you gasping.

Our first piece of software was a really simple program we found at some computer store for ten bucks. It erected a chart in about sixty seconds. There it was—rising, moon, sun, planets, the houses—everything set up on the computer screen as if by magic. In the late 1990s, we bought our first really terrific astrology software from Matrix for about $300. In the years since, http://www.astrologysoftware.com has supplied us with endless data and information and revolutionized the study of astrology.

But it's not just enough to have a great piece of software. When your computer crashes, when you receive updates that screw up, when windows updates to a new system, you call the Matrix help line and their people walk you through it until everything works. The employees on their help lines aren't outsourced. You won't reach India. You'll talk to someone in Michigan who is not only an astrologer, but a computer geek who knows how to fix your problem. If by some fluke they can't fix your problem, they'll credit you for one of their other terrific programs.

The only complaint we have about Matrix is that to activate the software, you have to call or contact them through the Internet to receive a special code. If your computer crashes, if you buy a new PC or laptop . . . well, it's annoying. When you pay this much for software, you shouldn't have to obtain a special access code.

Another great piece of software is SolarFire. Astrologers are as dedicated to this program as they are to Matrix's software. Check out http://www.alabe.com for current prices. While the two programs offer similar features and capabilities, preferences seem to be individual. Both Matrix's Winstar and astrolabe's SolarFire offer many alternative features—like reports for natal, transit, and progressed interpretations.

Kepler's astrology program—http://www.astrosoftware.com—is beautiful in its rendition of charts, interpretations, and just about anything any astrologer could use or need. We like it for its ease, its beauty. But it's not a Winstar or SolarFire.

If your exploration of astrology takes you deeper, there are other software programs that take you there. Bernadette Brady is the undisputed mistress of fixed stars. Her software program, Starlight, is remarkable not only for its accuracy, but for its presentation. You will never think of fixed stars in the same way once you play with this program. What won't make sense in a natal-chart interpretation suddenly snaps into clarity when you use Brady's software. Be sure to download a print to file version for the software—through a PDF file—so that you can maximize usage. Their Web site: http://www.zyntara.com.

Lois Rodden's AstroDatabank is the software that Lois Rodden developed. It contains over thirty thousand birth records, "carefully documented and coded for accuracy with the popular Rodden Rating system. AstroDatabank includes intriguing biographies, revealing personality traits, important life events, and significant relationships." For the curious, the researcher, the neophyte and pro alike.

Both Winstar and SolarFire produce computerized report software. These reports are handy for when a friend of a friend is in a fix and you don't have the time to interpret transits and progressions for the person's birth chart. Winstar also produces software on the tarot and numerology.

Day Watch, another Winstar program, is forecasting software that is invaluable for astrologers. From their site: "Certainly it creates personalized astrological calendars, a great tool for professional astrologers and those who have an understanding of astrological terms, symbols, and technique. But Day Watch also contains a full range of onscreen and printable interpretations of events that even someone with absolutely no astrological training can read, understand, and immediately put to use in their daily lives."

At the beginning of every month, we bring up our personalized calendars that tell us what is happening daily in our natal charts and also lists which planets are changing signs in that month, on what date, and which planets are turning retrograde or direct. Each month includes an ephemeris and lunar charts for the new and full moon. The program also offers various types of reports.

## Getting a Reading

So now you're ready for an astrological reading. But where do you start? Which astrologer should you use?

The best way to find an astrologer is through soeone who has gotten a reading and recommends the individual. If you don't know anyone who has had an astrological reading, then the next best course is to head over to the nearest bookstore and look through the astrology books. Browse through titles that interest you. Note the author's style. If the author uses a lot of astro jargon or seems to write in a depressing or heavy-handed way, move on. Once you find an author whose book you like, check to see if he or she has a Web site and get in touch with the person.

Rates for a reading vary from one astrologer to another and usually depend on what you want. Would you like just an interpretation of your natal chart? Would you like a forecast for the next six months or a year? Do you want a compatibility chart for you and your partner? Some astrologers prefer to do phone readings and record the reading. Others prefer to work through e-mail. If the astrologer you've chosen lives close to you, all the better. Have the reading done in person.

## What to Expect During a Reading

Every astrological reading begins with your natal chart, so an accurate birth time is essential. It should come from your birth certificate or a parent's memory. An approximate time means the entire reading won't be as accurate.

This reading differs from a daily horoscope you find in a newspaper or on a Web site because it's tailored to your specific chart rather than just to your sun sign. If you're getting a reading only on your birth chart, then the astrologer interprets the entire chart, not just pieces of it. The astrologer looks at the signs and house placements of the various planets and the angles the planets make to each other.

Think of a natal chart as a holographic depiction of who you are. It's an organic blueprint, where the parts fit together in certain ways. In a reading, the signs of your sun, moon, and rising are where most astrologers begin. The sun represents your total personality, the moon symbolizes your inner world, and your rising sign is the doorway to your chart—the portal through which all your experiences enter. So an astrologer would look at the mix of these planets and then look at how they meld or oppose, facilitate or challenge other planets in your chart.

In addition to planets and aspects, astrologers also look at some other things in natal charts: the Nodes of the moon, part of fortune, various asteroids, Chiron, Vertex, and Sabian symbols. The Nodes are discussed in the next chapter, so let's go through the other parts of the list.

**Part of fortune ⊗ :** This is the most commonly used Arabic part, of which there are dozens. Its placement by sign and house designates where your "pot of gold" lies. It's your luck factor.

**Asteroids:** There are probably hundreds of asteroids, but astrologers use only a handful of them. Thanks to the work of astrologer Demeter George, four asteroids are the most commonly used: Vesta, Ceres, Athena, and Juno. Here are their general meanings:

**Vesta ⚶:** This asteroid's position in a natal chart describes where we are dedicated and how we can use our energies to bring about the greatest change in the larger world.

**Ceres ⚳:** How were we nurtured and how do we nurture others? That's what Ceres shows us, according to the sign and house position.

**Pallas Athena ⚴:** How do you fight for what you want? How do you pursue what you desire? Pallas, the warrior queen, describes the battles we choose to fight.

**Juno ⚵:** The asteroid of marriage. It generally describes the romantic/marriage partner we need and get.

**Chiron ⚷:** Known as the wounded healer, this planetoid describes where we are wounded and how healing this wound, which often stems from early childhood, can lead to greater wisdom and the healing of others.

**Vertex:** It's a point that describes agreements we made prior to being born into this life, a point of destiny. Since we have free will, we can choose not to keep these appointments, but it's probably a good idea if we do. Often the sign of our Vertex is the sign of someone to whom we're close—parent, partner, child, friend, mentor.

**Sabian Symbols:** Back in the early part of the twentieth century, astrologer Marc Edmund Jones spent hours with a clairvoyant, Elsie Wheeler, who gave him psychic impressions of each of the 360 degrees of the zodiac. The impressions are usually couched in metaphors, but over the years have proven to be eerily accurate. To test it, go to one of the sites listed in this chapter and get a free birth chart. Then go to www.cafeastrology.com, search for Sabian symbols, and look up the degree of your sun sign.

There are other points and asteroids that astrologers use, but when you're just starting out in your interpretation of your own chart—or of someone else's—keep the chart as clean as possible. Stick to the planets. Once you've got those meanings down, start adding other elements to the chart.

CHAPTER 11

# Your Soul's Agenda

## The Soul

There are various ways to look for spiritual aspects in a chart. Some astrologers use Neptune and the angles it makes to other planets. Others use the moon and its aspects. We use the North and South Nodes of the moon.

The Nodes aren't planets. They're points formed by the moon's orbit around Earth that intersect with the Earth's path around the sun. They're always separated by 180 degrees, so they form an axis of energy. If your North Node falls in Gemini, then your South Node falls in Sagittarius, the sign that is six away from Gemini. If you haven't done so already, turn to the appendix, locate the time span that includes your birth date, and find out the sign of your North Node. Then look at the table below to find your South Node.

The South Node represents our comfort zone, the accumulation of characteristics, attitudes, and talents that we bring into this life from other lives or—if you don't believe in reincarnation—that are laid down early in childhood. We retreat to our South Node when we're hurt, feel sick or threatened, or perhaps when we're in a new relationship and aren't sure yet where things are going. We also retreat here when we feel unsure of ourselves. The South Node is the psychological equivalent of comfort food.

The North Node symbolizes the direction we should move in this life to fulfill our talents and potential and to evolve spiritually. It represents the soul's agenda this time around, the qualities, traits, and experiences our higher selves felt that we need to evolve spiritually and to reach our potential.

## LUNAR NODES

| *If your north node is in* | *your south node is in* |
|---|---|
| Aries | Libra |
| Taurus | Scorpio |
| Gemini | Sagittarius |
| Cancer | Capricorn |
| Leo | Aquarius |
| Virgo | Pisces |

The sign of your North Node describes the types of experiences you should strive for in this life. It can also describe the psychological bent, potential, and talents that you should try to develop, to reach for, in order to attain your soul's agenda and to achieve your creative and spiritual potential. The sign of the South Node describes all of the above, but from previous lives. It's "been there, done that, and still feel comfortable here."

The house placement of your South Node describes the area that is your comfort zone. The house placement of your North Node describes the area where your greatest potential and talent can be achieved and the way in which you can evolve spiritually.

Take a look at the natal chart at the end of chapter 9. The woman's South Node in Leo—☋12♌32—falls in her fourth house of the home, her domestic environment. Her North Node in Aquarius—☊12♒32—falls in her tenth house of career. These signs suggest that to evolve spiritually, to achieve her full potential, she should strive to create a career that helps others. Aquarius is the sign of the humanitarian, who often works with groups to achieve a common goal.

She feels most comfortable when she's in the spotlight, or when she's involved in some drama involving her family and personal environment. She's such a warm, caring person that she's a people magnet (South Node in Leo). The house placement of her South Node suggests that she feels most comfortable in her personal environment. But the path to her spiritual evolution and to her achievement lies in the public arena.

# Nodes Through the Signs

## Aries North Node

Your soul craves independence. But your comfort zone lies in the embrace of others. You're at ease in most relationships, within groups, and seek balance in everything you do. Sometimes your need for balance is so great that you bend over backward to accommodate others and end up compromising your own values. That's your comfort zone—Libra South Node—speaking.

It's your South Node, too, that constantly sends you off in search of the perfect partner, the elusive soul mate. But you probably won't find the ideal partner until you know who *you* are and what you believe separate from your parents, family, authority figures, and anyone else who seeks to define you. That's where your Aries North Node comes in, where you must reach for your independence and freedom.

This node is about *you*—your independence rather than your codependence, about following your impulses, passions, and hunches rather than pressing the pause button on all that and doing something to please someone else. You're here this time to develop independence in thought, action, words, deeds. You're here to define your values according to who *you* are rather than through group consensus. Don't hesitate to take risks. Live like the *Star Trek* motto, boldly going where no man (or woman!) has gone before. Spiritually, you must sprout your wings and fly.

Easier said than done because it begins with solitude, a state of being that is foreign to you. As you begin to carve time for yourself, your Libra South Node may throw a major tantrum and urge you to get out and about, to hurry to that party, that get-together, that crowd of friends and strangers so that you can work the room. Resist those temptations, regardless of the comfort they promise. Ignore the criticisms of others—a difficult challenge because Libra South Node can't abide disapproval. The moment it detects disapproval, it causes you to run around apologizing to everyone, making excuses, laughing, oh, you were just kidding, really, and how about if we all get together tomorrow night for another party?

While your Libra South Node seeks to smooth things over with family, friends, coworkers, and everyone else who disapproves, your Aries North Node coaxes you to continue following impulses and forging your own path. It urges you to be spontaneous, to take off at a moment's notice with just a backpack and your ATM card and head for parts unknown. It demands that you become an individual separate from the collective called family, relationships, the community. It pushes you beyond consensus reality to test the limits of your soul. Once you're able to do that, you can successfully draw on your Libra South Node for harmony and balance.

Examples: Ram Dass, Jay Leno, Neil Armstrong.

## Taurus North Node

Your soul seeks stability. With this fixed earth-sign node, your mission this time around is to define your values and realize your potential through everything the physical universe has to offer. It's a magnificent banquet of sensual delights, glittering beauty, unimagined riches. Your playground is physical reality, and you're supposed to build something meaningful and lasting while you're here. You're supposed to do it patiently, with resilience to any obstacles in your way, and whatever you tackle isn't done until it's done!

But your Scorpio South Node resists. It demands that you merge with whatever you're doing, that you become the project, the relationship, the ideal, and that you control it. It urges you to work privately, in secrecy, never letting on what your real agenda is. Your South Node investigates, researches, digs for answers and truth, and does it with a kind of terrible impatience and intensity. Your North Node asks that you take some things on faith and trust, that you let your soul speak, and allow events to unfold naturally, organically.

The Scorpio South Node suggests that in past lives, you've dealt with crisis, calamity, excessive sexuality, suspicion, deceit, profound transformation. This time around, one of your callings is to find the calm center of the storm. While everything is collapsing around you, while people you care for are losing their minds and swept up in high drama, you are as still and centered as Buddha.

To achieve this requires enormous practice and patience. Start meditating. Have a physical exercise routine that grounds you completely in physical reality. Yoga, running, swimming, tai chi, biking, the gym: do anything that heightens your awareness of your physical body. And be selfish. Yes, that last part sounds strange because we're taught from a young age to practice the opposite. But for the Taurus North Node, selfishness is self-empowerment. It means you put your own needs and desires first. You're a survivor. Once you do that, you won't feel the need to manipulate and control others.

The sensuality part of the Taurus North Node can be

troublesome because all too often you're working from the raw sexuality of your Scorpio South Node. Try to balance your sensuality. Instead of leaping into sexual relationships, ease yourself into sensual relationships. Experiment, follow your passions in areas other than sex. Otherwise, the seductiveness of the Scorpio North Node takes you into the really dark places—excessive sex, drugs, eating, spending, booze. Kurt Cobain, heroin addict and suicide, is the dark example of this nodal axis. Jacques Cousteau, underwater explorer, and J. R. R. Tolkien, author and creator of the Hobbit world, are more evolved examples. They built legacies and worlds and touched the lives of millions.

Other examples: Greg Allman, Lucille Ball, Pearl Buck, Harry Houdini

## Gemini North Node

Your soul seeks diversity and wants to tell everyone about the journey. It is as if you're searching for a unified theory of the universe. Why, why, why? Your insatiable curiosity urges you to gather information to answer these burning questions and then to disseminate what you learn in any way you can, through many venues simultaneously. That's why you're here this time around. As one of the two signs symbolized by two of something, you multitask with ease.

Your Sagittarius South Node practically guarantees that you have a worldview or belief system that serves as a solid foundation in your life. It enables you to take in other people's belief systems and to compare and contrast them with your own. But when you're deep inside this comfort zone, you may think *your* belief system is the only truth. You may become intolerant of other people's spiritual and political beliefs and become a self-righteous stick in the mud.

It's likely that someone in your immediate circle of family and friends holds a belief system radically opposed to yours—parent, friend, partner, sibling, other relative, neighbor, coworker. This opposition probably leads to heated discussions and arguments. You're intent on convincing the other person that you're right, but this only creates further dissension. Instead, look at this person as your teacher. What can you learn from him or her? Listen with an open mind—and *really* listen. Also listen to what your soul whispers in the silence of your own mind and body. All too often, you're so intent on what you're going to say next that you're deaf to what the other person is saying and dismiss the whispers of your soul as nonsense.

Once you're aware of this pattern within yourself, you can catch yourself before it happens. Here are some guidelines to help you along:

Maintain your curiosity. It's one of your most valuable resources. When someone says something that pushes your buttons, ask yourself why you feel the way you do. Resistance is usually a clue to something within yourself that you should explore and strive to understand.

Always believe in yourself. Yes, this can be challenging for a Gemini North Node person. The twins that symbolize Gemini indicate a duality in your personality. One twin urges you to reach for the seemingly impossible and the other twin is laughing into her hands, snickering, *Yeah, right.* The best way to reconcile this duality is to develop a firm certainty about your talents that gets you through both good times and bad.

Examples: Susan Sarandon, Deepak Chopra, Bill Clinton

## Cancer North Node

Your soul searches endlessly for someone or something to nurture—a person, a cause, a mission. You're here to navigate the world of your emotions and intuition, to learn to nurture others as you have nurtured yourself in past lives. You need to discover what makes you feel emotionally secure and to establish that security in your life in order to achieve your potential.

Your Capricorn South Node brings clear goals and ambitions. But because work, goals, and ambition are your comfort zone, you may feel you have to control everything and everyone within your environment. You have a heightened sense of responsibility too, believing that you must assume all the responsibility—at work, at home, with your family. Your desire to achieve and be recognized for those achievements suggests that you work extremely hard. But since these traits come from your South Node, you may not make significant progress until you're living from a centered, emotionally secure place.

If you can stay in tune with your emotions, they will act as an infallible guide. When a negative emotion surfaces, don't just shove it aside, but don't obsess about it, either. Take note of it—then release it and let it flow out of you. In the same way, you should release your need for control too. Control of others is an illusion fostered by your South Node. The only person you can control is yourself—your own thoughts, actions, choices, your home and personal environments. You can't control what others think, and do, and believe.

The Cancer/Capricorn axis is about how we live our private and public lives. Home and family versus career and profession, right brain versus left brain, the inner world versus the outer world. The Cancer North Node urges you to open your heart, to listen to the whispers of your intuition, to lower your defenses. As a cardinal water sign, this node also urges you to explore the unknown.

Examples: Elisabeth Kübler Ross, Erma Bombeck, Daphne du Maurier

## Leo North Node

Your soul craves recognition, so baby, let the good times roll! You're here this time around to explore all forms of creative expression. You're supposed to learn what you love, what you truly desire, to have fun and be happy and how to manifest all of it. Along the way, you're also supposed to learn how to give and receive unconditional love. Sounds like a Disney movie, right?

Thanks to your Aquarius South Node, you're tolerant of people who are different from you, understand group dynamics, believe that we're all created equal. Your comfort zone is the world of ideas, the mind, the intellect. In fact, you may be more comfortable with ideas than you are with people or more comfortable putting the group before the individual, friends before partner and family. But your Leo North Node urges you to reach beyond ideas, beyond the group, to plunder the depths of your creativity and express yourself as an individual.

To navigate your Leo North Node successfully, here are some essentials:

- Nurture your creativity on a daily basis—not just whenever the spirit moves you. Once you learn to do this out of sheer enjoyment, your heart opens wide, and you start to realize that it's okay to be recognized for your achievements. It's okay to stand out from the group, to step out into the limelight and announce who you are.
- Ignore peer pressure. Whether this is difficult or easy depends on your age, of course, and the type of work you do.
- Create your life consciously. This requires awareness of your internal patterns. If you dislike some of the patterns you find, then reshape them or break them altogether.
- Don't depend on others to make you happy. Whenever you find yourself doing this, break the habit by

making a conscious decision to create your own joy. Then go do exactly that.

The beauty of the Leo North Node is about *you*—as an individual separate from any collective, any tribe. Love yourself first so that you're whole enough to love others.

## Virgo North Node

Details, perfection: that's what your soul hopes to find this time around. You're the Swiss watchmaker, immersed in the details of creating the best watch in the world. All those intricate levers, the beveled glass face, the tiny little hands. Somehow you bring all these parts together and do it with utter perfection. Now apply the watchmaker analogy to your life. Somehow you're supposed to bring all these disparate bits and pieces together, analyze your experiences, and then manifest your beliefs and ideals in a practical way. The heart of your journey is self-perfection.

Your Pisces South Node offers some of the tools you need—a deep compassion, magnificent imagination, excellent intuition and healing ability. But when your inner critic is screaming, and you retreat into your Pisces South Node out of fear, then it's easy to become trapped in a victim consciousness. You know the routine—you're not good enough, not quite up to the task, there are others more qualified . . . and so on. First, silence the inner critic and resolve not to quit. Once you do that, the rest becomes easier.

When you feel that coiled serpent of fear in the pit of your stomach, tackle it. When you feel unable to make a decision, take a few deep breaths and try to explore your resistance. Don't obsess about the fear or tear it apart, scrutinizing every bit of it. Just acknowledge it and try to move through it.

Share your knowledge and skills with others, without

thought of compensation, but do so only because you want to, not because you feel obligated. By performing a service out of compassion rather than obligation, you mitigate the risk of victim consciousness.

Remain in the moment. Or, as Ram Dass said, *Be here now.* By being fully rooted in the moment, fear can't choke you. Read Eckhart Tolle's *The Power of Now.* By doing this, you also mitigate self-criticism. Any time you find yourself falling into this frame of mind, tell yourself that you're perfect as you are. *Love and approve of yourself.*

Your Virgo North Node urges you to navigate your daily life with reason, logic, and attention to detail. Once you're able to do this, you can draw on the South Node's power of imagination and intuition and can manifest virtually anything you desire.

Examples: Harrison Ford, Michael J. Fox, Kurt Vonnegut Jr.

## Libra North Node

Your soul seeks balance: that's what this lifetime is about. Specifically, you're here to learn how to balance your needs with those of your partner, kids, friends, parents, and just about everyone else. You do it by walking in the other person's shoes.

Your comfort zone, of course, is the exact opposite of everything in the first paragraph. When you're afraid or uncertain, hurt or not feeling well, you retreat into an independent, *I can do it myself* frame of mind. You become selfish, intolerant of people who are different from you, and aren't open to any kind of compromise.

This *me first* attitude can be tough to overcome. But a good first step is to put others first. Yes, balk all you want, but it's the perfect place to start. Try it in small increments at first. Perhaps your partner needs the car at the same time that you're scheduled to have lunch with someone. Instead of insisting that you should get the car, make other arrangements. Or once a week or once a month, put someone else before yourself—let someone else go before you in the grocery store line, at the theater, the gas station. When you start doing this on a regular basis, then you're moving along the path of your North Node.

The Aries South Node prompts you to act decisively, impulsively, rashly because you assume you know what's going on, that you've got the right information and the right answers, and it inadvertently hurts someone. Better to pace yourself, ask questions, interact with people around you, and gather the information you need. Use tact and diplomacy rather than the blunt force of words and actions.

Once you're able to embrace the art of relating to others, then you can successfully draw on the independence and fearlessness of your Aries South Node.

Examples: Madonna, Frédéric Chopin, Anaïs Nin

## Scorpio North Node

Your soul cries out for personal power. You're here to learn about using that personal power and magnetism in a positive, constructive way. Through intense experiences, you learn to purge your life of the nonessential or of whatever is stagnant in any area—relationships, jobs, careers, belief systems, habits. Then you can draw on your Taurus South Node to build what is durable, lasting.

You've got plenty of help on this journey. Your South Node gives you ample physical energy, practicality, and a stubborn determination that can see you through anything. Your Taurus South Node urges you to collect things—old books, stamps, art, jewelry—and it whispers, *I want to be surrounded by comfort and beauty.* But when you become obsessively attached to these possessions, to comfort and beauty for their own sake, you may attract a situation that teaches you possessions are just stuff we own.

Your work ethic is stellar, nose to the ground, immersed in whatever you're doing, for as long as it takes. But you make some things harder than they need to be. That's when you know you're being resistant to change. Yet change is part of what you're here to learn.

When change knocks at your door, invite it in for coffee and a chat. If you can't learn to do that, then circumstances will force change and it will be something profoundly transformative and probably not pleasant. Again, take small steps. Once a week, do something you've never done before. If you're terrified of heights, then the step could be something as dramatic as skydiving or as small as walking to the end of a high diving board.

Empower others by supporting their creative endeavors, spiritual values, raises and promotions, or anything else that is important to them. Use your exceptional intuition to gain insight into others—who are they in the privacy of their own hearts? What are their dreams, motives, and hopes? Use your intuition as often as you can. It's like a muscle. The more you use it, the stronger it becomes.

When you feel fear that threatens to send you scampering back to your comfort zone—to the nearest mall to shop for anything, to the comfort of rich foods, booze, drugs, the entire physical spectrum of sensual delights—stop. Breathe. Then investigate. What are you afraid of? Has it happened yet? Or are you afraid of something that *may* happen? Once you become aware of the pattern, you can break it, and when you break it, you're truly advancing along the path of your Scorpio North Node.

Examples: Tiger Woods, Edgar Allan Poe, Francis Ford Coppola

## Sagittarius North Node

Your soul is seeking truth—specifically, your personal truth. It may sound like a major undertaking, but you can achieve it by using your intuitive ability to grasp the big picture rather than collecting endless, disconnected facts. The emphasis for you in this lifetime is on right brain, intuition, and imagination rather than logic and reason.

Your comfort zone—the Gemini South Node—is about information, facts, and figures. You can talk to anyone about anything, have terrific communication skills, and are one of the most social creatures in the zodiac. But when you feel threatened and afraid, you retreat into the darker aspects of your South Node—you talk when you should be listening, second-guess what people are thinking and feeling, make up facts, change rules in the middle of the game.

To use your North Node energy successfully, learn to trust yourself. To trust that inner voice of your intuition rather than the voices of everyone you consult before you make a decision. Strive to be more spontaneous. By allowing yourself freedom to take off at a moment's notice for an exotic port, to call in sick to work so you can attend your kid's play at school, to run off and get married in Vegas—well, it's part and parcel of the Sadge North Node. Honor it! Spontaneity is the manifestation of your intuition.

Strive to be more patient. Yeah, your Gemini South Node won't want to hear about it, but patience leads you to realize there are no quick fixes, and what's the big rush about, anyway?

Your North Node urges you to explore the unknown, to delve into spiritual, political, and metaphysical issues that people around you may not want to discuss. Just resist the temptation for self-righteousness and go about your business. This journey doesn't belong to anyone else. It's *yours.*

Examples: Drew Barrymore, Colin Powell, Zelda Fitzgerald, Angelina Jolie

## Capricorn North Node

This time around, your soul seeks to control its own destiny. That's it in a nutshell, that's why you're here this time around. Already, your Cancer South Node is sobbing in a corner for that orphan on the news tonight, for the starving animals roaming the ruins of the latest disaster, for the most recent genocide somewhere. She doesn't want to hear about your ambitions, about you taking charge, about you controlling your destiny. So she pouts, she plunges you into a depression, and here *you* now sit, worrying yourself into a frenzy about stuff that hasn't even happened yet.

Let's back up. Your Cancer South Node offers plenty of tools for your journey—intuition and compassion, a sense of personal history, deep emotions that are your gauge to what's really going on in your life. Your South Node knows how to comfort anyone and anything in need that's hurting, that needs a shelter for the night—or for a year. This includes strays—cats, dogs, birds, whatever finds its way to your doorstep. The problem arises when you nurture and heal at the expense of your own needs or when you nurture others without first nurturing yourself. That's when your South Node becomes an impediment to achieving your potential. That's when you become like Rapunzel, trapped in her tower.

Your Capricorn North Node urges you to reach for everything you want and to achieve your potential through careful planning, strategizing, and hard work. But your Cancer South Node keeps hurling up images of your past mistakes, the issues you dealt with in childhood, how your mom or dad or family might object to what you're doing. You stop in your tracks, suddenly paralyzed and filled with doubt.

So your first order of business is to release the past.

The present is your point of power. The present is the place from which you write the script of your life. Honor the past, certainly, but recognize that your childhood, your parents, the bully in the sixth grade have no say over your life now.

Your second order of business—and imagine this as a Power Point presentation—is to stay tuned in to your feelings. But don't use your emotions to manipulate or control others. When you feel negative, don't dwell on it. Let the negativity wash through you, put one foot in front of the other, and move forward again.

Third point? Always express what you feel, when you feel it. Don't keep it all bottled up inside, as your South Node would like. Let it all out. Not only will you feel better, you'll be advancing on the path of your North Node.

By the way, you are in illustrious company! Examples: Indira Gandhi, Robert Redford, Oprah Winfrey

## Aquarius North Node

Your soul searches for the collective experience, so this time around, you're here to learn about the importance of groups. Whether it's your family group, your community, a social circle, a political or spiritual movement, or some massive humanitarian effort that impacts the family of man, you're supposed to learn you can't always be the center of attention.

Your Leo South Node won't be happy about this development. It basks in applause and recognition. Yet your South Node also confers a terrific personality, great warmth and magnetism, and such radiant joy for life that if you can direct those qualities toward something larger than yourself, you will succeed at everything you do.

Your ego is well developed, thanks in large part to your Leo South Node. But ego alone won't do the job this time around. You're called upon to reach beyond the self, to extend yourself into the larger world, into the family of man, where you can make a tremendous difference, an integral component in a paradigm shift. You may do this through any number of creative venues, through your career, through volunteering, through your family life or the way you earn your living. But there are some definite steps you can take toward embracing your North Node, and foremost among them is to minimize drama.

Your South Node, see, is all about drama—in temperament, relationships, activities. In every single phase and area of your life there may be drama that your South Node stirs up, stokes. So strip away the drama, and what do you have? Someone with great talents and potential who can achieve that potential through shifting focus from self to the group, the tribe, the community, whatever it is.

Use your Leo South Node to cultivate and nurture your creative passions. If you can pour your emotions into a creative outlet, especially one that brings insights and pleasures to a larger group, you're well on your journey into your North Node.

Examples: Leonard Cohen, F. Scott Fitzgerald

## Pisces North Node

Your soul wants to sink into the depths of imagination and intuition to discover the larger spiritual and creative picture that governs your life. This lifetime is about unearthing everything that is hidden in your life—power you have disowned, secrets that are kept in family vaults, in genealogy books, in the deepest reservoirs of your DNA. Your life is about bringing all this stuff into the light of day.

Your Virgo South Node brings a lot to the table for this journey—a discriminating intellect, a penchant for details, a remarkable ability to connect the dots in any situation, event, crisis, relationship. You name it, the Virgo South Node grasps how all the connections are made. Your South Node is terrific in any situation where rapid solutions are needed, where connections must be made at the speed of light, and where everything—all the information and details—are *correct.*

But, *correct* aside, this is the life where you go with the flow, avoid self-criticism, trust the universe to deliver what you need and desire, and develop your spiritual beliefs. All of this can be done through your daily work, but in terms of the big picture, the larger canvas of possibilities, the forest as opposed to the trees. Maybe you blog about your experiences. Maybe you set up a Web site that sells a particular product or service that helps others to reach their highest potential. The bottom line about the Pisces North Node is, ultimately, unknown and unknowable, too mystical to penetrate unless it's your conscious path, and too complex to decipher unless your intuitive skills are remarkably developed.

But remember this. When your Virgo South Node slaps its ruler across your desk in ninth grade and demands that you memorize how to conjugate the verb "to be" in Latin, Spanish, French, and German, it's your Pisces North Node that hurls your arm upward, knocking that ruler away, and says, "Chill. I'm on my own path to enlightenment."

Examples: Matt Damon, Naomi Campbell, Isadora Duncan

CHAPTER 12

# By the Numbers

Even though this is an astrology book, we use numbers in some of the daily predictions because we're attempting to remain true to what Sydney Omarr did. The legendary astrologer was also a numerologist and combined the two forms in his work. So let's take a closer look at how the numbers work.

If you're familiar with numerology, you probably know your life path number, which is derived from your birth date. That number represents who you were at birth and the traits that you'll carry throughout your life. There are numerous books and Web sites that provide details on what the numbers mean regarding your life path.

But in the daily predictions, what does it mean when it's a number 9 day, and how did it get to be that number? In the dailies, you'll usually find these numbers on the days when the moon is transiting from one sign to another. The system is simple: add the numbers related to the astrological sign (1 for Aries, 2 for Taurus, etc.), the year, the month, and the day.

For example, to find what number June 14, 2011, is for a Libra, you would start with 7, the number for Libra, add 4 (the number you get when you add 2011 together), plus 6 for June, plus 5 (1+4) for the day. That would be 7+4+6+5 (sign + year + month+ day) = 22= 4.

So June 14, 2011, is a number 4 day for a Libra. It would be a 5-day for a Scorpio, the sign following Libra. So on that number 4 day, Libra might be advised that her organizational skills are highlighted, that she should stay focused, get organized, be methodical and thorough. She's building a creative future. Tear down the old in order to rebuild. Keep your goals in mind, follow your ideas.

Briefly, here are the meanings of the numbers, which are included in more detail in the dailies themselves.

1. Taking the lead, getting a fresh start, a new beginning
2. Cooperation, partnership, a new relationship, sensitivity
3. Harmony, beauty, pleasures of life, warm, receptive
4. Getting organized, hard work, being methodical, rebuilding, fulfilling your obligations
5. Freedom of thought and action, change, variety, thinking outside the box
6. A service day, being diplomatic, generous, tolerant, sympathetic
7. Mystery, secrets, investigations, research, detecting deception, exploration of the unknown, of the spiritual realms
8. Your power day, financial success, unexpected money, a windfall
9. Finishing a project, looking beyond the immediate, setting your goals, reflection, expansion.

Simple, right?

CHAPTER 13

# Love and Timing in 2012 for Libra

Ah, Libra. You're the true romantic of the zodiac, the one who wants moonlight and roses, beautiful music and equally beautiful surroundings. Ruled by Venus, the planet that symbolizes love and beauty, you just can't help it! You have this image in your head about what romance should be, and when the real thing doesn't pan out that way your disappointment is palpable.

As a cardinal air sign, though, you always bounce back quickly from your disappointments and move right along to the next romantic interest. If you're in a committed relationship, then any disappointments you feel are brushed aside. Like Scarlett, you tell yourself that tomorrow is another day.

How do the stars stack up in the romance department in 2012? Let's take a closer look.

Whether you're flying solo or in a committed relationship, timing is often the crux on which success and happiness rest. The faster-moving planets—Mercury, Venus, and Mars—tend to have less of an impact on our lives because of the speed at which they move. Venus, for instance, stays in a sign for about three weeks, unless it's moving retrograde, then the transit can last several months. The transit of Venus through Libra, for example, lasts from October 28 to November 21. But Venus in Gemini, where it turns retrograde this year, extends from April 3 to June 27.

Mercury, unless retrograde, zips through a sign in just under three weeks. Mars, unless retrograde, takes about forty-five days to move through a sign. Compare this to the snail of the zodiac—Pluto, which enters Capricorn in 2009 and won't leave until 2024.

Venus rules love and romance, Mars governs sexuality, Mercury rules communication. Beneficial angles among these three planets or from these planets to your sun sign usually indicate a winning combination for relationships. We'll include new and full moons in the love and romance equation, too, since the moon rules our emotions and intuitive selves. New moons generally usher in new opportunities, and full moons bring insights, news, and a touch of moon madness!

## For the Single Libra

You're a social butterfly, so meeting people is rarely your challenge. In fact, you meet so many people that making a choice or decision about romance and matters of the heart is usually difficult for you. You bend over backward to accommodate a potential partner—and in the end, that only works to your detriment.

Like fellow air sign Gemini, you're an excellent communicator. You're usually able to express your ideas and feelings clearly. For any relationship to get off the ground, there must be a commonality in belief systems, attitudes toward relationships, and ideas and strong communication.

The best times for connecting with a potential partner at that level are when Mercury is in your own sign, in a fellow air sign, or in a compatible fire sign. The first period to watch for is between January 27 and February 13, when Mercury is in fellow air sign Aquarius, in the romance and love section of your chart. During this transit, be sure to get out and about, so that you're meeting new people. Accept all social invitations. Do whatever you enjoy the most. The more enjoyment you experience, the likelier it is that you'll attract exactly the right person at the right time. Romance is on your mind, and you're able to speak your mind.

Between May 24 and June 7, Mercury is in fellow air sign Gemini, in your solar ninth house. This transit is great for discussing your worldview and spiritual beliefs. You might meet your potential romantic interest at a workshop or seminar, at some sort of spiritual gathering, on a college campus, at a publishing function, or even while traveling.

Mercury will be in your sign between September 16 and October 5, an ideal time for a mind link with someone who interests you. Your head and heart are in complete agreement.

When Mercury is in a fire sign, your conscious mind is fired up with ideas that you're eager to share with a partner. Those dates? June 25 to August 31, when Mercury is in Leo and your solar eleventh house, and October 29 to December 10. However, during both of these periods, Mercury is retrograde for a time. With Leo, the retrograde occurs between July 14 and August 8. With Sagittarius, it's retrograde between November 6 and 26. Best not to begin a relationship during a retrograde. Be aware that people from your past may resurface.

When Mercury is in Aries, your opposite sign, your mind is sharp, restless, and innovative, and you're looking for the new and different. Those dates: March 2 to April 4, April 16 to May 9. However, since all Mercury retrogrades this year are in fire signs, note the retro periods for Mercury in Aries: March 12 to April 4.

The most romantic time occurs when Venus is in your sign or fellow air signs. Your sex appeal and self-confidence soar; others find you enormously appealing. Those dates: September 16 to October 5. Again, be sure to make yourself available during this time period. You never know where you may meet the love of your life!

A great backup date for romance and love and sheer enjoyment falls between April 3 and August 7, when Venus transits fellow air sign Gemini. However, be aware that Venus is retrograde in this sign between May 15 and June 27. While in direct motion, this transit suggests you may meet someone special while traveling or in school. You've got the gift of gab now, too.

Even if Venus doesn't transit Aquarius and your romantic sector this year, Mars does, between December 25 and February 2, 2013. This transit heats up your sex life and brings a lot of activity generally to romance and whatever you do for fun and pleasure. It's also a great transit for socializing and striking a balance in your life between two opposing factors.

From January 1 to June 11, Jupiter transits Taurus and your solar eighth house, where it has been since June 2011. By now, you have some idea of just how expansive this transit is—making it easier for you to obtain mortgages and loans and expanding your knowledge of metaphysics. It also increases the chances that your partner's income goes up. That trend continues until June 11.

From June 11 to June 25, 2013, Jupiter transits Gemini and forms a beneficial angle to your sun. During this period, everything in your life expands—including your romantic options. You may be traveling more frequently, particularly to overseas locales, and may decide to go to college or graduate school. For hints about what this transit may bring, look back twelve years, to 2000–2001, when Jupiter was last in Gemini. When Venus is in your sign between October 28 and November 21—a transit mentioned earlier—be aware that it is forming a beneficial angle to Jupiter in Gemini, a combination that really delivers.

Although we're going to talk more about Uranus in Aries in chapter 15, let's look at this transit in terms of love and romance. Until March 2019, Uranus in compatible fire sign Aries transits your solar seventh house of partnerships and is opposed to your sun.

This transit brings enormous unpredictability into your partnerships—both business and romantic. The journey is exciting, tumultuous, electrifying, and chaotic. There's one certainty about this transit: any relationship that restricts your freedom or doesn't allow you to express who you really are will rapidly become history. If you have stayed in a relationship just because you don't want to confront what's wrong or because you dislike conflict, that will change. You'll find it increasingly difficult to be what you are not.

This year, Uranus and Venus connect between February 8 and March 5, so anyone you meet during this period is going to appeal to you on a wildly visceral level. You may not have a clue why you're attracted to this person, but attracted you will be.

Mercury (communication) turns retrograde three times a year, so be sure to note those dates and ramifications in the Big Picture section for Libra. A relationship that begins under any of those retrograde periods will be messed up in the communication department. Those dates:

March 12–April 4, in Aries
July 14–August 8, in Leo
November 6–26, in Sagittarius

## For the Committed Libra

The dates listed above for the single Libra also apply to the committed Libra, but for different reasons. When Venus transits Aquarius and your solar fifth house between January 1 and 14, your relationship with your partner is apt to run more smoothly, and there will be greater camaraderie between you. Your creativity will be heightened, too, as will your need for enjoyment. So this would be the perfect time to get away with the one you love!

The time between April 3 and May 15 and June 27 and August 7 favors overseas travel with the one you love. You and your partner may be conducting research or on a spiritual quest together. Or you may pick some far-flung location where neither of you has been and make an adventure of it. The key word here is *enjoyment.*

When Venus transits Aries and your solar seventh house—February 8 to March 5—you and your partner may decide to deepen your commitment to each other in some way. Maybe you move in together, get engaged or married, or start a family. Perhaps you buy a home together.

If you're looking for a home, one of the best times falls between November 21 and December 15, when Venus transits Scorpio and your financial sector. You should have the money then to buy a place. Another favorable period for home buying falls between January 8 and 27, when Mercury will be moving through the home section of your chart. There will be a lot of discussion then about what you're looking for.

So let's look for some dates this year that favor marriage and which dates you might want to avoid:

- Avoid the Mercury retrograde dates mentioned above
- When Venus is in your sign between October 28 and November 21
- On or after the new moon in your sign on October 15
- On or after the full moon in your sign on April 6
- On or after a new or full moon in your partner's sign
- Avoid eclipse dates
- Any time between September 16 and October 5, when Mercury is moving direct in your sign

## For All Libras

Your consciousness is a powerful tool. Use it this year to reach for what you desire. Learn to go with the flow when Uranus starts creating chaos in your partnerships. Don't worry and fret; maintain an upbeat attitude.

CHAPTER 14

# Career Timing in 2012 for Libra

One of the best career indicators for you is Jupiter's transit through Gemini from June 11, 2012, to June 25, 2013. This transit expands your beliefs, personal philosophy, spirituality, and communication abilities. When your personal beliefs and worldview expand, you begin to realize that you live in a universe of infinite possibilities. It's smart to start actively visualizing your career goals, to ferret out those long-held beliefs that may be blocking you from attaining what you desire. Meditation, journaling, and blogging are all excellent ways to utilize this energy.

As your beliefs expand to accommodate new ideas and experiences, your options in every area of your life—including your career—multiply. In a sense, you're seeding your life during this transit for a professional payoff up the road. Here are some possible ramifications of this transit:

- Frequent overseas travel connected to your career
- You start your own business
- You change jobs/career for something more in alignment with your values
- Your products and services expand to overseas markets
- You write a novel

- You start a blog promoting your services and products
- You build a Web site
- You do more public speaking

While Jupiter is transiting Gemini, it forms a beneficial angle to Uranus in Aries, which brings an element of surprise and unpredictability in all the areas mentioned above. You attract unusual individuals who are helpful to you professionally.

From January 1 to June 11, Jupiter transits earth sign Taurus and forms a beneficial angle to that section of your chart that governs your daily work routine and the maintenance of your health. This transit indicates that the former will be broader in scope than it has been before. You could be dealing with more responsibility, more stuff to get done, more employees, more coworkers, more work. But you have the drive to get it all done.

In 2012, when paradigms are shifting, take stock early on. Are you happy in your job? Is your career satisfying? What kind of work would you do if you had the opportunity? Would you like to go to graduate school to study something else? Is there a talent or interest you would like to develop more fully? Does your job just pay your bills, or is it a focal point in your life?

Once you answer these questions, you can start putting the energies of 2012 to work for you. So let's take a closer look at how you can create a professional life that you love. If you already have that, then let's see how you can improve what is nearly perfect.

## Why 2012?

Most metaphysical teachers talk about the importance of being fully present, fully grounded in the moment. In *The Power of Now*, *The Law of Attraction, and Seth*

*Speaks,* the message is the same: our point of power is the present. We may cling to the past and yearn for the future, but neither will bring us the power we have in this moment, in this breath, in a present action.

So before this year is already behind you, make a list of your professional goals and dreams. If you haven't attained all of them, what's holding you back? Chances are that the only thing holding you back is . . . well, *you.* Perhaps you think you might fail at something new. Maybe you think you lack the proper education or skills. In other words, your insecurity could be your obstacle to attaining your goals.

As a cardinal air sign, you're focused but not rigid in your beliefs. You're willing to change as needed. That will be an asset this year.

## Dates to Watch For

In addition to the Jupiter transits, let's take a look at the new and full moons this year and how you can use their energies to your benefit.

New moons generally mean new opportunities. Full moons are usually equated with news, insights, and a tad of craziness tossed in just to keep things interesting!

The October 15 new moon in your sign is the most important one for you all year. It's worth preparing for—through visualizing, making lists of your wishes and desires, laying out a left-brain strategy for attaining what you want. Mercury forms a beneficial conjunction to this new moon, suggesting a lot of communication and activity generally. Your daily life could be very busy around the time of this new moon, and you are likely to feel pressed for time! In terms of your career, expect new opportunities to surface that will please you.

The new moon in fellow air sign Aquarius on January 23 should be beautiful for you. It gets your creative adrenaline pumping, and there should be new opportunities surfacing to use your creativity in new ways. Another terrific new moon is also a solar eclipse in fellow air sign Gemini, on May 20. This one could bring opportunities for more frequent travel abroad, to get a book published, or for more education. Since it occurs in your solar ninth house, you may also have new opportunities to broaden your worldview and spiritual beliefs. You get another new moon in this sign on June 19.

The new moon in Cancer and your career area on July 19 will usher in new opportunities professionally and creatively.

## What the Planetary Transits Reveal

We've talked about some of the transits and the moons in 2012 that are favorable for career matters. Now let's take a look at some other things that are going on that will impact your professional life.

Venus rules your sign, so its transits are important for you. When Venus transits Cancer and your career area, you've got a great opportunity to really speak your mind. It's a favorable time to pitch ideas, garner support among coworkers and bosses, and generally finish up projects that require sharp communication skills. It's also a favorable time to create a Web site or blog for your company or services. The dates? August 7 to September 6.

Another favorable period, particularly for brainstorming with coworkers about cutting edge ideas and technologies, falls between February 13 and March 2. Mercury transits Pisces then and forms a beneficial angle to your career area.

From May 24 to June 7, Mercury transits Gemini and your solar ninth house. This could be the period when your client base expands to overseas markets, you travel abroad for business, or you have increased contact with people overseas.

During any of the Mercury retrograde periods mentioned in the previous chapter, avoid pushing forward on new projects. Review and revise is the best way to navigate these periods.

## Saturn's Movements

Until October 5, Saturn is in your sign. It's been there since October 2009, so by now you have a strong sense of how it impacts your life. Saturn rules structure, restrictions, obligations. Throughout its transit through Libra, there may be restrictions placed on your personal freedom and delays in obtaining what you desire; you'll need to meet your responsibilities and obligations to others. If you can do that, then the transit will help you build strong structures—in your relationships, career, finances, family, creative ventures.

On October 5, Saturn enters Scorpio and the financial area of your chart, where it will be for the next two and a half years. During this period, you'll be urged to pay closer attention to your money. You may find the right structure for handling your money or may encounter restrictions and delays with money. Or both. But with Saturn forming a beneficial angle to your career area, chances are good that a raise could be in the offing, and this will urge you to pay closer attention to what you earn, how you spend it and save it, and what your deeper beliefs are about money.

## Parting Thoughts About Career Matters

Whenever you feel discouraged about your career or anything else this year, get out and do something you enjoy. Libras are social beings, who love beauty—art, music, lovely, dramatic landscapes. Do what you love. Do what makes your heart sing.

The more you do what you enjoy, the better you feel. The better you feel, the more likely it is that you'll attract experiences and people and situations that increase that feeling. The law of attraction.

CHAPTER 15

# Navigating Uranus in Aries in 2012

Even though we talked about Uranus in Aries in the last chapter, as it relates to your career, let's take a general look here at its impact on your life generally.

Uranus's transit through Aries until early March 2019 will be forming a challenging angle to your sun that will call for attitude adjustments. This transit stimulates that area of your chart related to your partner's income, to mortgages, loans, income tax. This area of your chart also governs large questions—life after death, communication between the dead and the living, and just about anything else that goes bump in the night.

With Uranus in this section, you may have sudden psychic experiences that prompt you to question the fundamentals of your belief system. Your partner's income may soar or plunge, and he or she will find innovative ways of making money. It may be more difficult to obtain a mortgage or other loan or you have sudden opportunities to get these loans and will have to act quickly.

With any Uranus transit, there's always a thrust for independence and freedom, so it's possible that you'll want to be free of a mortgage and will be able to purchase a home with cash or pay off your existing mortgage. You won't want to be burdened by any debt, especially credit card debt, and will work hard to pay it off.

One repercussion of Uranus's transit is that your psychic ability increases. You may have prophetic dreams or experiences with telepathy and clairvoyance, or you may take seminars and workshops on honing your abilities. You may take up the study of astrology or start using divination systems like the I Ching and runes.

In any area where your life is stuck in a rut or routine, Uranus is going to shake things up, sweep things clean. When the dust settles, you'll be amazed that you have arrived in a better place.

During these seven years, Uranus will be forming a beneficial angle to that area of your chart that governs your daily work routine and the maintenance of your health. This means there will be plenty of excitement and unpredictability in your daily work that will stimulate your creativity. During tumultuous times, meaningful coincidences—synchronicities—are frequent. Pay attention to these nudges from the universe, decipher their messages, and know that every time you experience one of these, you're on the right track or are being warned that a particular path isn't in your best interest.

What's particularly notable about the Uranus transit is that from June 11, 2012, to June 25, 2013, it fits in nicely with Jupiter's transit through Gemini and your solar ninth house—your career area. The two planets form harmonious angles to each other. The unpredictability that accompanies Uranus allows Jupiter to expand your professional opportunities. Until October 5, Saturn in Libra is moving in opposition to Uranus. If we look at Saturn as representing the established way of doing things and Uranus as the new way, there can be some significant tug-of-wars. Just let the new win!

Here are some possibilities that may unfold with this Uranus transit. The abrupt changes can be troubling, but the end result seven years from now will be beneficial to you.

## Possibilities

1. You change jobs
2. Your career heads in a new direction
3. Your partner's income increases or plunges
4. Relationships end
5. New relationships begin
6. New, exciting experiences are the norm
7. You take more risks
8. The risks pay off
9. You start your own business
10. You sell a novel or screenplay
11. You're recognized in some way by your peers
12. The people around you are confused by your behavior
13. Loss of a loved one
14. You inherit money
15. You win or lose an insurance settlement
16. You find innovative ways to perform your job
17. Your marital status changes
18. You pay off your home
19. Your need for personal freedom and self-expression increases
20. You start meditating, take up yoga
21. You encounter people from past lives

These possibilities are just that—merely possibilities. To really grasp how the transit will affect you, get out your natal chart. Look at the house where Aries is found in your chart. Look for any planets you have in Aries. These areas—plus your sun—are the ones that will be impacted most strongly by Uranus's transit through Aries.

Turn to the natal chart at the end of chapter 9. This woman is a Capricorn with a tenth-house sun, has a Leo moon in the fifth house, and has Aries rising at 19 degrees and 54 minutes—19♈54. The rising is the cusp of her first house, which governs the self. So Uranus has been in her twelfth house since it was at 17 degrees and 16 minutes of Pisces—17 ♓ 16—the cusp of her twelfth house.

During this period, with Uranus stirring up all the hidden stuff in her unconscious, she got married and divorced, landed a great job in an assisted living facility as the wellness director (she's an RN), was nearly forced to resign by an abusive boss, fought it, held onto her job, and got a raise. All three of her sons from her first marriage left home during this transit—to jobs and college. She moved twice.

As of this writing, in 2010, she is now accustomed to this Uranian energy and is planning to branch out as a consultant in her field, helping other men and women to navigate the labyrinth of health care and options for their aging parents and grandparents. In other words, she sees a gap in the health-care market and is figuring out ways she might fill that gap. That's the innovation part of the equation.

Once Uranus enters Aries in March 2011, it will be on its approach to her rising—an important, major life transit. The rising, as the portal to our charts, is where our experiences enter into our lives. The closer Uranus gets to her ascendant, the more unpredictable, exciting, and high energy her life will become. The conjunction is exact in March 2016, but she may start feeling it as early as the summer of 2012, when Uranus reaches 8 degrees Aries (eleven degrees from her rising) before it turns retrograde. It turns direct again in early December 2012 and gets to within 7 degrees of her ascendant by July 2013, before it retrogrades again. By July 2014, Uranus gets to within 3 degrees of her rising before it retrogrades once more. In late May 2015, it hits her rising.

What all this means is that each year as Uranus inches closer to that exact hit on her rising sign, she feels a progressively stronger urge to break free of any restrictions that are holding her back. The closer it gets to her rising, the closer it also gets to forming beautiful angles—trines—to her South Node in Leo (fourth house)—☋12♌32, and her natal moon and Pluto in Leo in the fifth house—☽21♌48 and ♇22♌54. So while she's feeling this tremendous urge for freedom, Uranus is making it easier for her to bring about major changes in her emotional, inner life (moon). A new relationship could enter the picture, and it will be one wild, wonderful ride, different from anything she has experienced before. She might move.

With Pluto thrown into the mix, she has a marvelous opportunity to understand her innermost being—the unconscious beliefs and attitudes that have resulted in negative situations or relationships in the past. The trine to Pluto from Uranus gives her enormous personal power. One of her sons (fifth house) may get married. She might do or create something so innovative that she is recognized for it by peers. The trine to her South Node and sextile to her North Node in Aquarius in the eleventh house—☊12♒32—suggests that people she has known in the past (this life or others) may surface. She will have an opportunity to attain her dreams.

These possibilities are due to the transit of just one planet, Aries. So when you look at your natal chart to see where Uranus's impact will be felt most strongly, look beyond your sun sign. Look at other planets and points, too.

Notice, for instance, that in this same chart the woman has Jupiter in Taurus in her first house—♃10♉59. This means that during the first six months of 2012—as well as the last six months of 2011—this woman enjoys a Jupiter return. This is when Jupiter returns to the place it was when you were born, which happens every twelve years. It marks the beginning of a new cycle. So even while Uranus is upsetting the apple cart, she's benefiting tremendously from her Jupiter return during the first six months of 2012. New opportunities will surface in her personal life, she may have opportunities to travel internationally, she might get married.

In addition, see her Capricorn sun up there in the tenth house—☉13♑ 03? Pluto in Capricorn is now transiting her tenth house—her career area—creating profound change in her professional path. In March 2014, Pluto will conjunct her sun, so as it approaches the changes will become more intense. She'll feel a greater urge to alter her path and will gain insight into her own motives and psyche.

So when you look at your own chart, study how the other transiting planets are affecting your natal blueprint. You probably will find there's a balance. If one area of your life is chaotic, there will be other areas where life is truly exciting and prosperous.

## Dates to Watch For

**March 22:** On or around this new moon in Aries, life is going to get chaotic. A new partnership—business or romantic—may surface. Uranus will be close to this moon, suggesting sudden, unexpected events that catch you by surprise.

**May 20:** Solar eclipse in Gemini, in your solar ninth house. This one attracts new opportunities for foreign travel, education, and for expanding your spirituality and worldview.

**June 4:** Lunar eclipse in fire sign Sagittarius, in your solar third house. Any news you hear on or around this eclipse date should be positive.

One powerful period this year occurs between **July 3 and August 23,** when Mars joins Saturn in your sign. Mars endows you with all the physical energy you need to accomplish something, and Saturn brings the structure with which to do it. During this same period, Mercury transits compatible fire sign Leo, so your communication skills are sharp and dramatic, and people are paying attention.

Between **February 8 and March 5,** Venus and Uranus are traveling together in Aries, a surefire combination that revs up your love life. During this period, a business or romantic partner may enter your life suddenly, unexpectedly. An exciting, unpredictable time.

From **October 28 to November 21,** Venus transits your sign, a wonderful period for meeting someone new, socializing, for creative work. Others find you appealing and are open to your ideas.

Venus is retrograde in Gemini between **May 15 and June 27,** a period when there may be some bumps in traveling or your education or with legal issues. The bumps are annoyances, not headaches!

CHAPTER 16

# Libra and Mars in 2012

Mars and Martians. In movies and books from the 1950s, the Martians were usually the bad guys, and they were invading Earth. They looked bad, too—green blobs with tentacles or very tall beings with multiple arms that resembled old rubber. The invaders had powers we humans lacked and were obviously more technologically advanced, but they could be brought down by simple science: Earth germs against which they had no immunity.

These days, of course, the bad aliens might be from anywhere. In ABC's remake of *V*, the aliens look like us, talk like us, and are all attractive and cultured, but they have an insidious agenda. We don't really know what the true physical appearance is of these "visitors." Mars is never mentioned.

Our cultural fascination with invading aliens and Mars probably began with the publication of H. G. Wells's *War of the Worlds* in 1898. The novel's story idea is simple: Mars is dying and the Martians flee their world and invade Earth, planning to take over the planet and all its resources. Their first attack, on London, with advanced weaponry seems to ensure their victory. But they're defeated by—you guessed it!—germs.

Edgar Rice Burroughs had a thing or two to say about Mars, too. In 1911, he wrote *A Princess of Mars,* the first of eleven novels about the red planet. The protagonist was John Carter, a confederate Civil War veteran who ends up being transported to Mars. Over the course of the eleven books, he settles into life on his adopted planet—gets married, involved in Martian politics, fights the good fight.

In 1951, Ray Bradbury's *Martian Chronicles* twisted the idea of Martian as invader in a new way. Human settlers arrive on Mars, and the Martians are killed by the bacteria that the humans bring with them. But these Martians capture our hearts because they are beautiful people of an ancient civilization.

Robert Heinlein, with his 1961 publication of *Stranger in a Strange Land*, brought another curve into the Martian theme. His story centers on a human born on Mars, the only survivor of the first manned space mission to the planet. The protagonist, Valentine Michael Smith, is raised and educated by Martians, then is returned to Earth when he's a young man with the sensibilities of a human, the perspective of an alien, and incredible psychic powers.

In addition to *V,* television has mined the alien and Mars theme, too. There was *My Favorite Martian, Alien Nation, Battlestar Galactica,* and of course, *X-Files.* In film, there were a host of many forgettable movies, but an exception was *Total Recall,* based on a Philip K. Dick short story. Arnold Schwarzenegger plays a man haunted by suppressed memories—specifically, journeys to Mars. The story has all the complex hallmarks of Philip K. Dick—paranoia, duplicity, deep and powerful secrets, and plenty of corrupt bad guys. The ending takes place on Mars, when atmospheric gases and water are freed from deep within the planet's rocks. Spielberg never told us where ET came from, but it probably wasn't Mars!

What do we actually know about the red planet? We know that it bears some similarities to Earth and may have been habitable at one time in the past—and may be in the future. Its surface has been dramatically altered by volcanism, impacts by asteroids and meteors and other celestial bodies, violent movements in its crust, and great cyclonic dust storms that frequently swallow the entire planet. Its polar ice caps grow and recede, like ours, with the change of seasons. Near the poles, the layered soil indicates that the planet's climate has changed more than once. Its ancient volcanoes, once powered from the heat of the Martian core, rise against the starkness with a kind of fierce purity. The largest volcano, Olympus Mons, is seventeen miles high and may be the largest in the solar system. There's also a titanic canyon about the size of the distance between New York and L.A.

Due to several unmanned missions to Mars, our knowledge about the planet is growing. Thanks to the Mars Odyssey spacecraft, launched in 2001, it's now believed that billions of years ago Mars was inundated by the largest floods in the solar system. No one knows where all that water went, but the Mars Odyssey detected substantial quantities of water mixed into the soil about three feet down, near the Martian south pole.

On August 12, 2005, the Mars Reconnaissance Orbiter was launched, and it entered the orbit of Mars on March 10, 2006. After five months of a technique called aerobraking—a three-step procedure that cuts in half the fuel needed to achieve a lower, more circular orbit—the orbiter started its scientific tests. These lasted until November 2008. Since then, NASA has released thousands of high-resolution photos of the Mars surface that have broadened our knowledge about the fourth planet from the sun. The photos may answer the basic questions about whether Mars had water, if it was once inhabited and if so, was it destroyed by a catastrophe? Can it sustain human life in the future?

Images of recent impact craters on Mars have revealed subsurface ice midway between the planet's north pole and equator. A geologist with the U.S. Geological Survey claims he has found evidence of an extensive cave system among ancient volcanoes at Mars's equator. He believes the depressions visible in the high-resolution photos are consistent with lava flows on Earth that produce caves. Some of these depressions are more than 60 miles long and 150 feet across. If the geologist is right, then caves may provide early colonists with protection from the harsh environment and lethal cosmic rays.

On a clear night at certain times of the year, you can walk outside after dark and glimpse Mars in the sky, a speck of rose-tinted light between 56,000,000 and 399,000,000 kilometers from Earth. Its diameter is a little more than half that of Earth, the length of a Martian day is 24.6 Earth hours, a Martian year is 1.88 Earth years, and gravity on the surface is about a third of Earth's. Ninety-five percent of the atmosphere consists of carbon dioxide. It has two moons, both so small that they may not be moons but just rock that has gotten trapped in the planet's gravitational pull. They are named after the two squires who served Ares, the Greek god of war: Phobos—which means "fear," and Deimos—"panic."

## Mars in Astrology

To the ancient Greeks, he was Ares, a savage god who was little more than a bloodthirsty SOB. In the *Iliad,* Zeus says it like he sees it, that he finds Ares, his son, completely odious because he enjoyed nothing but "strife, war, and battles." On Olympus, he was intensely disliked for his blind violence and brutality.

This theme is beautifully illustrated in the movie *Gladiator.* Times are brutal, and brute strength is held in such high esteem that the populace turns out to watch men kill each other in the stadium. Not surprisingly, Aries Russell Crowe won an Oscar for his performance. Now skip ahead a couple thousand years. In *The Running Man,* one of the novellas that Stephen King wrote as Richard Bachman, this same theme is repeated, but now the protagonist (Arnold Schwarzenegger in the film) is running for his life on national TV and surviving by his wits and brute strength. Same theme, different century.

But aggression, survival, and war are only one side of Mars. The Greek side. On the Roman side, he was called by the name we know him—Mars. He was first and foremost the god of agriculture—the protector of cattle, the preserver of corn—and was associated with the woodpecker, the horse, and the wolf. As the husband of Rhea Silvia, a vestal virgin, he fathered Romulus and Remus, who were suckled by a wolf.

The connection between Mars and sex probably came about as a result of Ares's affair with the goddess Aphrodite. She was married to a cripple, Hephaestus, and compared to him Ares was handsome, dashing, courageous, all the things the Olympians looked for in a mate. Ares, of course, took advantage of the situation, and their lustful encounters on the "marriage couch" became well known to the other gods when Hephaestus ensnared the adulterous couple in an invisible net.

In 2012, Mars makes it through six signs and spends less than a week in a seventh. Let's take a look at what these transits mean for you, Libra.

## Important Dates

**January 1–July 3:** Mars in Virgo, your solar twelfth house. This area is the most secretive part of your chart, so you'll do plenty of digging around in your own psyche. Your motives will be obvious to you. It's possible you'll meet up with people you have known in past lives. A lot is going on underneath the surface, out of sight, behind the scenes. Therapy, meditation, yoga can all be beneficial.

During this transit, Mars forms a beneficial angle to Pluto, which is in Capricorn, and helps you to set and attain realistic goals.

**July 3 to August 23:** Mars in your sign. This transit accentuates all the qualities for which you're known—your need for balance and harmony, sociable personality, ability to communicate and to attract the helpful people you need. You're able to achieve a lot under this transit. Use the time wisely.

**August 23 to October 6:** Mars in Scorpio, in your solar second house of finances. You may be working harder to make ends meet or simply because you love what you're doing. Mars in Scorpio is an intense combination and may bring up issues and situations concerning your values. You may have to defend your values to someone. Or someone expects you to do so—and you refuse. Budgetary issues may surface, too. Are you sticking to yours? One way or another, your money and values are highlighted during this transit.

**October 6 to November 16:** Mars in Sagittarius, your solar third house of communication. You're doing more writing and talking during this transit, more e-mailing; perhaps you even start a blog or build a Web site. You may be checking out new neighborhoods in anticipation of a move. This transit also brings more frequent contact with siblings, other relatives, neighbors. A romance is possible with someone who may live as close to you as your own neighborhood!

**November 16 to December 25:** Mars in Capricorn, your solar fourth house of home and family. Unless you have natal planets in earth signs, this probably won't be your favorite transit of the year. It may create friction at home as you feel pulled between responsibilities there and obligations at work. That said, consider using this energy for refurbishing your home in some way—fresh paint on the walls, new floors, or just general cleaning out of the garage, attic, closets. Practice Feng Shui to bring greater balance into your home and thus into your life.

**December 25 to February 13, 2013:** Mars in Aquarius, your solar fifth house. Mars now forms a beneficial angle to your sun sign and enables you to accomplish quite a bit. Your creative projects take on new life and energy, you make more time for enjoyable activities, and your love life (and sex life!) also improves.

Aquarius's energy is familiar to you. It enables you to focus more clearly on your goals and to think outside the box.

CHAPTER 17

# The Big Picture for Libra in 2012

Welcome to 2012, Libra. It's a year of innovation, intellectual curiosity, research, communication. It's also a year when your closest partnerships in business and romance undergo abrupt change. Let's take a closer look.

Pluto, the slowest-moving planet in the zodiac, starts off the year in Capricorn, in your solar fourth house, where it has consistently been since November 2008. You're accustomed to its energy now. Its transit, which lasts until 2024, is bringing profound and permanent change globally, evident in the economic challenges that now face the U.S. Most institutions are in the throes of great change—the health-care industry, the petroleum and insurance industries, mortgages/lending, housing, aviation, even the Internet. You name it, and Pluto's fingerprint can be found.

On a personal level, this planet's transit through that area of your chart that represents home and family will continue to transform these things at profound levels. You may start a family, or your kids leave home as adults. One of your parents moves in with you or needs additional help and support. You move. Get married or divorced. The specifics that unfold with this transit depend on your age and circumstances. But profound change is certain.

Neptune entered Pisces and your solar sixth house on

April 4, 2011. But by early August 2011, it had slipped back into Aquarius. On February 3, 2012, it enters Pisces again and won't move on until January 2026. This transit forms an angle to your sun that demands an attitude adjustment with your daily work routine. For hints about what this may mean for you, look back to that period in 2011 when Neptune was in Pisces.

Neptune symbolizes our higher ideals, escapism, fiction, spirituality, and our blind spots. It seeks to dissolve boundaries between us and others. One possible repercussion of this transit is prolonged religious wars, which proliferated during Uranus's transit in Pisces from early 2003.

On a personal level, though, Neptune's transit through your solar sixth house indicates that you will try to integrate your ideals and spiritual beliefs more readily into your daily work routine. Since the sixth house also deals with the maintenance of your health, you may be trying alternative therapies for health stuff—anything from acupuncture to homeopathy. If you are diagnosed with any ailment, get a second opinion. Neptune lends itself to plenty of confusion, and a misdiagnosis is possible during this transit.

Uranus entered Aries and your solar seventh house in March 2011. This transit is discussed at some length in chapter 15, on Uranus's transit through Aries, so take a look there for in-depth information. But know that one repercussion of this transit is that unusual and exciting people are going to be entering your life and shaking things up. Your business and personal partnerships are about to undergo radical and unexpected changes.

Saturn begins the year in your sign. It has been there since the summer of 2010 and will be there until October 2012. This transit brings greater structure to your life, but can also indicate delays, restrictions. You are urged to live up to your responsibilities and obligations.

Once Saturn enters water sign Scorpio on October 5, your attention turns toward finances—what you earn, what you spend, your budget, your values. This transit is apt to be emotionally intense, as is the nature of Scorpio, but also intuitive, psychic. You may have hunches about how to earn more money, about creating a financial niche for yourself. Follow those hunches.

One of your best periods falls between June 11, 2012, and June 25, 2013, when Jupiter transits fellow air sign Gemini. This transit provides an expansive foundation for what will follow when Jupiter enters Cancer and your solar tenth house of career in 2013. Every seed you plant during this period, every thought you change, every belief you fine-tune will produce results down the road, but will also broaden your outlook about what is possible in your life overall.

It highlights higher education, publishing, overseas travel, foreign cultures. It's possible that your company's products or your services/products expand to overseas markets. You may be traveling overseas more frequently, which opens your consciousness to new experiences, thoughts, ideas.

From January 1 to June 11, when Jupiter transits earth sign Taurus and your solar eighth house, everything connected to mortgages, loans, taxes, and insurance will go your way. Nice change, right? Also, your partner's income should expand in a major way. Your own psychic and intuitive abilities will deepen. Other people will be ready and willing to share their time, expertise, and money with you.

They say that timing is everything, so with that in mind let's look at some specific areas in your life in 2012.

## Romance/Creativity

The most romantic and creative time for you all year falls between October 28 and November 21, when Venus transits your sign. Think: appeal, seduction, popularity, artistic flow. You feel more sensual, your self-confidence soars. Other people pick up what you radiate and respond accordingly. If you're in a committed relationship, then you and your partner rediscover each other. Plan a trip out of town to some secluded, romantic spot. Spend time together doing whatever you both enjoy.

Other good dates: April 3 to May 15 and June 27 to August 7, when Venus is moving direct in fellow air sign Gemini. Your communication abilities are ramped up; you're in your creative groove, Libra. The best time for serious involvement and deepening commitment in an existing relationship occurs when Venus transits Aries and your solar seventh house of partnerships. This happens between February 8 and March 5. You and your partner may decide to move in together, get engaged, or get married. Just be sure that you don't do any of this under a Mercury retrograde period. Take a look under the appropriate section below to find out when Mercury will be retrograde this year.

Other good backup dates: September 16 to October 5, when Mars transits your sign.

## Career

Career timing is covered in chapter 14, but here's some additional information about professional matters. Usually, Venus and Jupiter transits to your career area are the times to look for. Jupiter doesn't transit that area this year, but in 2013 it will, so now is the time to sow the seeds for whatever you desire professionally in 2013.

Between August 7 and September 6, Venus transits Cancer and your career area. This is the time to pitch your ideas and garner support among coworkers for your projects. Others are open and receptive to your insights and ideas, and it's much easier to move ahead with specific projects. A raise or promotion could be in the offing, too. Fortunately, Mercury turns direct on August 8, so you enjoy the full benefit of Venus's transit.

Even though Jupiter doesn't transit your career area until 2013, during its transit through Taurus it forms a beneficial angle to this area. Your professional responsibilities expand, your worldview deepens and broadens, and the people you meet and draw into your professional sphere will be experts.

Another nice period is when Mercury transits your career area between June 7 and 25. This is the time to pitch ideas, push your agenda forward, travel related to work, and socialize with peers. It also favors all professional communication.

Between July 3 and August 23, Mars transits your sign, linking up with Saturn in your sign, too. Read more about the possible ramifications in chapter 16.

## Best Times For

***Buying or selling a home:*** November 16 to December 25, when Mars transits Capricorn and your solar fourth house. Between January 8 and 27, Mercury transits the same sign and house.

***Family reunions:*** Any of the dates above or when Venus is in your sign between October 28 and November 21.

***Financial matters:*** The period from November 21 to December 15, when Venus transits Libra and your solar second house.

***Signing contracts:*** When Mercury is moving direct!

## Mercury Retrogrades

Every year, Mercury—the planet of communication and travel—turns retrograde three times. During this period, it's wise not to sign contracts (unless you don't mind renegotiating when Mercury is moving direct), to check and recheck travel plans (or, better yet, don't travel), and to communicate as succinctly as possible. Refrain from buying any large-ticket items or electronics during this time, too. Often, computers and appliances go on the fritz, cars act up, data is lost . . . you get the idea. Be sure to back up all files before the dates below:

***March 12–April 4:*** Mercury retrograde in Aries, your seventh house—partnerships.

***July 14–August 8:*** Mercury retrograde in Leo, your solar eleventh house—groups, friends.

***November 6–26:*** Mercury retrograde in Sagittarius, your solar third house of communication, travel, siblings.

## Eclipses

Solar eclipses tend to trigger external events that bring about change according to the sign and house in which they fall. Lunar eclipses trigger inner, emotional events according to the sign and house in which they fall. Any eclipse marks both beginnings and endings. The solar and lunar eclipse in a pair falls in opposite signs. If you're interested in detailed information on eclipses, take a look at Celeste Teal's excellent and definitive book, *Eclipses: Predicting World Events & Personal Transformation.*

If you were born under or around the time of an eclipse, it's to your advantage to take a look at your birth chart to find out exactly where the eclipses will impact you.

Most years feature four eclipses—two solar, two lunar, with the set separated by about two weeks. In November and December 2011, there were solar and lunar eclipses, so this year the first eclipses fall during May and June.

***May 20:*** Solar eclipse at 0 degrees Gemini. This one should bring in new opportunities for foreign travel, education, publishing, and expressing your spiritual beliefs and worldview.

***June 4:*** Lunar eclipse in Sagittarius, your solar third house. News that arrives around this time is positive.

***November 13:*** Solar eclipse in Scorpio, in your solar second house. New financial opportunities.

***November 28:*** Lunar eclipse, Gemini. Jupiter forms a five-degree conjunction to the eclipse degree, suggesting that news you receive around this time will be cause for celebration!

## Luckiest Day of the Year

Every year, there's one day when Jupiter and the sun meet up and luck, serendipity, and expansion are the hallmarks. This year, that day falls on May 13, with a conjunction in Taurus.

CHAPTER 18

# Eighteen Months of Day-by-Day Predictions: July 2011 to December 2012

***Moon sign times are calculated for Eastern Standard Time and Eastern Daylight Time. Please adjust for your local time zone.***

## JULY 2011

***Friday, July 1 (Moon in Cancer)*** With the new moon in your tenth house, opportunities that can move you ahead in your career appear. Meanwhile, Jupiter forms a nice angle to the moon, suggesting that you can expand whatever you're doing in your profession. It could also mean an elevation in prestige or a raise in pay.

***Saturday, July 2 (Moon into Leo, 5:44 p.m.)*** Mercury moves into your eleventh house. Your mind is quick, and your interests vary. You're willing to talk about your ideas with anyone who will listen, and you don't really care what they think. You're friendly toward others, but somewhat impersonal and nonemotional as you express your thoughts and exchange ideas.

***Sunday, July 3 (Moon in Leo)*** You're very organized, and you feel best when you're in control. Be aware of a tendency to be somewhat bossy—a remarkable shift for you, Libra. Don't worry. These are just passing notions. Toot your horn, but avoid being overly impressed with your accomplishments.

***Monday, July 4 (Moon into Virgo, 9:16 p.m.)*** Venus moves into your tenth house. A marriage or partnership boosts your career. You thrive in any creative work, such as the arts, diplomacy, and entertainment. You gain public favor in whatever you're doing.

***Tuesday, July 5 (Moon in Virgo)*** The moon is in your twelfth house. Work behind the scenes and stay out of public view. Childhood issues come to the surface. Take time to focus on your dreams and consider past lives.

***Wednesday, July 6 (Moon into Libra, 11:54 p.m.)*** A domestic adjustment works out for the best. Be understanding and avoid confrontations. Be diplomatic, resourceful, and helpful, but avoid scattering your energies. Focus on making people happy.

***Thursday, July 7 (Moon in Libra)*** The moon is in your first house. You get your batteries recharged. You're physically vital, Libra; you get along well with the opposite sex. You're also malleable, and you can easily change your mind. You're restless and uncertain what to do.

***Friday, July 8 (Moon in Libra)*** With the moon in your sign, it's a great day for romance, Libra. Art, music, and film are highlighted. You're seeking harmony and peace. Your creativity, personal grace, and magnetism are emphasized.

***Saturday, July 9 (Moon into Scorpio, 2:32 a.m.)*** Uranus goes retrograde in your seventh house. You could encounter some erratic behavior in relationships, especially with a spouse or partner. Money issues could arise, especially related to whatever you share. Be generous. Try to avoid any feelings of wanting it all for yourself. An inheritance or investments could be at the source of any conflict. Expect some financial ups and downs until mid-December.

***Sunday, July 10 (Moon in Scorpio)*** Yesterday's energy flows into your Sunday. Finances and money issues take center stage, Libra. You identify emotionally with your possessions or whatever you value. Watch your spending. You feel best when surrounded by familiar objects, especially in your home environment. It's not the objects themselves that are important, but the feelings and memories you associate with them.

***Monday, July 11 (Moon into Sagittarius, 3:47 a.m.)*** You have the chance to work cooperatively with others, Libra. Be aware that tensions could flare, but you have the talent to keep everything on an even keel. There could be some soul-searching about a relationship.

***Tuesday, July 12 (Moon in Sagittarius)*** The moon is in your third house. You get your ideas across, but try not to get too emotional, especially with siblings and neighbors. A female relative plays an important role. Follow your hunches. You write from a deep place.

***Wednesday, July 13 (Moon into Capricorn, 10:14 a.m.)*** Control your impulses. Fulfill your obligations. You're building a base for an outlet for your creativity. Persevere to get things done, and don't get sloppy. Be methodical and thorough.

***Thursday, July 14 (Moon in Capricorn)*** Spend time with your family and loved ones. Stick close to home, if possible. Do something to beautify your home. Remember your home is a reflection of who you are. Retreat to a private place to consider everything that has been taking place. A parent plays a role.

***Friday, July 15 (Moon into Aquarius, 4:30 p.m.)*** There's a full moon in Capricorn. You gain insight and illumination related to a domestic matter. You reap what you've sown. You feel a close tie to your roots. Change a bad habit.

***Saturday, July 16 (Moon in Aquarius)*** The moon is in your fifth house. You're in touch with your creative side, but your emotions tend to overpower your intellect. There's great depth to a love relationship. You might be somewhat possessive of loved ones, particularly children.

***Sunday, July 17 (Moon in Aquarius)*** You find strength in numbers and meaning through friends and groups. You have deep contact with friends and other like-minded individuals who join you in a project for the common good. Help others, but keep an eye on your wishes and dreams.

***Monday, July 18 (Moon into Pisces, 1:13 a.m.)*** It's about beginnings and endings. Finish what you've been working on, and get ready for something new. Take time to assimilate what you've learned. Look for ways to expand. Look beyond the immediate. It's all part of a cycle.

***Tuesday, July 19 (Moon in Pisces)*** You're at the top of your cycle. You get an opportunity to take the lead, and there's no need to be afraid of trying something new. Don't let the doubters get in your way. You attract creative and positive people to your side.

***Wednesday, July 20 (Moon into Aries, 12:26 a.m.)*** Yesterday's energy flows into your Wednesday. Try not to get impatient with others who don't quite see your vision yet. A partner will be important in the process. Pursue your goals, but stress cooperation as well as individuality and creativity. New relationships form. Show your appreciation to others.

***Thursday, July 21 (Moon in Aries)*** Your high energy and creative partnership continue. You're extremely persuasive, especially if you're passionate about what you're doing, selling, or trying to convey. You get along well with your partner, especially if he or she is a Cancer or Capricorn. Others are more accepting. You can fit in just about anywhere.

***Friday, July 22 (Moon into Taurus, 12:59 p.m.)*** More hard work is called for. Stay grounded. Control your impulses to promote rather than create. Now is the time to fulfill your obligations. Be methodical and thorough. Emphasize quality. It's not an especially good day for romance.

***Saturday, July 23 (Moon in Taurus)*** Security is an important issue with you right now. It can affect your feelings about your possessions, as well as things that you share with others. Deal with mortgages, insurance, and investments. Issues of the day also could include matters of sex, death, rebirth, rituals, and relationships.

***Sunday, July 24 (Moon in Taurus)*** Cultivate new ideas, but make sure that they're down-to-earth. Get involved in a worthwhile cause aimed at improving living conditions for large numbers of people. You're opinionated and also highly sensual.

***Monday, July 25 (Moon into Gemini, 12:35 a.m.)*** You're a searcher, a seeker of truth. You venture out into the unknown. Secrets, intrigue, and confidential information play roles. Be aware of decisions made behind closed doors. Knowledge is essential to success. You work best on your own.

***Tuesday, July 26 (Moon in Gemini)*** The moon is in your ninth house, the home of higher learning. You communicate well, Ideas and philosophies are important. Plan a trip or sign up for a seminar or workshop. A foreign country or person of foreign birth could play a role. Publicity and advertising are emphasized.

***Wednesday, July 27 (Moon into Cancer, 9:12 p.m.)*** Clear up odds and ends. Take an inventory of where things are going in your life. It's a good day to make a donation to a worthy cause. Make room for something new. Use the day for reflection, expansion, and concluding projects. Don't start anything new until tomorrow.

***Thursday, July 28 (Moon in Cancer)*** Venus moves into your eleventh house, indicating that you get along well with others. You can find romance with someone in a group, but it might take help from friends. Meanwhile, with Mercury moving into your twelfth house, subconscious influences affect your decisions. You tend to go with your emotions over logic, and you're feeling somewhat shy.

***Friday, July 29 (Moon in Cancer)*** Professional concerns take on importance. You could get a promotion, a raise, or a pat on the back. You're more responsive to the needs and moods of a group and of the public in general. You move up the ladder.

***Saturday, July 30 (Moon into Leo, 2:16 a.m.)*** Yesterday's energy flows into your Saturday as a new moon appears in your eleventh house. Opportunities come your way through your work with others, especially a group. Friends play a surprisingly important role, especially Gemini and Aquarius. Focus on your wishes and dreams. Examine your overall goals, and make sure that they're still an expression of who you are.

***Sunday, July 31 (Moon in Leo)*** You're feeling particularly passionate. You're impulsive and honest. Drama is highlighted; you're at center stage. Dress boldly. Romance and love feel majestic. Let others know who you are.

## AUGUST 2011

***Monday, August 1 (Moon into Virgo, 4:42 a.m.)*** Use your intuition to get a sense of your day. Be kind and understanding. Your intuition focuses on relationships. Marriage could play a key role. Don't make waves. Don't rush or show resentment; let things develop.

***Tuesday, August 2 (Moon in Virgo)*** Mercury goes retrograde in your twelfth house and stays there until August 26. Over the next three weeks, you could meet one or more people from your past lives. You also could be dealing with personal power issues during this time that you thought were resolved. Expect some delays in short-distance travel, some possible computer glitches.

***Wednesday, August 3 (Moon into Libra, 6:05 a.m.)*** Mars moves into your second house. You put a lot of energy into money issues this month. You have a strong drive to increase your earnings. Be aware that you'll also have an urge to spend as well. You're competitive and not afraid to take risks.

***Thursday, August 4 (Moon in Libra)*** The moon is on your ascendant. You're recharged for the month ahead, and this makes you more appealing to the public.

It's a great day for starting something new. Your appearance and personality shine. Your feelings and thoughts are aligned. Dealings with the opposite sex go well.

***Friday, August 5 (Moon into Scorpio, 7:57 a.m.)*** It's a number 6 day, a service day. You offer advice and support. Diplomacy wins the day. Be sympathetic and kind, generous and tolerant. Focus on making people happy, but avoid scattering your energies.

***Saturday, August 6 (Moon in Scorpio)*** With the moon in your second house, expect emotional experiences related to money. You feel best when surrounded by familiar objects in your home. It's not the objects themselves that are important, but the feelings and memories you associate with them. Put off making any major purchases.

***Sunday, August 7 (Moon into Sagittarius, 11:21 a.m.)*** You're in the power seat. It's your day to play it your way. You have a chance to gain recognition, fame, and power. Be courageous. Be yourself; be honest. Expect a windfall.

***Monday, August 8 (Moon in Sagittarius)*** The moon is in your third house. You write from a deep place. It's a good day for journaling. Your mental abilities are strong, and you have an emotional need to reinvigorate your studies, especially regarding matters of the past. You're attracted to historical or archaeological matters. A female relative plays a role.

***Tuesday, August 9 (Moon into Capricorn, 4:38 p.m.)*** It's a number 1 day, and that means you're at the top of your cycle again. You get a fresh start and attract creative people to your cause. Avoid naysayers, and don't be afraid to turn in a new direction. In romance, a flirtation could turn serious.

***Wednesday, August 10 (Moon in Capricorn)*** Spend time with your family and loved ones. You're dealing with your roots. Stick close to home, if possible. You're dealing with the foundations of who you are and who you are becoming. How about buying something to beautify your home?

***Thursday, August 11 (Moon into Aquarius, 11:48 p.m.)*** Your attitude determines everything. Spread your good news. You communicate well. Your charm and wit are appreciated. Friends play an important role in your day. Take time to relax, enjoy yourself, and recharge your batteries. You can influence people with your upbeat attitude.

***Friday, August 12 (Moon in Aquarius)*** Social events and group activities are on tap. Your individuality is stressed. You have a great sense of freedom. You're dealing with new ideas, new options, originality. You get a new perspective. Play your hunches. Look beyond the immediate.

***Saturday, August 13 (Moon in Aquarius)*** There's a full moon in your fifth house. You gain insight and illumination related to a love interest. You might be somewhat possessive of loved ones, particularly children. But eventually you need to let go. Take a gamble; buy a lottery ticket. Your emotions tend to overpower your intellect, and your creative energies or romantic inclinations are strong.

***Sunday, August 14 (Moon into Pisces, 8:55 a.m.)*** Service to others is the theme of the day, and diplomacy wins the day. Do a good deed for someone. Visit someone who is ill or in need of help. Be sympathetic, kind, and compassionate. A domestic adjustment works out for the best.

***Monday, August 15 (Moon in Pisces)*** Yesterday's energy flows into your Monday. You improve, edit, and refine the work of others. Help others, but don't deny your own needs. Keep your resolutions about exercise, and watch your diet. Attend to details related to your health.

***Tuesday, August 16 (Moon into Aries, 8:03 p.m.)*** It's a number 8 day—your power day and your day to play it your way. You can go far with your plans and achieve financial success. Be aware that fear of failure or fear that you won't measure up will attract tangible experiences that reinforce the feeling.

***Wednesday, August 17 (Moon in Aries)*** It's a great time for initiating projects, launching new ideas, and brainstorming. However, emotions could be volatile. You're passionate but impatient. You're extremely persuasive, especially if you're passionate about what you're doing, selling, or trying to convey. Avoid self-deception.

***Thursday, August 18 (Moon in Aries)*** You could be negotiating or signing a contract, possibly for the sale of your house. You're taking the initiative, along with your partner, and, like yesterday, emotions could get volatile. You're looking for security, but you have a hard time going with the flow.

***Friday, August 19 (Moon into Taurus, 8:37 a.m.)*** Cooperation and partnerships are highlighted. You work well with others. Your intuition focuses on relationships—either a new one that's developing or a current one. Don't make waves; let things develop. Show your appreciation to others.

***Saturday, August 20 (Moon in Taurus)*** Health and physical activity are highlighted. Go to the gym or take a yoga class. It's a good time for gardening, cultivating ideas, and doing practical and healthy things. Go hiking, have a picnic, get out into nature. Tend to money issues.

*Sunday, August 21 (Moon into Gemini, 8:53 p.m.)* With Venus moving into your twelfth house, you have a love of secrecy. You feel best staying out of the public eye. It's a good day for meditation. Focus on ideals: universal truth, love, and compassion. Your emotions are controlled by the subconscious mind.

*Monday, August 22 (Moon in Gemini)* The moon is in your ninth house. Your mind is active, and you yearn for new experiences. You can create positive change through your ideas. A publishing project takes off. Publicity and advertising are emphasized.

*Tuesday, August 23 (Moon in Gemini)* Yesterday's energy flows into your Tuesday. You're mentally stimulated and feeling restless. Get away; a change of scenery would do you good. You communicate well and make your point, especially with family members and neighbors.

*Wednesday, August 24 (Moon into Cancer, 6:31 a.m.)* You're a spy for your own cause. Gather information, but don't make any absolute decisions until tomorrow. Go with the flow. Knowledge is essential to success. Make sure that you see things as they are, not as you wish them to be. Express your desires, but avoid self-deception. Maintain your emotional balance.

*Thursday, August 25 (Moon in Cancer)* The moon is in your tenth house. Professional concerns take on more importance. You could get a promotion, a raise, or a pat on the back. You're more responsive to the needs and moods of a group and of the public in general. You move up the ladder.

***Friday, August 26 (Moon into Leo, 12:09 p.m.)*** Mercury goes direct in your eleventh house. Misunderstandings and miscommunication with friends and members of a group recede into the past. Also, you can move ahead with your wishes and dreams. The delays and confusion are over. You get along well with others now.

***Saturday, August 27 (Moon in Leo)*** The moon is in your eleventh house, Libra. Your friendships expand as new people come into your life. You find strength in numbers and meaning through friends and groups. Focus on your wishes and dreams. But take a close look at your responsibilities and obligations, and follow through on them. Make sure that you're not hurting anyone with whatever your doing.

***Sunday, August 28 (Moon into Virgo, 2:13 p.m.)*** There's a new moon in your twelfth house. That means opportunities that could allow you to work at home or behind the scenes come your way. You're in touch with your subconscious, and you're dealing with love relationships from the past. You can turn it all into creative fodder.

***Monday, August 29 (Moon in Virgo)*** The moon is in your twelfth house. Withdraw and work behind the scenes. Hide your emotions and moodiness. Things associated with the past play a role. Avoid any self-destructive behavior. There's a tendency to undo all the positive actions you've taken.

***Tuesday, August 30 (Moon into Libra, 2:26 p.m.)*** Jupiter goes retrograde in your eighth house and stays there until December 25. You become more introspective about things that go bump in the night, about your worldviews, about spiritual beliefs. There also could be some delay and confusion related to an expansion of your role in managing shared property or possessions. Insurance, an inheritance, or taxes play a role.

***Wednesday, August 31 (Moon in Libra)*** The moon is in your first house. It's all about your health and your emotional self. Your feelings and thoughts are aligned. You get recharged for the coming month. It's a good day for pursuing romance and the arts. You keep everyone around you in balance, Libra, but make sure you take care of your duties and responsibilities.

## SEPTEMBER 2011

***Thursday, September 1 (Moon into Scorpio, 2:48 p.m.)*** You can influence people with your upbeat attitude. Play your hunches. Your charm and wit are appreciated. In business dealings, diversify. Insist on all the information, not just bits and pieces.

***Friday, September 2 (Moon in Scorpio)*** The moon is in your second house. Money issues and your emotions are on your agenda. You equate your financial assets with emotional security. Look at your priorities in handling your income. Look for an investment, pay your bills, and collect what's owed to you.

***Saturday, September 3 (Moon into Sagittarius, 3:04 p.m.)*** Think freedom, no restrictions. Variety is the spice of life. Think outside the box. Take risks and experiment. Travel and variety are highlighted. Release old structures; get a new point of view. You're versatile and changeable.

***Sunday, September 4 (Moon in Sagittarius)*** Share what you know with others. However, keep conscious control of your emotions when communicating, especially with siblings. Your thinking is unduly influenced by the past. You accept an invitation to a social event.

***Monday, September 5 (Moon into Capricorn, 10:04 p.m.)*** Explore something mysterious. You investigate, analyze, or simply observe what's going on. You quickly come to a conclusion and wonder why others don't see what you see. Keep any secrets entrusted to you. Maintain your emotional balance.

***Tuesday, September 6 (Moon in Capricorn)*** Your ambition and drive to succeed are highlighted. Your responsibilities increase. You may feel stressed and overworked, but don't ignore your exercise routine. Self-discipline and structure are key.

***Wednesday, September 7 (Moon in Capricorn)*** The moon is in your fourth house. Spend time with your family and loved ones. Stick close to home, if possible. You could be dealing with parents now. You feel close to your roots. It's a good day for dream recall.

***Thursday, September 8 (Moon into Aquarius, 5:43 a.m.)*** It's a number 1 day, and you're at the top of your cycle again. Get out and meet new people; have new experiences. You're inventive; you make connections that others overlook. You get a fresh start. Trust your hunches.

***Friday, September 9 (Moon in Aquarius)*** Mercury goes back into your twelfth house. Subconscious influences affect your thoughts. You're somewhat reticent about speaking out. Matters from the past are difficult, and your thinking is more influenced by feelings than by logic.

***Saturday, September 10 (Moon into Pisces, 3:27 p.m.)*** You communicate well. Your popularity is on the rise.

Your charm and wit are appreciated today. Make time to listen to others. Relax, enjoy yourself, and recharge your batteries.

***Sunday, September 11 (Moon in Pisces)*** You're creative and imaginative, but you're also a dreamer and you can be somewhat unrealistic. You respond emotionally to whatever is happening now. Don't fall into a trap of self-deception.

***Monday, September 12 (Moon in Pisces)*** There's a full moon in your sixth house. It's harvesttime, Libra. You get good news related to your health. Your diet and exercise program pays off. Others respect you and turn to you for help. You improve, refine, and edit their work. But don't ignore your own needs.

***Tuesday, September 13 (Moon into Aries, 2:50 a.m.)*** It's a number 6 day, a service day. Be diplomatic, especially with someone who is giving you trouble. Do a good deed for someone. Visit someone who is ill or in need of help. Be sympathetic, kind, and compassionate, but avoid scattering your energies.

***Wednesday, September 14 (Moon in Aries)*** Venus moves into your first house. Your personal grace is recognized and appreciated, and it can help you in business dealings, especially if you avoid any appearance of vanity. You can create new friendships. A romance blossoms.

***Thursday, September 15 (Moon into Taurus, 3:25 p.m.)*** Focus on a power play. Unexpected money arrives. You can go far with your plans and achieve financial success. Be aware that you're playing with power, so try not to hurt anyone.

***Friday, September 16 (Moon in Taurus)*** Pluto goes direct in your fourth house. You feel very attached to your home or land, and that feeling will continue for years. At the same time, there could be some tension in the home, and it could be a continuing concern. Be aware of power struggles, and see if you can defuse them before they get out of control.

***Saturday, September 17 (Moon in Taurus)*** With the moon in your eighth house, your experiences are more intense than usual. You have a strong sense of duty; you feel obligated to fulfill your promises. An interest in metaphysics plays a role in your day. You could take a deeper look into astrology.

***Sunday, September 18 (Moon into Gemini, 4:06 a.m.)*** Mars moves into your eleventh house. You put a lot of energy into a cause. You can excite people to support your goals, especially if you are working for the common good. You initiate action, and you are able to organize the masses. However, your strong sense of independence can make you your own worst enemy. Try not to disrupt the flow.

***Monday, September 19 (Moon in Gemini)*** The moon is in your ninth house today. You're a dreamer and a thinker. You may feel a need to get away. You yearn for a new experience. Plan a long trip or sign up for a workshop or seminar.

***Tuesday, September 20 (Moon into Cancer, 2:54 p.m.)*** Tear down the old in order to rebuild. Be methodical and thorough. Revise, rewrite. Persevere to get things done. Romance goes on the back burner.

***Wednesday, September 21 (Moon in Cancer)*** You're loving and caring. Your family is what counts. You're sensitive to the moods of others and tend to keep your concerns to yourself. You're intuitive and nurturing; your home life is important to you.

***Thursday, September 22 (Moon into Leo, 9:56 p.m.)*** Diplomacy wins the way. Focus on making people happy. Service to others is the theme of the day. Do a good deed for someone. Visit someone who is ill or in need of help.

***Friday, September 23 (Moon in Leo)*** Friends play an important role in your day, especially Gemini and Aquarius. Focus on your wishes and dreams. Examine your overall goals for the year and beyond. Make sure those goals are an expression of who you are.

***Saturday, September 24 (Moon into Virgo, 10:50 p.m.)*** It's another power day for you, Libra. You're well grounded and ready to gain financially. Friends play a role in your success. You can go far with your plans, especially if you get friends and members of a group involved. Be aware that you're playing with power, so try not to hurt anyone. Act with courage and honesty.

***Sunday, September 25 (Moon in Virgo)*** Mercury moves into your first house. You have a strong mental presence, an inquiring mind. You're talkative, and you communicate your ideas easily. You're quick-witted and you adapt smoothly to changing circumstances. You can grasp ideas on a wide variety of subjects.

***Monday, September 26 (Moon into Libra, 12:51 a.m.)*** You're at the top of your cycle again. You can take the lead and turn in a new direction. Trust your hunches. Stress originality. In romance, something new is developing. You express your opinions dynamically.

***Tuesday, September 27 (Moon in Libra)*** There's a new moon in your first house. That means new opportunities appear for you personally. You can connect and network with others, possibly through social networking sites. This new moon happens once a year and sets the tone for the next twelve months. Make a wish board and back your wishes with emotion.

***Wednesday, September 28 (Moon into Scorpio, 12:06 a.m.)*** Your charm and wit are appreciated. Make time to listen to others. Relax, enjoy yourself, and recharge your batteries. In business dealings, diversify. Insist on all the details, not just bits and pieces.

***Thursday, September 29 (Moon in Scorpio)*** The moon is in your second house. You can expect emotional reactions related to money and finances. You identify emotionally with your possessions or whatever you value. Watch your spending. Look at your priorities in handling your income.

***Friday, September 30 (Moon into Sagittarius, 12:42 a.m.)*** It's a number 5 day. That means you're open to change and variety, and you desire to loosen any restrictions. You're willing to take a risk and experiment. Variety is the spice of life, and change is good. Think outside the box.

## OCTOBER 2011

***Saturday, October 1 (Moon in Sagittarius)*** The moon is in your third house. You get your ideas across, Libra, especially when you're talking to family members and neighbors. You could be taking one or more short trips. Take time to check up on your mother.

***Sunday, October 2 (Moon in Sagittarius)*** Look for the big picture, not just the details. It's all about growth and expansion. You're restless, impulsive, and inquisitive. Don't limit yourself. There's passion in relationships, but making a commitment might be a problem.

***Monday, October 3 (Moon into Capricorn, 4:16 a.m.)*** The moon moves into your fourth house. Your ambition and drive to succeed are highlighted. Your responsibilities increase, and you might feel overburdened. But take time to exercise and watch your diet. Be conservative; don't speculate or take any unnecessary risks. Maintain emotional balance.

***Tuesday, October 4 (Moon in Capricorn)*** Stick close to home. Take care of domestic issues. Spend time with your family. Work on a home-repair project, or buy something special for your home.

***Wednesday, October 5 (Moon into Aquarius, 11:19 a.m.)*** It's a number 8 day, and you're at the top of your cycle. You're in the power seat now. Business discussions go well, especially if you open your mind to a new approach that could bring in big bucks. You pull off a financial coup.

***Thursday, October 6 (Moon in Aquarius)*** Be yourself; be emotionally honest. In love, there's greater emotional depth to a relationship. Creativity is emphasized. You're emotionally in touch with your artistic talents. You feel strongly attached to loved ones, particularly children. You can be somewhat possessive.

***Friday, October 7 (Moon into Pisces, 9:14 p.m.)*** You're at the top of your cycle. Take the lead. Get out and meet new people; have new experiences. Express your opinions dynamically. Explore, discover, and create. In romance, a flirtation turns more serious.

***Saturday, October 8 (Moon in Pisces)*** With the moon in your sixth house today, the emphasis turns to helping others. Trust your hunches. Your intuition is highlighted. Be careful not to overlook any seemingly minor matters that could take on importance. Attend to details related to your health. Make a doctor or dentist appointment that you've been putting off. Go to the gym or take a yoga class.

***Sunday, October 9 (Moon in Pisces)*** Venus moves into your second house. You can make money through the arts, Libra. You have a love of security and the better things in life. You take an interest in nice clothes and jewelry. Whatever represents the better side of life appeals to you. A desire to climb the social ladder plays a role.

***Monday, October 10 (Moon into Aries, 8:57 a.m.)*** It's a number 4 day. Your organizational skills are highlighted. Control your impulses. Set aside romantic notions for the time being. Persevere and fulfill your obligations. You're building foundations for your creativity. Emphasize quality.

***Tuesday, October 11 (Moon in Aries)*** There's a full moon in your seventh house. You gain insights or illumination related to a relationship or partnership. You get along well with others. You can fit in just about anywhere. You comprehend the nuances of a situation, but it's difficult to go with the flow.

***Wednesday, October 12 (Moon into Taurus, 9:35 p.m.)*** Focus on making people happy. Be sympathetic, kind, and compassionate. Service to others is the theme of the day. You offer advice and support.

***Thursday, October 13 (Moon in Taurus)*** With Mercury moving into your second house, come up with moneymaking ideas. Your values are more about material wealth than about ideals. You can also teach others about finances.

***Friday, October 14 (Moon in Taurus)*** Cultivate new ideas, but make sure that they're down-to-earth.

You could be somewhat stubborn and fixed in your opinions. Health and physical activity are highlighted. Your senses are highly developed. You're opinionated and highly sensual.

***Saturday, October 15 (Moon into Gemini, 10:15 a.m.)*** Finish what you started. Make room for something new. Visualize the future; set your goals, and then make them so. Accept what comes your way now. It's all part of a cycle. Don't start anything new today.

***Sunday, October 16 (Moon in Gemini)*** The moon is in your ninth house. Your experiences are more intense than usual, especially when dealing with matters related to your home. Take time to meditate or study a metaphysical subject, such as life after death or past lives.

***Monday, October 17 (Moon into Cancer, 9:39 p.m.)*** It's a number 2 day. Use your intuition to get a sense of your day. Be kind and understanding. Cooperation, especially with partners, is highlighted. Don't make waves. Don't rush or show resentment; let things develop. Marriage or a partnership plays a key role.

***Tuesday, October 18 (Moon in Cancer)*** The moon is in your tenth house. It's a good day for sales and dealing with the public. You're more responsive to the needs of others, and you're more emotional and warm toward coworkers. You get a boost in prestige. However, avoid mixing your professional life with your personal life.

***Wednesday, October 19 (Moon in Cancer)*** You're feeling somewhat moody and sensitive to other people's moods. Keep any negative comments to yourself. Tend to loved ones. Do something with your children or a sweetheart.

***Thursday, October 20 (Moon into Leo, 6:07 a.m.)*** Promote new ideas; follow your curiosity. Approach the day with an unconventional mindset. Let go of old structures; get a new point of view. Think freedom. Variety is the spice of life.

***Friday, October 21 (Moon in Leo)*** The moon is in your eleventh house. You have deeper contact with friends and could join a group of like-minded individuals. Social consciousness plays a role. You work for the common good, but keep an eye on your own wishes and dreams.

***Saturday, October 22 (Moon into Virgo, 10:42 a.m.)*** Secrets, intrigue, and confidential information play a role today. You might feel best working on your own. You investigate, analyze, or simply observe what's going on now. You quickly come to a conclusion and wonder why others don't see what you see. It's best to hold off on making any final decisions for a couple days.

***Sunday, October 23 (Moon in Virgo)*** Yesterday's energy flows into your Sunday. Again you feel comfortable remaining behind the scenes and out of public view. Meditate, recall your dreams, and look for meaning in any uncanny coincidences. Matters of the past might surface. Unconscious attitudes can be difficult. Keep your feelings secret.

***Monday, October 24 (Moon into Libra, 11:50 a.m.)*** It's a number 9 day. Visualize the future; set your goals, and then make them so. Complete a project. Clear up odds and ends. Take an inventory of where things are going in your life. It's a good day to make a donation to a worthy cause.

***Tuesday, October 25 (Moon in Libra)*** You're at the top of your cycle, and the moon is on your ascendant, Libra. The way you see yourself is the way others see you.

Your face is in front of the public. You get a fresh start. You take the lead in something new. You're recharged for the month ahead, and this makes you more appealing to the public. You're physically vital, and relations with the opposite sex go well.

***Wednesday, October 26 (Moon into Scorpio, 11:09 a.m.)*** There's a new moon in your second house, which speaks to opportunities related to finances coming your way. Whatever it is makes you feel joyful and more financially secure. However, think carefully before you go out and spend what's coming your way. Your values play an important role.

***Thursday, October 27 (Moon in Scorpio)*** Intense, emotional experiences are likely. You're passionate, and your sexuality is heightened. You look deeply into a matter, and you could become aware of things happening in secret and of possible deception. Forgive and forget, and try to avoid going to extremes.

***Friday, October 28 (Moon into Sagittarius, 10:46 a.m.)*** Your organizational skills are highlighted. Control your impulses. Tear down the old in order to rebuild. Be methodical and thorough. Persevere and fulfill your obligations. You're building foundations for your creativity. Emphasize quality.

***Saturday, October 29 (Moon in Sagittarius)*** The moon is in your third house. Your mind is sharp, and you communicate well. Take what you know and share it with others. You send out e-mails or make an entry on a blog. Your thinking is unduly influenced by things of the past. Family members play a role in your day. Do your best to avoid arguing with siblings or neighbors.

***Sunday, October 30 (Moon into Capricorn, 12:39 pm)*** Be sympathetic, kind, and compassionate on this Sunday. Do a good deed for someone. Visit someone who is ill or in need of help. Focus on making people happy. Take time to dance to your own tune. Domestic purchases are highlighted.

***Monday, October 31 (Moon in Capricorn)*** Authority figures play a role in your day. So do banks and financial institutions. Self-discipline and structure are key. You're feeling financially flush, but don't speculate or take unnecessary chances. Maintain emotional balance. Spend time with your family. Your domestic scene needs attention.

## NOVEMBER 2011

***Tuesday, November 1 (Moon into Aquarius, 6:08 p.m.)*** As the new month begins, the focus is on travel, adventure, and meeting new people. You're seeking new horizons. Freedom of thought and action is key. But so is moderation; avoid excess in whatever you're doing. You're motivated and inspired.

***Wednesday, November 2 (Moon in Aquarius)*** Mercury moves into your third house. You're witty and clever, adaptable and versatile. Your mind is active, and you express yourself smoothly and effectively. Your artistic abilities are also enhanced, with Venus joining Mercury. You get along well with family members. You're socially active and willing to compromise.

***Thursday, November 3 (Moon in Aquarius)*** The moon is in your fifth house. Dive into a creative project. Make use of your imagination and intuition. Likewise, there's greater emotional depth in a relationship. Children play a role in your day, and so do pets.

***Friday, November 4 (Moon into Pisces, 3:18 a.m.)*** It's your power day. Expect a financial coup. Open your mind to a new approach that will pay off. You have a chance to gain recognition, fame, and power. It's a good day to buy a lottery ticket.

***Saturday, November 5 (Moon in Pisces)*** Imagination is highlighted. Watch for psychic events, synchronicities. It's a time of deep healing. Your imagination is strong. Universal knowledge, eternal truths, and deep spirituality are the themes of the day.

***Sunday, November 6—Daylight Saving Time Ends (Moon into Aries, 2:02 p.m.)*** It's another service-oriented day. Help others, but don't deny your own needs. You could be feeling emotionally repressed. Keep your resolutions about exercise, and watch your diet.

***Monday, November 7 (Moon in Aries)*** With the moon in your seventh house, you get along well with others. You can fit in just about anywhere. Loved ones and partners are more important than usual. Women play a particularly prominent role. Be careful that others don't manipulate your feelings.

***Tuesday, November 8 (Moon in Aries)*** You're extremely persuasive, especially if you're passionate about what you're doing, selling, or trying to convey. It's a great time for initiating projects, launching new ideas, and brainstorming. Imprint your style. Wear bright colors. You're passionate but impatient.

***Wednesday, November 9 (Moon into Taurus, 2:46 a.m.)*** Neptune goes direct in your fifth house and stays there until April 5. That means you'll be more intuitive and also highly sensitive over the coming months. You become more romantic than usual, and fantasy plays a role in your life. You're attracted to romance, science fiction, and fantasy novels. You have a love of the theater and movies.

***Thursday, November 10 (Moon in Taurus)*** There's a full moon in your eighth house. You reap what you've sown regarding shared money or possessions; you could receive an inheritance. You're dealing with security issues. Alternately, you could be gaining recognition for your work with a social movement dedicated to helping others. You also might gain illumination and understanding related to a metaphysical subject, such as synchronicity.

***Friday, November 11 (Moon into Gemini, 3:11 p.m.)*** Mars goes into your twelfth house. You have a strong sense of mission, but you keep many of your ideas to yourself to avoid criticism. You're somewhat secretive; you prefer working alone. You need to deal with any anger that you've buried. Once you bring it into the open, you can understand it better.

***Saturday, November 12 (Moon in Gemini)*** With the moon in your ninth house, there's a fascination with philosophy or religion, mythology, or intellectual interests. You want an escape from the routine, Libra. Plan a long trip for pleasure or play a computer game. In romance, a flirtation with a foreign-born person could turn serious.

***Sunday, November 13 (Moon in Gemini)*** It's a good day for socializing. You're talkative, and you tend to jump from one subject to the next. Get out and have fun; flirt. A change of scenery does wonders. A short trip to visit family members or friends works to your benefit.

***Monday, November 14 (Moon into Cancer, 2:20 a.m.)*** It's a number 9 day. Complete a project. Clear your desk for tomorrow's new cycle, but don't start anything new. Use the day for reflection, expansion, and concluding projects.

***Tuesday, November 15 (Moon in Cancer)*** Your efforts pay off, and you get a fresh start. Business is highlighted. Your prestige is bolstered as you are offered a chance to take the lead on a new project. It's a good day for dealing with the public. Get out and meet new people; have new experiences.

***Wednesday, November 16 (Moon into Leo, 11:18 a.m.)*** Cooperation and partnerships are highlighted. You're diplomatic and capable of fixing whatever has gone wrong. As usual, you're concerned about keeping everything in balance, Libra. That's your native energy. You excel in working with a group. You're playing the role of the visionary. Be honest and open.

***Thursday, November 17 (Moon in Leo)*** Yesterday's energy flows into your Thursday. You work well with others. You work for the common good. Your individuality shines through. Focus on your wishes and dreams.

***Friday, November 18 (Moon into Virgo, 5:20 p.m.)*** Hard work and diligence are called for today. It's not the best day for romance. Stay focused and avoid wandering off task. Be methodical and thorough. You're building foundations for a creative future.

***Saturday, November 19 (Moon in Virgo)*** Take care of details as well as helping others. Tend to your health and exercise; watch your diet. It's a good day to take a yoga class and to write in a journal. You write from a deep place with lots of details and colorful descriptions.

***Sunday, November 20 (Moon into Libra, 8:17 p.m.)*** It's another service day as yesterday's energy flows into your Sunday. You offer advice and support. Help others, but don't overlook your own needs. Diplomacy wins the day.

***Monday, November 21 (Moon in Libra)*** With the moon in your first house, Libra, you're sensitive to other people's feelings. You may feel moody—withdrawn one moment, happy the next, then sad. It's all about your emotional self. The way you see yourself is the way others see you. Your feelings and thoughts are aligned.

***Tuesday, November 22 (Moon into Scorpio, 8:59 p.m.)*** It's your power day. You're feeling aligned, engaged, empowered. You can go far with whatever you're pursuing. Look for a windfall to come your way. Business dealings go well.

***Wednesday, November 23 (Moon in Scorpio)*** Expect intense emotional experiences. You're passionate about what you want and somewhat suspicious of others. Investigate and dig deep for information. But in the end, forgive and forget. Move on.

***Thursday, November 24 (Moon into Sagittarius, 8:58 p.m.)*** Mercury goes retrograde in your third house and stays there until December 13. That means you can expect some delays and glitches in communication over the next three weeks. Allow more time for short trips. When dealing with someone you are trying to help, especially relatives and neighbors, be sure to make yourself clearly understood. There also could be some miscommunication related to the past.

***Friday, November 25 (Moon in Sagittarius)*** There's a new moon in your third house and a solar eclipse. Watch for new opportunities that appear during your everyday activities. Something comes your way that has eluded you in the past. You'll recognize it when it happens.

***Saturday, November 26 (Moon into Capricorn, 10:05 p.m.)*** Venus moves into your fourth house. There's a lot of love and affection in the home. Beautify your home. Buy something nice for your house, change the decor, or just add a bouquet of flowers. You feel close to your roots and family members.

***Sunday, November 27 (Moon in Capricorn)*** You need to spend time with family again. Take care of a domestic situation. Self-discipline and structure are key. Maintain emotional balance. You may feel stressed and overworked. Retreat to a private place. Relax, stretch your tight muscles, and meditate.

***Monday, November 28 (Moon in Capricorn)*** Your ambition and drive to succeed are highlighted. Your responsibilities increase. You're dealing with the foundations of who you are and who you are becoming. Be conservative. Don't speculate or take any unnecessary risks. You're good at balancing everyone around you, Libra, but just make sure that you stay balanced yourself.

***Tuesday, November 29 (Moon into Aquarius, 2:02 a.m.)*** Focus on making people happy. You're a natural, Libra. It's another service day, so direct your energy toward helping others. Do a good deed. Be generous and tolerant, kind and understanding.

***Wednesday, November 30 (Moon in Aquarius)*** The moon is in your fifth house. Your love life soars. There's an idealistic turn to whatever you do for pleasure. It's a great time for a creative project, especially fiction writing. You could be somewhat possessive of loved ones, especially children. Get a pet!

## DECEMBER 2011

***Thursday, December 1 (Moon into Pisces, 9:46 a.m.)*** It's another service day, Libra. Of course that's no surprise for you. You offer advice and support. Be aware that you could face emotional outbursts by someone making unfair demands. Be understanding, but dance to your own tune.

***Friday, December 2 (Moon in Pisces)*** With the moon in your sixth house, the emphasis turns to your daily work and service to others. Attend to all the details, Libra. Be careful not to overlook any seemingly minor matters that could percolate into something more important. Keep up with your exercise plan, and watch your diet.

***Saturday, December 3 (Moon into Aries, 8:52 p.m.)*** It's your power day and business dealings go well. You can go far with your plans and achieve financial success, especially if you open your mind to a new approach. You have a chance to gain recognition, fame, and power. You're playing with power, so be careful not to hurt others. Be yourself; be honest.

***Sunday, December 4 (Moon in Aries)*** With the moon in your seventh house, the focus turns to relationships, business and personal ones. You get along well with others. You comprehend the nuances of a situation, but it's difficult to go with the flow. Be careful that others don't manipulate your feelings.

***Monday, December 5 (Moon in Aries)*** It's a great time for initiating projects, launching new ideas, and brainstorming. You're extremely persuasive, but emotions could be volatile. Try to avoid reckless behavior. Be careful about accidents.

***Tuesday, December 6 (Moon into Taurus, 9:36 a.m.)*** It's all about cooperation and partnerships. You're diplomatic and capable of fixing whatever has gone wrong. As usual, you're willing to keep everyone in balance, Libra. You're ambitious in pursuing a partnership. You excel in working with others. You're playing the role of the visionary. Be honest and open.

***Wednesday, December 7 (Moon in Taurus)*** Cultivate new ideas, but make sure that they're down-to-earth. An interest in shamanism could play a role. You also could be managing shared resources, as well as taking care of issues related to mortgages, taxes, and insurance.

***Thursday, December 8 (Moon into Gemini, 9:54 p.m.)*** Some of yesterday's energy flows into your Thursday as you need to remain focused and organized. Be methodical and thorough in whatever you're doing. Tear down the old in order to rebuild. You're at the right place at the right time.

***Friday, December 9 (Moon in Gemini)*** Communication is highlighted as you're anxious to express yourself. You've got a lot to say today. You e-mail, send text messages, blog, and talk on the phone. A change of scenery will work wonders.

***Saturday, December 10 (Moon in Gemini)*** There's a lunar eclipse in your ninth house. That means new opportunities come your way related to higher education or long-distance travel. With Uranus going direct in your seventh house, you can expect some disruption in a partnership over the coming months. But disruptions can actually enhance your relationship.

***Sunday, December 11 (Moon into Cancer, 8:27 a.m.)*** You journey into the unknown and investigate something hidden that's going on behind the scenes. You dig deep. You're exploring a mystery. Knowledge is essential to your success.

***Monday, December 12 (Moon in Cancer)*** The moon is in your tenth house. Your focus turns to professional matters. You could be dealing with a matter related to your reputation, and it works out for the better. You get a boost in prestige. You are received well by others, but avoid making emotional displays in public.

***Tuesday, December 13 (Moon into Leo, 4:49 p.m.)*** Mercury goes direct in your third house. You communicate your ideas well to relatives, especially related to matters from the past. Misunderstandings are resolved. You and relatives or neighbors feel reunified. Delays related to communication or travel are over.

***Wednesday, December 14 (Moon in Leo)*** With the moon in your eleventh house, friends play an important role, especially Aquarius and Gemini. Take a look at your goals, and make sure that they're still an expression of who you are. You do well in a group setting. You could be dealing with an issue involving social consciousness.

***Thursday, December 15 (Moon into Virgo, 10:59 p.m.)*** It's all about partnerships again. The spotlight shines on cooperative efforts. If you're married, your marriage takes on more significance. If you're not married, there could be some soul-searching related to a relationship, or a new relationship develops. Like yesterday, help comes through friends.

***Friday, December 16 (Moon in Virgo)*** Take care of details, especially related to your health. Stick close to home, focus on tidying up the house, and tend to loose ends. Everything doesn't have to be perfect. Relax. Take time to write in a journal. You write from a deep place with lots of details and colorful descriptions.

***Saturday, December 17 (Moon in Virgo)*** Remain out of public view, and work behind the scenes. Keep your feelings secret. Follow your intuition. You communicate your deepest feelings to another person. Pursue a mystical or spiritual discipline. Take time to reflect and meditate.

***Sunday, December 18 (Moon into Libra, 3:07 a.m.)*** It's a number 5 day. A change of scenery would work to your advantage. You could be moving to a new location. You're seeking new horizons, travel, and adventure. Promote new ideas; follow your curiosity. You're versatile, changeable. Be careful not to spread out and diversify too much.

***Monday, December 19 (Moon in Libra)*** With the moon in your first house, you're sensitive to the feelings of others. It's all about your health and your emotional self. You may feel moody one moment, happy the next, then withdrawn and sad. You're dealing with the person you are becoming.

***Tuesday, December 20 (Moon into Scorpio, 5:33 a.m.)*** With Venus moving into Aquarius, you project a romantic nature that is somewhat cool and detached. You tend to make your own rules on behavior. Others consider you charming, but you don't display your emotions openly. You're enjoying your freedom, and you don't want to be committed. You reject anyone who is acting possessive of you.

***Wednesday, December 21 (Moon in Scorpio)*** In spite of yesterday's sense of independence and nonemotional tendencies, your emotions can ignite at any time, especially when the issue is money. You identify closely with your possessions or whatever you value. It's not the objects themselves that are important, but the feelings and memories you associate with them. Money and material goods give you a sense of security.

***Thursday, December 22 (Moon into Sagittarius, 7:03 a.m.)*** Finish what you started. Clear up odds and ends. Use the day for reflection, expansion, and concluding projects. Visualize the future; set your goals, and then make them so. Look beyond the immediate and make room for something new. But don't start anything until tomorrow.

***Friday, December 23 (Moon in Sagittarius)*** The moon is in your third house. As the holidays grow closer, you're in contact with relatives. You make your opinions known, but try to control your emotions when expressing yourself. Your thinking may be unduly influenced by the past. You accept an invitation to a social event.

***Saturday, December 24 (Moon into Capricorn, 8:48 a.m.)*** There's a new moon in your fourth house. Spend time with your family and loved ones. Stick close to home. A doorway opens, and you get a new opportunity. A parent plays a role. You're dealing with the foundations of who you are and who you are becoming.

***Sunday, December 25 (Moon in Capricorn)*** Jupiter goes direct in your eighth house. Partnership and marriage play a role in your day. You share possessions; gifts come your way. An inheritance could play a role. You have an opportunity to expand and move ahead. Spiritual values arise. Merry Christmas!

***Monday, December 26 (Moon into Aquarius, 12:15 p.m.)*** With the moon in your fifth house, take a chance and speculate. Your emotions tend to overpower your intellect. You might be somewhat possessive of loved ones, particularly children. You're also more involved with creative facets of your life. Be yourself; be emotionally honest. In love, there's great emotional depth to a relationship.

***Tuesday, December 27 (Moon in Aquarius)*** Your individuality is stressed. Your visionary abilities are heightened. You're dealing with new ideas, new options, originality. You find a new perspective. It's another good day to play your hunches. Your wishes and dreams come true.

***Wednesday, December 28 (Moon into Pisces, 6:46 p.m.)*** Focus on making people happy. Be sympathetic, kind, and compassionate. You offer advice and support. Diplomacy wins the day. Domestic purchases are highlighted.

***Thursday, December 29 (Moon in Pisces)*** The moon is in your sixth house. Yesterday's energy flows into your Thursday. It's a service day. Others rely on you. You're the one they go to for assistance. You improve, edit, and refine the work of others. Help them, but don't deny your own needs. Your personal health occupies your attention.

***Friday, December 30 (Moon in Pisces)*** Your imagination is highlighted. You respond emotionally to whatever is happening. Watch for psychic events, synchronicities. Keep track of your dreams, including your daydreams. Ideas are ripe. You're compassionate and sensitive. Turn inward for inspiration, universal knowledge, and eternal truths.

***Saturday, December 31 (Moon into Aries, 4:49 a.m.)*** Clear up odds and ends. Take an inventory of where things are going in your life. Make a donation to a worthy cause. Make room for something new. Make a list of goals for 2012. Use the day for reflection, expansion, and concluding projects. Don't start anything new today.

HAPPY NEW YEAR!

***Sunday, January 1 (Moon in Aries)*** The moon is in your seventh house. The year begins with a strong focus on relationships, partnerships, or marriage. You have a tendency, Libra, to try to keep everyone around you in balance, but your challenge today is to keep yourself in balance! There's a tendency today to be somewhat aggressive in making your point. Happy New Year!

***Monday, January 2 (Moon into Taurus, 5:17 p.m.)*** It's a number 6 day. That means you need to remain firm but diplomatic, especially in dealing with a situation in your home. A domestic adjustment or readjustment is needed now. Don't put off the situation. That will only aggravate the problem. However, avoid becoming stubborn when issues arise in the evening. Be understanding and avoid confrontations.

***Tuesday, January 3 (Moon in Taurus)*** Your experiences are more intense than usual today, Libra. Security is an important issue with you right now. It can affect your feelings about your possessions, as well as things that you share with others, such as a spouse. An interest in astrology or another metaphysical subject plays a role in your day.

***Wednesday, January 4 (Moon in Taurus)*** Cultivate new ideas today, but make sure that they're down-to-earth. Your senses are highly developed and attuned today. You're sensual and opinionated. Again, avoid any urge to act in a stubborn manner. Health and physical activity are highlighted.

***Thursday, January 5 (Moon into Gemini, 5:45 a.m.)*** Finish whatever you've been working on. Look beyond the immediate. Visualize the future; set your goals, then make them so. You'll probably find that old ways have outlived their usefulness. Find a new approach, a new perspective, but don't start anything new today.

***Friday, January 6 (Moon in Gemini)*** You're a dreamer and a thinker today. Higher education and the higher mind are highlighted. You may feel a need to get away now, a break from the usual routine. You yearn for a new experience. It's a great time to improve your skills with a foreign language. A foreign-born person or a foreign country could play a role.

***Saturday, January 7 (Moon into Cancer, 4:06 p.m.)*** Partnerships and cooperation are highlighted today, Libra. Your intuition focuses on relationships, and you're playing the role of the visionary now. Don't make waves. Don't rush or show resentment. Let things develop, even if other people are nagging. Marriage plays a key role.

***Sunday, January 8 (Moon in Cancer)*** Mercury moves into your fourth house today. New ideas are being discussed in your home now. You could be talking about home schooling or setting up a home office. A parent could play a role. There also could be changes in the home, a renovation project, or a move to a new home.

***Monday, January 9 (Moon into Leo, 11:35 p.m.)*** There's a full moon in your tenth house today. You gain insight related to your career. You reap what you've sown, and that could be an advancement, a raise, a boost in your prestige. You get along well with coworkers now.

***Tuesday, January 10 (Moon in Leo)*** With the moon in your eleventh house today, yesterday's energy flows into your Tuesday. Friends and associates play an important role. You find strength in numbers. You find meaning through friends and groups. You could get involved with a group of like-minded individuals. Focus on your wishes and dreams, because now they can come true.

***Wednesday, January 11 (Moon in Leo)*** You're at center stage today, Libra, keeping everyone in balance around you. Expect lots of drama, perhaps involving children. You're creative and passionate, impulsive and honest. Romance feels majestic. Dress boldly; showmanship is emphasized.

***Thursday, January 12 (Moon into Virgo, 4:44 a.m.)*** It's a number 7 day, your mystery day. You venture into the unknown. You're a searcher, a seeker of truth. You investigate, analyze, or simply observe what's going on now. Knowledge is essential to success. Gather information, but don't make any absolute decisions until tomorrow.

***Friday, January 13 (Moon in Virgo)*** The moon is in your twelfth house today. You might feel a need to withdraw and work on your own. Things associated with the past and your childhood play a role. You could be dealing with an institution now, a hospital or government office. Unconscious attitudes can be difficult. Keep your feelings secret. Take time to reflect and meditate.

***Saturday, January 14 (Moon into Libra, 8:29 a.m.)*** With Venus moving into your sixth house today, you could be feeling emotionally attached to the workplace. Is that why you're working on Saturday? There's also the possibility of romance in the office, if that's what you want. You're good at mediating a dispute now, Libra. You work well with women.

***Sunday, January 15 (Moon in Libra)*** The moon is on your ascendant today, and that makes more appealing to the public. You're physically vital, and relations with the opposite sex go well. Your appearance and personality shine. Your feelings and thoughts are aligned, and you're recharged for the rest of the month.

***Monday, January 16 (Moon into Scorpio, 11:34 a.m.)*** Use your intuition to get a sense of your day. Be kind and understanding. Don't make waves. Don't rush or show resentment; let things develop. A relationship plays a key role. The emphasis is on cooperation today, even if others are nagging.

***Tuesday, January 17 (Moon in Scorpio)*** With the moon in Scorpio and your second house today, you can expect emotional experiences related to money. Money and material goods are important to you now and give you a sense of security. You identify emotionally with your possessions or whatever you value. Put off making any major purchases now. Look at your priorities in handling your income.

***Wednesday, January 18 (Moon into Sagittarius, 2:30 p.m.)*** It's a number 4 day. Your organizational skills are highlighted. Persevere to get things done today. Don't get sloppy; be methodical and thorough. Tear down the old in order to rebuild. Keep your goals in mind; follow your ideas. Be tenacious.

***Thursday, January 19 (Moon in Sagittarius)*** With the moon in your third house today, your speaking and writing skills are enhanced. You communicate well and in a variety of ways, possibly including text messages, e-mail, a blog entry. However, there's a tendency to become overly emotional. Best to keep the lid on your emotions. That's especially true if you're dealing with siblings or neighbors.

***Friday, January 20 (Moon into Capricorn, 5:42 p.m.)*** It's a service day. Adjust to the needs of loved ones. Diplomacy wins the day. Be understanding and avoid confrontations. Focus on making people happy, but avoid scattering your energies. An adjustment in your domestic life may be necessary now.

***Saturday, January 21 (Moon in Capricorn)*** Spend time with your family and loved ones. Stick close to home. You're dealing with the foundations of who you are and who you are becoming. Retreat to a private place for meditation. It's a good day for dream recall.

***Sunday, January 22 (Moon into Aquarius, 9:54 p.m.)*** It's your power day, your day to play it your way. Think big and act big! You have a chance to expand, to gain recognition, fame, and power. You can go far with your plans and achieve financial success. Be aware that you're playing with power, so try not to hurt anyone.

***Monday, January 23 (Moon in Aquarius)*** There's a new moon in your fifth house today. Be yourself; be emotionally honest. In romance, there's greater emotional depth to an existing relationship or an opportunity for starting a new one. It's also a good time to get a fresh start on a creative project. Sex for pleasure is on your agenda—or should be!

***Tuesday, January 24 (Moon in Aquarius)*** Groups and social events are highlighted now. Your individuality is stressed. Your visionary abilities are heightened. You get a new perspective. You have a greater sense of freedom. You're dealing with new ideas, new options, originality.

***Wednesday, January 25 (Moon into Pisces, 4:12 a.m.)*** Some of yesterday's energy flows into your Wednesday. You excel in working with others now. You're playing the role of a visionary today. Take time to consider the direction you're headed and your motivation for continuing on this path. The spotlight is on cooperation.

***Thursday, January 26 (Moon in Pisces)*** The moon is in your sixth house today. It's a service day. You improve, edit, and refine the work of others. Help others, but don't deny your own needs. It's a good day to clarify any health or work issues. It's best if you follow a regular schedule now.

***Friday, January 27 (Moon into Aries, 1:29 p.m.)*** With Mercury moving into your fifth house today, your artistic and creative expression flourishes. Your writing and speaking abilities are strong now. In romance, you tend to be somewhat critical and analytical now about a relationship. It's as if you're thinking, what's this worth for me?

***Saturday, January 28 (Moon in Aries)*** It's a great time for initiating projects, launching new ideas, brainstorming. Emotions could be volatile. You're passionate, but impatient. It's a good day to attend an athletic event. Get out; have an adventure.

***Sunday, January 29 (Moon in Aries)*** The moon is in your seventh house today. Relationships take on more importance. A legal matter comes to your attention. You comprehend the nuances of a situation, but it's difficult to go with the flow. You might have trouble now getting in touch with your own feelings.

***Monday, January 30 (Moon into Taurus, 1:29 a.m.)*** It's a number 7 day, your mystery day. You're a searcher and a seeker. Secrets, intrigue, confidential information play a role. You investigate, analyze, or simply observe what's going on now. You quickly come to a conclusion and wonder why others don't see what you see. You detect deception and recognize insincerity with ease.

***Tuesday, January 31 (Moon in Taurus)*** With the moon in your eighth house today, your experiences are more intense than usual. You have a strong sense of duty and feel obligated to fulfill your promises. You could be getting involved in managing or controlling someone's assets. Security is an important issue with you right now. Alternatively, it's a good time to help out in a cause aimed at improving living conditions for large numbers of people.

## FEBRUARY 2012

***Wednesday, February 1 (Moon into Gemini, 2:15 p.m.)*** Do a good deed for someone. Visit someone who is ill or in need of help. Focus on making people happy, but avoid scattering your energies. A domestic adjustment works out for the best.

***Thursday, February 2 (Moon in Gemini)*** You can create positive change through your ideas. Your mind is active, and you yearn for new experiences, a break from the routine, a change from the status quo. Foreign places and worldviews are emphasized. Your thoughts run wild today. You're a dreamer and a thinker, and your thoughts tend to rattle the status quo. You jump easily from one idea to another.

***Friday, February 3 (Moon in Gemini)*** With Neptune moving into your sixth house today, you could be creating illusions of grandeur about your place in the scheme of things at work. You might not feel inclined to handle routine or menial tasks assigned to you. This attitude could result in some trouble for you by the end of the year. Be cautious regarding any intake of drugs or alcohol. You could be especially sensitive this year.

***Saturday, February 4 (Moon into Cancer, 1:04 a.m.)*** It's a number 9 day. Use the day for reflection, expansion, and concluding projects. Accept what comes your way now, but don't start anything new. Strive for universal appeal.

***Sunday, February 5 (Moon in Cancer)*** The moon is in your tenth house today. Professional concerns are on your mind on this Sunday. You're thinking about a raise, a bonus, or a commendation. You're more responsive to the needs and moods of a group and of the public in general. Be careful about blurring the boundary between your personal and professional lives.

***Monday, February 6 (Moon into Leo, 8:24 a.m.)*** Partnerships are highlighted today. Your intuition focuses on relationships. The spotlight is on cooperation. Flow with the current; accept what comes your way. But also take time again today to consider the direction you're headed and your motivation for continuing on this path.

***Tuesday, February 7 (Moon in Leo)*** Saturn turns retrograde in your eleventh house today and stays there until June 25. It's a good time for dental work or an exercise program that will strengthen your bones as well as muscles. There's also a full moon in your eleventh house, and that means you gain new perspective related to higher education or long-distance travel. A foreign-born person could play a role in your day.

***Wednesday, February 8 (Moon into Virgo, 12:33 p.m.)*** Venus moves into your seventh house today. Marriage and partnerships take on new importance. There's harmony in a relationship. You might be socializing with associates from the workplace today, and you get along well.

***Thursday, February 9 (Moon in Virgo)*** The moon is in your twelfth house today. Think carefully before you act. There's a tendency now to undo all the positive actions you've taken. Avoid any self-destructive tendencies. Be aware of hidden enemies. You might feel a need to withdraw and work on your own.

***Friday, February 10 (Moon into Libra, 2:55 p.m.)*** It's a service day, and time to deal with the needs of loved ones. A change in the home, an adjustment or readjustment, is needed now. Don't put off the situation. That will only aggravate the problem. Diplomacy wins the way.

***Saturday, February 11 (Moon in Libra)*** The moon is in your first house today. You're sensitive to other people's feelings. You may feel moody one moment, happy the next, then withdrawn and sad. It's all about your health and your emotional self: how you feel and how you feel about yourself. You focus on how the public relates to you and how you can improve yourself.

***Sunday, February 12 (Moon into Scorpio, 5:02 p.m.)*** It's a number 8 day, your power day, so focus on a power play. Open your mind to a new approach that could bring in big bucks. Be courageous. Be yourself; be honest. But also be aware that fear of failure or fear that you won't measure up will attract tangible experiences that reinforce the feeling.

***Monday, February 13 (Moon in Scorpio)*** Mercury moves into your sixth house today. Let your imagination run wild on whatever you're working on. Meanwhile, you're methodical and thorough in your approach to work. You want to make sure everything is just right and everyone is working toward the same goals. You're efficient and capable, but you can get flustered easily by disorder. You might be overly concerned about your health and diet now.

***Tuesday, February 14 (Moon into Sagittarius, 7:57 p.m.)*** Get out and meet new people, have new experiences, do something you've never done before. Explore and discover. Creativity is highlighted. You get a fresh start, a new beginning. Happy Valentine's Day.

***Wednesday, February 15 (Moon in Sagittarius)*** You're busy interacting with neighbors, relatives, or siblings, possibly at a social gathering. You get your ideas across and you're very expansive in your approach, but try not to get too emotional. A female relative plays an important role.

***Thursday, February 16 (Moon in Sagittarius)*** Make use of your sense of humor. You're restless, impulsive, and inquisitive. Spiritual values arise. Worldviews are emphasized. You see the big picture, not just the details. Publishing or the law plays a role.

***Friday, February 17 (Moon into Capricorn, 12:04 a.m.)*** It's a number 4 day. Tear down the old in order to rebuild. Be methodical and thorough. Your organizational skills are emphasized. Revise, rewrite. Persevere to get things done today. Romance goes onto the back burner for now.

***Saturday, February 18 (Moon in Capricorn)*** The moon is in your fourth house today, the house of the home. It's a good day to stay home and spend time with your family. Work on a home-repair project. Beautify your home. You could be dealing with parents now. You feel a close tie to your roots.

***Sunday, February 19 (Moon into Aquarius, 5:29 a.m.)*** It's another power day. So it's time for a power play. You can go far with your plans and achieve financial success. Appear successful now, even if you don't feel that way. Financial gain is at hand; expect a windfall.

***Monday, February 20 (Moon in Aquarius)*** Pleasure and fun are called for today. Express your joy. It's a good day to take a chance, experiment. In love, there's greater emotional depth to a relationship now. Your creativity, personal grace, and magnetism are highlighted.

***Tuesday, February 21 (Moon into Pisces, 12:32 p.m.)*** There's a new moon in your sixth house. New opportunities come your way today in the workplace. You help others, keeping everyone in balance, Libra, and it pays off. Doors open. Make sure you keep yourself in balance. Exercise and watch your diet.

***Wednesday, February 22 (Moon in Pisces)*** The moon is in your sixth house today. Attend to details related to your health. Make a doctor or dentist appointment. Keep your resolutions about exercise, and watch your diet. It's best if you follow a regular schedule now. You could be feeling somewhat emotionally repressed.

***Thursday, February 23 (Moon into Aries, 9:48 p.m.)*** It's a number 1 day, and that means you're at the top of your cycle again. You get a fresh start today. Take the lead, follow your hunches, and don't be afraid to turn in a new direction. You attract creative people to your cause. In romance, a flirtation could turn serious now, if that's what you want.

***Friday, February 24 (Moon in Aries)*** Yesterday's energy flows into your Friday. It's a great day for brainstorming, coming up with new ideas, or launching a new project. Be aware that emotions can be volatile. You're extremely persuasive now, especially if you're passionate about what you're doing or selling or trying to convey. However, avoid reckless behavior.

***Saturday, February 25 (Moon in Aries)*** The moon is in your seventh house today. You get along well with others now. You can fit in just about anywhere. A marriage or partnership plays an important role in your day.

A legal matter comes to your attention now. You comprehend the nuances of a situation, but it's difficult to go with the flow. Be careful that others don't manipulate your feelings.

***Sunday, February 26 (Moon into Taurus, 9:30 a.m.)*** It's a number 4 day. Tear down the old in order to rebuild. Be methodical and thorough. Revise, rewrite. Persevere to get things done today. Romance goes onto the back burner for now.

***Monday, February 27 (Moon in Taurus)*** The moon is in your eighth house today. Your experiences are more intense than usual. Security is an important issue with you right now. It can affect your feelings about your possessions, as well as things that you share with others, such as a spouse. It's also a good day to explore a metaphysical subject, such as past lives or life after death.

***Tuesday, February 28 (Moon into Gemini, 10:28 p.m.)*** It's a service day. Adjust to the needs of loved ones. Diplomacy wins the day. Clear up a situation at home that has lingered too long. Be sympathetic and kind, generous and tolerant. Focus on making people happy, but avoid scattering your energies.

***Wednesday, February 29 (Moon in Gemini)*** The moon is in your ninth house today. You may feel a need to get away now, a break from the usual routine. You yearn for a new experience. It's a good time to plan a long trip or sign up for a workshop or seminar on a subject that interests you. A foreign country or foreign-born person could play a role.

***Thursday, March 1 (Moon in Gemini)*** The moon is in your ninth house today. You may feel a need to get away now, a break from the usual routine, Libra. Visit a museum exhibit or art gallery opening. Pursue a new idea. Are you ready to plan a long trip or sign up for a seminar?

***Friday, March 2 (Moon into Cancer, 10:09 a.m.)*** As Mercury moves into your seventh house today, your energy is focused on relationships. You tend to spend time with creative, witty, and well-spoken people now. You feel a need to communicate with intelligent or well-educated people, Libra. You get along well with others and can resolve any disagreements.

***Saturday, March 3 (Moon in Cancer)*** It's a good day for sales and dealing with the public. You gain an elevation in prestige now related to your career. Business dealings are highlighted. You're warmer and friendlier toward coworkers, but don't make any emotional displays in public.

***Sunday, March 4 (Moon into Leo, 6:19 p.m.)*** It's a number 1 day, so you're at the top of your cycle on this Sunday. Express your opinions dynamically. Get out and meet new people, have new experiences, do something you've never done before. Refuse to deal with people who have closed minds. In romance, a flirtation turns more serious, if that's what you want.

***Monday, March 5 (Moon in Leo)*** Venus moves into your eighth house. You could gain financially now through a partnership or marriage. An inheritance could be involved. Joint finances play a role. Be aware of any tendencies toward jealousy or possessiveness.

***Tuesday, March 6 (Moon into Virgo, 10:28 p.m.)*** Yesterday's energy flows into your Tuesday. Enjoy the harmony, beauty, and pleasures of life. Your imagination is keen now. You're curious and inventive. You communicate well. You're warm and receptive to what others say. Your attitude determines everything today.

***Wednesday, March 7 (Moon in Virgo)*** The moon is in your twelfth house now. Think carefully before you act today. It's best to work behind the scenes now. You're more sensitive than usual today, Libra. Avoid any self-destructive tendencies. You could be dealing with an institution now, a hospital or government office.

***Thursday, March 8 (Moon into Libra, 11:51 p.m.)*** There's a full moon in your twelfth house today. You gain new perspective related to your personal unconscious mind. Your dreams are more vivid. Pay attention to details. Take time to get away to a quiet place and meditate. You become your own best friend.

***Friday, March 9 (Moon in Libra)*** The moon is on your ascendant today. The way you see yourself now is the way others see you. Your appearance and personality shine, and your feelings and thoughts are aligned. Dealings with the opposite sex go well now.

***Saturday, March 10 (Moon in Libra)*** Romance is highlighted, Libra. Relationships issues figure prominently in your day. It's all about your health and your emotional self: how you feel and how you feel about yourself.

***Sunday, March 11—Daylight Saving Time Begins (Moon into Scorpio, 1:25 a.m.)*** It's your power day and your day to play it your way. A power play today could involve your generosity. You're in the power seat. You have a chance to expand, to gain recognition, fame, and power. Be aware that you're playing with power, so try not to hurt anyone.

***Monday, March 12 (Moon in Scorpio)*** Mercury goes retrograde in your seventh house today and stays that way until April 4. That means there could be some miscommunication or misunderstanding with partners, either business or personal. Your wishes and dreams might be stalled for the time being. Leave extra time when traveling. There also could be some confusion related to a group activity. Things will get better!

***Tuesday, March 13 (Moon into Sagittarius, 2:54 a.m.)*** It's a number 1 day, so you're at the top of your cycle. Trust your hunches today. Your intuition is highlighted. You're inventive and make connections that others overlook. You're determined and courageous. You attract creative people now.

***Wednesday, March 14 (Moon in Sagittarius)*** With the moon in your third house today, Libra, your thinking is influenced by matters from the past, especially related to siblings, relatives, or neighbors. You communicate well, but you tend to be quite opinionated. Control your emotions when you make your point. You'll probably be taking short trips. Be sure to drive carefully if you're talking on your cell while behind the wheel.

***Thursday, March 15 (Moon into Capricorn, 6:24 a.m.)*** It's a number 3 day. You're innovative, creative, and communicate well. Your attitude determines everything today. Spread your good news, and take time to listen to others. Ease up on routines. Your charm and wit are appreciated.

***Friday, March 16 (Moon in Capricorn)*** The moon is in your fourth house today. You feel close to your roots now. Spend time with your family and loved ones.

Stick close to home, if possible. A parent plays a role. It's a good day to work on a home repair project.

***Saturday, March 17 (Moon into Aquarius, 12:12 p.m.)*** Variety is the spice of life. You're seeking new horizons. Think outside the box. Take risks, experiment. Let go of old structures; get a new point of view. You're versatile and changeable now, Libra.

***Sunday, March 18 (Moon in Aquarius)*** The moon is in your fifth house today. It's a great day for pursuing a romance. There's greater emotional depth in whatever you pursue. Be yourself; be emotionally honest. You're creative now and have the ability to tap deeply into the collective unconscious. Children and pets could play a role.

***Monday, March 19 (Moon into Pisces, 8:05 p.m.)*** It's a number 7 day, your mystery day. Secrets, intrigue, confidential information play a role. Investigate activities taking place behind closed doors. You work best on your own today. Keep your own counsel. Knowledge is essential to success. Gather information, but don't make any absolute decisions until tomorrow.

***Tuesday, March 20 (Moon in Pisces)*** The moon is in your sixth house today. You're compassionate and sensitive, Libra. Help others, but don't ignore your own needs. You tend to think a lot about whatever you're doing at work, and you can get quite dramatic about it if things aren't the way you want them. Keep your resolutions about exercise, and watch your diet.

***Wednesday, March 21 (Moon in Pisces)*** Imagination is highlighted. Watch for synchronicities, psychic events. Keep track of your dreams, including your daydreams. Ideas are ripe. It's a day for deep healing. Universal knowledge, eternal truths, deep spirituality are the themes of the day.

***Thursday, March 22 (Moon into Aries, 5:58 a.m.)*** There's a new moon in your seventh house today. New opportunities arise; a doorway opens related to a partnership. Expect a contract. Cooperation is emphasized. It's a good time to begin a new project.

***Friday, March 23 (Moon in Aries)*** Yesterday's energy flows into your Friday. It's a good day for launching new ideas, brainstorming. You're passionate, but impatient. You're extremely persuasive now, especially if you're passionate about what you're doing, selling, or trying to convey.

***Saturday, March 24 (Moon into Taurus, 5:44 p.m.)*** Your popularity is on the rise. You communicate well. Your attitude determines everything today. Spread your good news, and take time to listen to others. Ease up on routines. Your charm and wit are appreciated.

***Sunday, March 25 (Moon in Taurus)*** The moon is in your eighth house today. Your experiences are more intense than usual. Your emotions could affect your feelings about belongings that you share with others. Finances or an inheritance could play a role. An interest in metaphysics or related rituals grabs your attention.

***Monday, March 26 (Moon in Taurus)*** It's a good day to use common sense and take a down-to-earth perspective on whatever you're doing. Health and physical activity are highlighted today. Go hiking, have a picnic, get out into nature. Enjoy the spring weather. You're more sensual and opinionated than usual today, Libra. But avoid any tendency toward stubborn behavior.

***Tuesday, March 27 (Moon into Gemini, 6:44 a.m.)*** It's a service day. You're the one others come to for help. You improve what they're doing. You offer advice and support. Focus on making people happy. Do a good deed for someone, but avoid scattering your energies.

***Wednesday, March 28 (Moon in Gemini)*** The moon is in your ninth house today. You're a dreamer and a thinker. You're keenly perceptive, and you understand how others feel. You yearn for a new experience, an escape, possibly with a special friend. You could be looking at a foreign destination, or maybe that friend is foreign-born. You can create positive change through your ideas.

***Thursday, March 29 (Moon into Cancer, 7:08 p.m.)*** It's a number 8 day, another power day. You're ambitious and goal-oriented. Remain confident and convinced that material success is within reach, if not already here. You're playing with power, so be careful not to hurt others.

***Friday, March 30 (Moon in Cancer)*** The moon is in your tenth house today. Business dealings are highlighted. You have a chance to expand your base. You gain responsibilities and prestige. You tend to put a lot of energy into your professional life, and that could mean that you're ignoring domestic obligations. Also, it's best not to bring your career concerns home now. That's your challenge today.

***Saturday, March 31 (Moon in Cancer)*** Beautify your home today. Take care of home repairs. But also tend to loved ones; do something with your children or sweetheart. You're sensitive to other people's moods. It's best to keep things to yourself to avoid arguments.

## APRIL 2012

***Sunday, April 1 (Moon into Leo, 4:37 a.m.)*** The month starts on a power day for you, Libra. It's your day to play it your way. You can go far with your plans and achieve financial success. That's especially true if you think big and act big. Be courageous. Be yourself, be honest. Appear successful now, even if you don't feel that way.

***Monday, April 2 (Moon in Leo)*** With the moon in your eleventh house today, friends play an important role in your day. You find strength in numbers and meaning through friends and groups. Focus on your wishes and dreams. Examine your overall goals. Those goals should be an expression of who you are.

***Tuesday, April 3 (Moon into Virgo, 9:54 a.m.)*** Venus moves into your ninth house today. You gain pleasure through the study of metaphysics, philosophy, art, or religion. You're in touch with your creative side. Your ideas probably challenge the status quo. You could be setting off or planning a long, romantic getaway. Emotions are powerful now, so try to stay in balance, Libra.

***Wednesday, April 4 (Moon in Virgo)*** With Mercury moving into your sixth house today, you're very concerned with details involving your daily work or your health and diet. Make a doctor or dentist appointment. You want to keep everything in order and everybody around you in balance. You improve, edit, and refine the work of others.

***Thursday, April 5 (Moon into Libra, 11:33 a.m.)*** Your attitude determines everything today. You communicate well. Spread your good news, and take time to listen to others. You're warm and receptive to what they say. Enjoy the harmony, beauty, and pleasures of life.

***Friday, April 6 (Moon in Libra)*** There's a full moon in your first house today. You pick up some news that relates to your personal life or insights into some issue of your life. Things are more hectic now; your social calendar heats up. There's more focus on relationships. It's a good night to get out and party with friends!

***Saturday, April 7 (Moon into Scorpio, 11:18 a.m.)*** It's a number 5 day. Variety is the spice of life today. Think freedom, no restrictions. Release old structures; get a new point of view. Promote new ideas; follow your curiosity. You can overcome obstacles with ease.

***Sunday, April 8 (Moon in Scorpio)*** With the moon in your second house, you could gain a financial boost that feels like a jolt of energy. While that will make you feel more secure, you need to decide what your priorities are in handling your income. Temper your spending for now, even if you've just received an increase in your finances.

***Monday, April 9 (Moon into Sagittarius, 11:13 a.m.)*** There's an unmistakable sense of mystery surrounding the day. You investigate a secret or confidential matter. Look beneath the surface for answers or explanations. See things as they are, not how you would like them to be. You might discover deception, but find that others still can't see what's so obvious to you.

***Tuesday, April 10 (Moon in Sagittarius)*** Pluto goes retrograde in your fourth house today and stays that way until September 17. If you're planning to renovate, repair, or beautify your home, things might not go exactly as hoped. Likewise, if you're dealing with family members, be aware that they won't necessarily agree with your plans. Expect delays in domestic matters of all sorts.

***Wednesday, April 11 (Moon into Capricorn, 1:02 p.m.)*** It's a number 9 day, your day to finish up what you've been working on and get ready for something new. Take time to reflect on what you've been doing, and look for a way to expand. Visualize the future; set your goals, then make them so.

***Thursday, April 12 (Moon in Capricorn)*** The moon is in your fourth house today. You're dealing with the foundations of who you are and who you are becoming now. Spend time with your family and loved ones. Take time to retreat to a private place for meditation. It's a good day for dream recall.

***Friday, April 13 (Moon into Aquarius, 5:48 p.m.)*** Partnerships take center stage, Libra. Your intuition comes into play as you focus on relationships. Don't make waves. Don't rush about or show resentment. Cooperation is stressed now.

***Saturday, April 14 (Moon in Aquarius)*** The moon is in your fifth house today. You're emotionally in touch with your creative side. Be yourself; be emotionally honest. In love, there's greater emotional depth to a relationship. You might be somewhat possessive of loved ones now, particularly children.

***Sunday, April 15 (Moon in Aquarius)*** Your individuality is stressed. Your visionary abilities are heightened. You get a new perspective and have a new sense of freedom. Play your hunches. Look beyond the immediate. Help others, but dance to your own tune. Your wishes and dreams come true.

***Monday, April 16 (Moon into Pisces, 1:38 a.m.)*** Mercury moves into your seventh house today. Expect lots of conversing now with partners, business or personal. You discuss travel plans or a contract. You promote your ideas and express yourself well.

***Tuesday, April 17 (Moon in Pisces)*** The moon is in your sixth house today. It's a service-oriented day. Help others, but be careful not to fall into a martyr syndrome. Take care of health issues. It's a good time to begin a new diet or exercise regimen. Don't let your fears hold you back.

***Wednesday, April 18 (Moon into Aries, 12:00 p.m.)*** It's another mystery day. You launch a journey into the unknown. Secrets, intrigue, confidential information play a role. You work best on your own today. Knowledge is essential to success. Gather information, but don't make any absolute decisions until tomorrow.

***Thursday, April 19 (Moon in Aries)*** With the moon in your seventh house today, your focus turns to a partnership. It's a great time for you and your partner to come up with new ideas. You can go far with your plans and achieve financial success. You get a fresh start, a new beginning. Ideas are ripe.

***Friday, April 20 (Moon in Aries)*** Yesterday's energy flows into your Friday. It's a great time for initiating projects or launching new ideas. You're extremely persuasive now, especially if you're passionate about what you're doing, selling or trying to convey. Imprint your style. Wear bright colors. However, avoid reckless behavior. It's a good day to attend a sports event.

***Saturday, April 21 (Moon into Taurus, 12:06 a.m.)*** There's a new moon in Taurus, your eighth house, today. New, solid opportunities come your way now, and they could relate to a mortgage, insurance, or an inheritance. Expect a windfall. With the sun, moon, and Jupiter in Taurus, you have a chance to expand whatever you're working on. Ideas are ripe. There's lots of action and activity around you, and possibly some chaos. But you can get things done.

***Sunday, April 22 (Moon in Taurus)*** It's a good day to use common sense and take a down-to-earth perspective on whatever you're doing. Go hiking, have a picnic, get out into nature. Your senses are highly developed. You're opinionated today, but avoid becoming stubborn if someone disagrees with you.

***Monday, April 23 (Moon into Gemini, 1:06 p.m.)*** It's a number 3 day. Intuition is highlighted. Spread your good news, and take time to listen to others. You can influence people now with your upbeat attitude. Have fun today in preparation for tomorrow's discipline and focus.

***Tuesday, April 24 (Moon in Gemini)*** The moon is in your ninth house today. Your mind is active, and you yearn for new experiences, a break from the routine, a change from the status quo. You can create positive change through your ideas now. A publishing project takes off. Publicity and advertising are emphasized. Stay focused today.

***Wednesday, April 25 (Moon in Gemini)*** Yesterday's energy flows into your Wednesday. You're feeling restless today and sending text messages to friends and associates to pass the time. Your mind moves quickly now from one thought to another. A change of scenery works to your benefit. Take a car trip to visit friends or relatives.

***Thursday, April 26 (Moon into Cancer, 1:43 a.m.)*** It's a number 6 day. It's all about service. Do a good deed for someone. Visit a sick family member. Focus on making people happy. A domestic adjustment works out for the best. Don't put it off any longer.

***Friday, April 27 (Moon in Cancer)*** The moon is in your tenth house today. Professional concerns are the focus of the day. You gain an elevation in prestige. Your life is more public. You feel close to coworkers, but don't blur the boundaries between your private and professional lives.

***Saturday, April 28 (Moon into Leo, 12:11 p.m.)*** It's another power day, Libra. It's your day to play it your way. Open your mind to a new approach. Unexpected resources arrive. You can go far with your plans and achieve financial success. It's a good day to buy a lotto ticket.

***Sunday, April 29 (Moon in Leo)*** The moon is in your eleventh house today. You get along better with friends and associates. Your sense of security is tied to your relationships. Your interests are so diverse now that others might think you lack depth. Work for the common good, but keep an eye on your own wishes and dreams.

***Monday, April 30 (Moon into Virgo, 7:03 p.m.)*** You're at the top of your cycle today. Stress originality. You attract creative people now. You're inventive and make connections that others overlook. You're determined and courageous. In romance, something new is developing.

## MAY 2012

***Tuesday, May 1 (Moon in Virgo)*** It's a number 9 day. Look beyond the immediate. Finish what you started. Visualize the future; set your goals, then make them so. Complete a project and make room for something new. But wait until tomorrow before beginning anything new.

***Wednesday, May 2 (Moon into Libra, 10:04 p.m.)*** It's a great day to begin a new project. You get a fresh start, a new beginning. Be independent and creative, and refuse to be discouraged by naysayers. Don't be afraid to turn in a new direction. Explore and discover. Creativity is highlighted.

***Thursday, May 3 (Moon in Libra)*** The moon is on your ascendant today. Your face is before the public and all over Facebook. You're recharged for the month ahead, and this makes you more appealing to the public. You're physically vital, and relations with the opposite sex go well. Your appearance and personality shine. Your feelings and thoughts are aligned.

***Friday, May 4 (Moon into Scorpio, 10:20 p.m.)*** You're warm and receptive to what others say. Your imagination is keen now. You're curious and inventive. Enjoy the harmony, beauty, and pleasures of life. You have a strong sense of duty and feel obligated to fulfill your promises.

***Saturday, May 5 (Moon in Scorpio)*** There's a full moon in your second house today. You gain insight, illumination, or news related to money issues. You reap what you've sown related to finances. You have a strong emotional need for security. You feel best when surrounded by familiar objects in your home environment. Look at your priorities in handling your income.

***Sunday, May 6 (Moon into Sagittarius, 9:40 p.m.)*** Approach the day with an unconventional mind-set. Release old structures; get a new point of view. Variety is the spice of life. Think freedom, no restrictions. Change and variety are highlighted now.

***Monday, May 7 (Moon in Sagittarius)*** The moon is in your third house today. You're busy interacting with neighbors, relatives, or siblings in a social gathering. You get your ideas across, but try not to get too emotional. A female relative plays an important role.

***Tuesday, May 8 (Moon into Capricorn, 10:01 p.m.)*** It's your mystery day, Libra. Secrets, intrigue, confidential information play a role. You might feel best working on your own. You investigate, analyze, or simply observe what's going on now. You quickly come to a conclusion and wonder why others don't see what you see. It's best to hold off on making any final decisions for a couple of days.

***Wednesday, May 9 (Moon in Capricorn)*** Mercury moves into your eighth house today. Yesterday's energy flows into your Wednesday. You investigate and dig deep to get to the bottom of a mystery that might involve an inheritance, insurance, or taxes. You could also be looking into the deeper mysteries of life, such as life after death or past lives.

***Thursday, May 10 (Moon in Capricorn)*** The moon is in your fourth house today. Get organized, Libra. You're dealing with the foundations of who you are and who you are becoming. Make an effort to change a bad habit. It's best today to work on your own. Stay focused and don't get distracted.

***Friday, May 11 (Moon into Aquarius, 1:04 a.m.)*** It's a number 1 day, and you're at the top of your cycle again. You're determined and courageous today. Stress originality in whatever you're doing. Refuse to deal with people who have closed minds. Explore, discover, create. In romance, something new could be brewing. A flirtation turns more serious.

***Saturday, May 12 (Moon in Aquarius)*** It's a good day to take a chance, experiment. Your emotions tend to overpower your intellect today, especially related to romance. You're emotionally in touch with your creative side now. You feel strongly attached to loved ones, particularly children, and can be somewhat possessive.

Friends are supportive and play an important role in your day.

***Sunday, May 13 (Moon into Pisces, 7:43 a.m.)*** You come out of your shell now, Libra. You communicate well. You're warm and receptive to what others say. Spread your good news. Ease up on routines. Your charm and wit are appreciated. Play your hunches. Enjoy the harmony, beauty, and pleasures of life.

***Monday, May 14 (Moon in Pisces)*** The moon is in your sixth house today. Service to others is the theme of your day. Look for ways to keep everyone around you in balance, Libra. You're seeking peace and harmony in the workplace. Be careful not to overlook any seemingly minor matters that could take on importance. Keep up with your exercise plan, and watch your diet.

***Tuesday, May 15 (Moon into Aries, 5:47 p.m.)*** Venus goes retrograde in your ninth house today. That means you have a strong desire for higher education or long-distance travel. A foreign-born person could be a love interest. However, be aware that you could face some delays and glitches in your plans. Things will straighten out after Venus goes direct on June 27.

***Wednesday, May 16 (Moon in Aries)*** The moon is in your seventh house. Marriage or partnerships are highlighted. Material gain connected to a significant relationship is likely. You have a strong sense of justice and treat others fairly.

***Thursday, May 17 (Moon in Aries)*** It's a great time for initiating projects, launching new ideas, brainstorming. You're extremely persuasive, especially if you're passionate about what you're doing, selling, or trying to convey. Be wary of reckless behavior, and avoid any tendencies toward self-deception.

***Friday, May 18 (Moon into Taurus, 6:04 a.m.)*** You're in the power seat today, so it's time for a power play. Business dealings go well. Unexpected money arrives. You can go far with your plans and achieve financial success. Be aware that you're playing with power, so try not to hurt anyone.

***Saturday, May 19 (Moon in Taurus)*** The moon is in your eighth house today. Like yesterday, you're on top of your game. You make use of your mind to explore deeper issues, a mystery that might be haunting you. Joint resources play a lead role in your day, and you could deal with taxes, insurance, or an inheritance.

***Sunday, May 20 (Moon into Gemini, 7:06 p.m.)*** There's a solar eclipse in your ninth house today. External events affect your worldview or plans for foreign travel. It's the end of something or the beginning of something new. New opportunities come your way, and they could involve a publishing project. Your mind is active, and you're ready for something new, a break from the routine, a change from the status quo.

***Monday, May 21 (Moon in Gemini)*** Yesterday's energy flows into your Monday. You're restless today and yearn for something new, whether it's long-distance travel to a foreign land or taking a seminar on a subject that attracts your interest. Mythology, philosophy, or religion plays a role in your day. Your beliefs are strong and sincere, but changeable now.

***Tuesday, May 22 (Moon in Gemini)*** You're restless and mentally quick today. You're busy contacting friends and associates—calling them, e-mailing, or texting. You're going on Facebook or Twitter, and you get your message across. It's a good day to socialize, go out for lunch, get out and have fun. In romance, it's a day for flirting and flitting about.

*Wednesday, May 23 (Moon into Cancer, 7:32 a.m.)* After yesterday's busy day of socializing, it's time to get focused. Tear down the old in order to rebuild. Be methodical and thorough. Revise, rewrite. Persevere to get things done today. Romance goes onto the back burner for now.

*Thursday, May 24 (Moon in Cancer)* With Mercury moving into your ninth house today, you express yourself well. It's a great day for teaching or writing. You're busy exchanging ideas. An interest in foreign countries or cultures is highlighted now. You could be planning a long trip.

*Friday, May 25 (Moon into Leo, 6:12 p.m.)* Service to others is the theme of the day. You offer advice and support. Be sympathetic and kind, generous and tolerant. Focus on making people happy. Diplomacy wins the way.

*Saturday, May 26 (Moon in Leo)* Friends play an important role in your day and help you in surprising ways. You work well with a group of like-minded people and keep everyone in balance. Focus on your wishes and dreams, and make sure that they are an expression of who you really are.

*Sunday, May 27 (Moon in Leo)* Drama is highlighted, perhaps involving children. Be wild, imaginative; be the person you always imagined you might be. Play with different personas. You're creative and passionate today, impulsive and honest.

*Monday, May 28 (Moon into Virgo, 2:07 a.m.)* It's a number 9 day. Use the day for reflection, expansion, and concluding projects. Take an inventory on where things are going in your life. Make room for something new, but don't start anything until tomorrow.

Romance feels majestic. Dress boldly; showmanship is emphasized.

***Tuesday, May 29 (Moon in Virgo)*** The moon is in your twelfth house today. Unconscious attitudes can be difficult, Libra. Keep your feelings secret. You might feel a need to withdraw and work on your own. You're good at keeping everyone in balance, but now you need to work on your own balance. Take time to reflect and meditate. It's a great time for pursuing a spiritual discipline.

***Wednesday, May 30 (Moon into Libra, 6:46 a.m.)*** It's a number 2 day. That means partnerships and cooperation are highlighted. Help comes through friends or loved ones, especially a partner. Don't make waves. Don't rush or show resentment; let things develop. You could be undergoing some soul-searching related to a relationship now.

***Thursday, May 31 (Moon in Libra)*** The moon is in your first house today, Libra. Your self-awareness and appearance are important now. You're dealing with your emotional self, the person you are becoming. You might feel moody—happy one moment, sad or withdrawn the next. However, your thoughts and feelings are aligned. You tend to search for ways to improve yourself.

## JUNE 2012

***Friday, June 1 (Moon into Scorpio, 8:32 a.m.)*** The month begins with a number 1 day. You're inventive and make connections that others overlook. You're determined and courageous today. Don't be afraid to turn in a new direction. Trust your hunches. Intuition is highlighted. Refuse to deal with people who have closed minds.

***Saturday, June 2 (Moon in Scorpio)*** The moon is in your second house today. You feel strongly about a money issue. Finances and material goods are important to you and give you a sense of security. You identify emotionally with your possessions or whatever you value.

***Sunday, June 3 (Moon into Sagittarius, 8:33 a.m.)*** You're innovative and creative and communicate well. Ease up on routines. Your attitude determines everything today. Spread your good news, and take time to listen to others. Have fun in preparation for tomorrow's discipline and focus. You can influence people now with your upbeat attitude.

***Monday, June 4 (Moon in Sagittarius)*** With Neptune going retrograde in your sixth house until November 10, your efforts to bring a more enlightened atmosphere to the workplace take longer than you had hoped. Meanwhile, you have trouble focusing on mundane tasks, getting organized, and attending to details. There's also a lunar eclipse today, and that means you have an emotional reaction related to events in your everyday world.

***Tuesday, June 5 (Moon into Capricorn, 8:32 a.m.)*** Change and variety are highlighted. Think freedom, no restrictions. Find a new point of view that fits current circumstances and what you know now. It's a good day to take a risk, experiment. Promote new ideas.

***Wednesday, June 6 (Moon in Capricorn)*** The moon is in your fourth house today. It's a good day to stay home, where you feel comfortable. The domestic scene plays a major role in your day. If possible, take the day off or work at home. You're feeling closer to your roots.

***Thursday, June 7 (Moon into Aquarius, 10:18 a.m.)*** Mercury moves into your fourth house today. There's a lot of activity in the home related to education. You could be helping a child with homework, considering home schooling, or looking into colleges for an older child. Things are definitely active and changing in your home life. Try to take time to relax.

***Friday, June 8 (Moon in Aquarius)*** The moon is in your fifth house today. Your love life takes off. There's an idealistic turn to whatever you do for pleasure. It's a great time for a creative project, especially fiction writing. You could be somewhat possessive of loved ones and children today. It's a good day to get a pet!

***Saturday, June 9 (Moon into Pisces, 3:23 p.m.)*** Finish up whatever you've been working on, and get ready for something new. Take time to reflect on everything that's been going on. Look for a way to expand your horizons, but don't start anything new until next week.

***Sunday, June 10 (Moon in Pisces)*** With the moon in your sixth house today, the emphasis turns to your daily work and service to others. Attend to all the details, Libra. Be careful not to overlook any seemingly minor matters that could take on importance. Keep up with your exercise plan, and watch your diet.

***Monday, June 11 (Moon in Pisces)*** Jupiter enters your ninth house today, where it will stay until June 25, 2013. That means that over the next year you'll be expanding in some way related to philosophy, higher education, or religion. You see the big picture now; you expand your vision. It's also a good time to travel, especially to a foreign country.

***Tuesday, June 12 (Moon into Aries, 12:22 a.m.)*** Ease up on your routines, and spread your good news. You communicate well. You're warm and receptive to what others say. Your imagination is keen now. You're curious and inventive. Enjoy the harmony, beauty, and pleasures of life. Beautify your home.

***Wednesday, June 13 (Moon in Aries)*** The moon is in your seventh house today. A marriage or partnership plays an important role. You could be dealing with a contract. You get along well with others, and can fit in just about anywhere. You comprehend the nuances of a situation, but it's difficult to go with the flow.

***Thursday, June 14 (Moon into Taurus, 12:22 p.m.)*** You're restless and looking for change, a new perspective. You're versatile and changeable, but be careful not to overcommit yourself. Stay focused as best you can. Take risks, experiment; pursue a new idea. Freedom of thought and action is key.

***Friday, June 15 (Moon in Taurus)*** With the moon in your eighth house, Libra, you could attract power people to you today. Your energy is more intense than usual, and drama plays a role. Your emotions could affect your feelings about belongings that you share with others. An interest in metaphysics or related rituals grabs your attention.

***Saturday, June 16 (Moon in Taurus)*** Health and physical activity are highlighted. It's a good time for gardening, cultivating ideas, or doing practical things. Tend to money matters. A partnership plays a role. Your senses are highly attuned today.

***Sunday, June 17 (Moon into Gemini, 1:24 a.m.)*** It's your power day and your day to play it your way. You get an opportunity to expand and grow. Be courageous. You're playing with power, so be careful not to hurt others. Be honest; be courageous.

***Monday, June 18 (Moon in Gemini)*** You're feeling restless, and a change of scenery would do you good. Get out and have some fun. You communicate well. It's a good day for writing or editing or publicizing what you're doing.

***Tuesday, June 19 (Moon into Cancer, 1:34 p.m.)*** New opportunities come your way. A doorway opens related to higher education or long-distance travel. You yearn for a new experience, and now is the time to go for it.

***Wednesday, June 20 (Moon in Cancer)*** The moon is in your tenth house today. You're focused on your professional life. You're looking for a boost in prestige, possibly a raise. You get along well with coworkers. Your life is more in public view now. Your hard work is appreciated, Libra.

***Thursday, June 21 (Moon into Leo, 11:48 p.m.)*** Your imagination is keen now. You're curious and inventive. It's a good day to visit a museum or take in an art gallery opening. Romance is highlighted. You're intuitive and communicate well. Spread your good news, and take time to listen to others. You're warm and receptive to what others say.

***Friday, June 22 (Moon in Leo)*** The moon is in your eleventh house today. Friends play an important role in your day, especially Gemini and Aquarius. You find strength in numbers and meaning through friends and groups. Focus on your wishes and dreams. Examine your overall goals. Make sure those goals should be an expression of who you are. Social consciousness plays a role.

***Saturday, June 23 (Moon in Leo)*** You're at center stage today, Libra. Be wild and imaginative; be the person you always imagined you might be. Play with different personas. Theatrics and drama are highlighted, especially with friends. It's a good day to publicize whatever you're doing. Showmanship is emphasized.

***Sunday, June 24 (Moon into Virgo, 7:43 a.m.)*** It's another service day. Diplomacy wins the day. A change in the home, an adjustment or readjustment, is needed now. Don't put off the situation. That will only aggravate the problem. Be understanding and avoid criticizing, condemning, and complaining.

***Monday, June 25 (Moon in Virgo)*** With Mercury moving into your eleventh house today, you spend a lot of time communicating with friends and associates. Meanwhile, Saturn goes direct in your first house. That means you find structures that work for your personal life. For example, you might place boundaries around a relationship or look at a relationship in a new way. You gain a more serious outlook and become more goal directed over the next couple of years.

***Tuesday, June 26 (Moon into Libra, 1:16 p.m.)*** It's another power day, so it's time for a power play. Business discussions go well. You pull off a financial coup. Be aware that fear of failure or fear that you won't measure up will attract tangible experiences that reinforce the feeling.

***Wednesday, June 27 (Moon in Libra)*** Venus goes direct in your ninth house today. Things work out for the best now related to any delays or disappointments you faced in higher education or long-distance travel. In the retrospect, you even see some benefits from the confusion or setbacks. It wasn't any fun at the time, but now that it's over you can see the positive side.

***Thursday, June 28 (Moon into Scorpio, 4:33 p.m.)*** You're at the top of your cycle now. Be independent and creative. You can take the lead in a new project, and you can turn in a new direction. Don't let people with closed minds hold you back. Stress originality. You attract creative people.

***Friday, June 29 (Moon in Scorpio)*** You have strong feelings today related to money matters. You identify emotionally with your possessions or whatever you value. You equate your financial assets with emotional security. Watch your spending. Pay your bills, and collect what's owed to you.

***Saturday, June 30 (Moon into Sagittarius, 6:05 p.m.)*** You're creative and express yourself well today. Play your hunches. Your artistic talents are highlighted. Your charm and wit are appreciated. Your attitude determines everything. Your popularity is on the rise.

## JULY 2012

***Sunday, July 1 (Moon in Sagittarius)*** The moon is in your third house today. Take what you know and share it with others. However, keep conscious control of your emotions when getting your ideas across. Your thinking can be unduly influenced by things of the past. Siblings, other relatives, or neighbors play a role. Drive carefully if you're talking on your cell phone as you go about your everyday business.

***Monday, July 2 (Moon into Capricorn, 6:52 p.m.)*** Your charm and wit are appreciated. Your attitude determines everything today. In romance, you're an ardent and loyal lover. Ease up on routines. Remain flexible. Take time to relax, enjoy yourself, recharge your batteries.

***Tuesday, July 3 (Moon in Capricorn)*** With Mars moving into your first house today, you're quite outgoing and assertive, letting others know exactly what you think and how you feel. Others see you as ambitious. There's also a full moon in your fourth house, and that means you get a better handle on domestic matters. You reap what you've sown.

***Wednesday, July 4 (Moon into Aquarius, 8:26 p.m.)*** Change and variety are highlighted now. Think outside the box. Take risks, experiment. Let go of old structures; get a new point of view. You're especially versatile and changeable today, Libra. Promote new ideas; follow your curiosity.

***Thursday, July 5 (Moon in Aquarius)*** The moon is in your fifth house today. Your emotions tend to overpower your intellect now. Be yourself; be emotionally honest. In love, there's greater emotional depth to a relationship. It's a good day to take a chance, experiment. Children and animals could play a significant role in your day.

***Friday, July 6 (Moon in Aquarius)*** You have a greater sense of freedom now. You're dealing with new ideas, new options, originality. You get a new perspective. Play your hunches. Look beyond the immediate. Help others, but dance to your own tune. Your wishes and dreams come true.

***Saturday, July 7 (Moon into Pisces, 12:29 a.m.)*** It's a power day, and your day to play it your way. Unexpected money arrives. Business discussions go well. It's a good day for buying a lottery ticket. Think big and act big! Be aware that fear of failure or fear that you won't measure up will attract tangible experiences that reinforce the feeling.

***Sunday, July 8 (Moon in Pisces)*** The moon is in your sixth house today. Others come to you for guidance; you're the "go to" person. They rely on you for information. Help others, but be careful not to fall into a martyr syndrome. Don't forget your own needs. Take care of any health issues. Exercise and watch your diet.

***Monday, July 9 (Moon into Aries, 8:14 a.m.)*** It's a number 1 day. You get a fresh start now, a new beginning like the phoenix rising from the ashes. Get out and make contacts today. Experiment, explore, discover, and express your opinions. Your originality is highlighted.

***Tuesday, July 10 (Moon in Aries)*** The moon is in your seventh house today. Make sure that you focus on relationships, business and personal ones. Loved ones and partners play a role. A legal matter comes to your attention. You comprehend the nuances of a situation, but it's difficult to go with the flow.

***Wednesday, July 11 (Moon into Taurus, 7:30 p.m.)*** Ease up a bit today, Libra. Focus on keeping yourself rather than those around you in balance. You're feeling vital and have a natural ability to express yourself. Your charm and wit are appreciated. You're innovative and communicate well. In romance, you're an ardent and loyal lover.

***Thursday, July 12 (Moon in Taurus)*** The moon is in your eighth house today. Things could get emotionally intense in your dealing with someone from the opposite sex. That's particularly true if you're facing issues related to shared belongings. You're sensitive and attuned to what's going on around you. You could take an interest in a metaphysical topic, such as past lives.

***Friday, July 13 (Moon in Taurus)*** Uranus goes retrograde in your seventh house today and stays there until December 13. Your intuitive and inventive nature feels bottled up during the last half of the year. From time to time, the pent-up energy explodes spontaneously, but the results are somewhat erratic. You seek freedom and rebel against all that has held you in place.

***Saturday, July 14 (Moon into Gemini, 8:27 a.m.)*** Mercury goes retrograde in your eleventh house today and stays there until August 8. That means there could be some miscommunication or misunderstanding with friends and associates. Your wishes and dreams are delayed. Leave extra time when traveling. You work for the common good, but others in a group seem to misunderstand your intentions. It will all clear up soon!

***Sunday, July 15 (Moon in Gemini)*** You're thinking and talking a lot about your philosophy of life, about your ideas on how things should work, about why certain things are happening. You analyze and scrutinize. While you lay it all out for friends or a group, you don't feel much emotional commitment to correcting the situation.

***Monday, July 16 (Moon into Cancer, 8:32 p.m.)*** It's another power day. Unexpected resources come your way. Business discussions go well. You have a chance to expand, to gain recognition, fame, and power. It's a good day to buy a lotto ticket.

***Tuesday, July 17 (Moon in Cancer)*** With the moon in your tenth house today, professional concerns are the focus of the day. You're more responsive to the needs and moods of a group and of the public in general, and more emotional and warm toward coworkers. However, don't blur the boundary between your professional and personal lives.

***Wednesday, July 18 (Moon in Cancer)*** You could be feeling moody today, so it's a good day to work at home, if possible. Water plays a prominent role; you might feel a need to get close to it. Tend to loved ones; do something with them, your children, or sweetheart. You're intuitive and sensitive to other people's moods now.

***Thursday, July 19 (Moon into Leo, 6:14 a.m.)*** There's a new moon in your tenth house today. That means new opportunities come your way related to your profession or career. You get an advancement, a new position, a boost in prestige. It's a good day for sales or dealing with the public.

***Friday, July 20 (Moon in Leo)*** The moon is in your eleventh house today. Friends play an important role in your day, especially Aquarius and Gemini. You find strength in numbers. You find meaning through friends and groups, especially a group of like-minded people working for the common good.

***Saturday, July 21 (Moon into Virgo, 1:25 p.m.)*** Your organizational skills are highlighted. Control your impulses. Fulfill your obligations. Keep your goals in mind, follow your ideas. You're building foundations for an outlet for your creativity. Revise, rewrite. Missing papers or objects are found.

***Sunday, July 22 (Moon in Virgo)*** The moon is in your twelfth house today. Unconscious attitudes can be difficult. Keep your feelings secret. You might feel a need to withdraw and work on your own. Take time to reflect and meditate. It's a great time for pursuing a spiritual discipline.

***Monday, July 23 (Moon into Libra, 6:39 p.m.)*** It's a number 6 day, a service day. Be diplomatic, especially with someone who is giving you trouble. Do a good deed for someone. Visit someone who is ill or in need of help. Be sympathetic, kind, and compassionate, but avoid scattering your energies.

***Tuesday, July 24 (Moon in Libra)*** The moon is on your ascendant as the month ends. You're recharged for the rest of the month and beyond, and this makes you more appealing to the public. You're physically vital, and relations with the opposite sex go well. The way you see yourself now is the way others see you. Your thoughts and emotions are aligned.

***Wednesday, July 25 (Moon into Scorpio, 10:30 p.m.)*** It's another power day and your way to play it your way. Open your mind to a new approach that could bring in big bucks. You attract financial success, Libra. Think big and act big! However, you're playing with power, so be careful not to hurt others.

***Thursday, July 26 (Moon in Scorpio)*** The moon is in your second house today, Libra, so it's a good day for dealing with money issues. Pay what you owe, and collect what others owe you. You equate your financial assets with emotional security now. Look at your priorities in handling your income.

***Friday, July 27 (Moon in Scorpio)*** You could experience intense emotions today. You're passionate now, and your sexuality is heightened. Investigate, research, and dig deep for information. Be aware of things happening in secret and of possible deception. Control issues might arise. Best advice: forgive and forget, and try to avoid going to extremes.

***Saturday, July 28 (Moon into Sagittarius, 1:18 a.m.)*** Use your intuition to get a sense of the day. Cooperation is highlighted. Don't make waves. Don't rush or show resentment; let things develop. The spotlight is on cooperation. Show your appreciation to others.

***Sunday, July 29 (Moon in Sagittarius)*** The moon is in your third house today. You have a strong emotional need to get your ideas across. You connect with siblings, and matters from the past are discussed. It's also a good day to write in a journal or study history or archaeology. The past intrigues.

***Monday, July 30 (Moon into Capricorn, 3:30 a.m.)*** It's a number 4 day. Tear down the old in order to rebuild. Be methodical and thorough. Revise, rewrite. Persevere to get things done today. Romance goes onto the back burner for now.

***Tuesday, July 31 (Moon in Capricorn)*** The moon is in your fourth house today, the house of the home. It's a good day to stay home and spend time with your family or work on a home-repair project. You could be dealing with parents now. You feel a close tie to your roots.

## AUGUST 2012

***Wednesday, August 1 (Moon into Aquarius, 5:56 a.m.)*** There's a full moon in your fifth house today. That means you get a fresh perspective regarding a love interest. You might be somewhat possessive of loved ones now, particularly children. But eventually you need to let go. It's a good day to take a gamble or buy a lotto ticket. Your emotions tend to overpower your intellect. Your creative energies or romantic inclinations are strong.

***Thursday, August 2 (Moon in Aquarius)*** Your individuality is stressed. At the same time, group activities or social events are highlighted. You have a greater sense of freedom now. You're dealing with new ideas, new options, originality. You get a new perspective. It's a good day to play your hunches and look beyond the immediate.

***Friday, August 3 (Moon into Pisces, 9:58 a.m.)*** It's a number 5 day. That means you're open to change and variety, and you want to loosen any restrictions. You're willing to take a risk and experiment. Variety is the spice of life, and change is good. Think outside the box, Libra.

***Saturday, August 4 (Moon in Pisces)*** With the moon in your sixth house today, the emphasis turns to helping others. Trust your hunches; your intuition is highlighted. Be careful not to overlook any seemingly minor matters that could take on importance. Attend to details related to your health. Make a doctor or dentist appointment that you've been putting off. It's a good day to go to the gym or take a yoga class.

***Sunday, August 5 (Moon into Aries, 4:59 p.m.)*** It's your mystery day, Libra. You venture into the unknown. Secrets, intrigue, confidential information play a role. Be aware of decisions made behind closed doors. You work best on your own today. Gather information, but don't make any absolute decisions until tomorrow.

***Monday, August 6 (Moon in Aries)*** The moon is in your seventh house today. You could be negotiating or signing a contract now, possibly for the sale of property. You're taking the initiative, and emotions could get volatile, especially if you don't inform your partner of everything you're doing. It's difficult to maintain an objective and detached point of view. Keep everyone in balance, Libra, and be careful not to let others manipulate your feelings.

***Tuesday, August 7 (Moon in Aries)*** Venus moves into your tenth house today. Romance in the workplace, or with someone in a similar career with similar goals, is possible now. You get along well with others, Libra, and your social skills allow you to get ahead in your profession this month.

***Wednesday, August 8 (Moon into Taurus, 3:28 a.m.)*** Mercury goes direct in your eleventh house today. Confusion, miscommunication, and delays, especially related to friends and associates, recede into the past. Things move more smoothly now. You get along with others better, and you get your message across. Everything works better, including computers and other electronic equipment. Others now appreciate all that you do.

***Thursday, August 9 (Moon in Taurus)*** The moon is in your eighth house today. Take care of any matters related to taxes, insurance, or investments. An inheritance could play a role. Be aware that emotions can get intense now, especially when dealing with shared resources. Metaphysics could play a role in your day. You could be dealing with a mystery of the unknown, such as past lives or what happens after death.

***Friday, August 10 (Moon into Gemini, 4:12 p.m.)*** Your imagination is keen now. You're curious and inventive. Enjoy the harmony, beauty, and pleasures of life. You're warm and receptive to what others say. You have a strong sense of duty and feel obligated to fulfill your promises.

***Saturday, August 11 (Moon in Gemini)*** The moon is in your ninth house today, the home of higher learning. You're considering ideas now on matters such as philosophy or religion, the law or publishing. You also have a strong interest in foreign travel or a foreign nation. Break away from your routine or the usual way you think about things. You can create positive change through your ideas, especially if you express them forcefully.

***Sunday, August 12 (Moon in Gemini)*** It's a good day to take a drive to visit friends or relatives. A change of scenery works well for you now. You also see two sides of an issue today, Libra, so you're in a position to help resolve a dispute. You're feeling creative and need to express yourself in writing or through speech. You're mentally quick, and easily get your message across.

***Monday, August 13 (Moon into Cancer, 4:29 a.m.)*** It's a number 6 day, a service day. A domestic adjustment works out for the best. You could face emotional outbursts by someone making unfair demands. Be understanding and avoid confrontations. Help others, but dance to your own tune.

***Tuesday, August 14 (Moon in Cancer)*** The moon is in your tenth house today. Your focus turns to professional matters, whether it's career or education. You could be dealing with a matter related to your reputation, and it works out for the best. You get a boost in prestige now. You're received well by others, but avoid making an emotional display in public.

***Wednesday, August 15 (Moon into Leo, 2:06 p.m.)*** It's another power day, Libra, and you're in the power seat. You can go far with your plans and achieve financial success. You have a chance to expand, to gain recognition even fame and power, especially if you open your mind to a new approach. Remember that you're playing with power, so avoid hurting others.

***Thursday, August 16 (Moon in Leo)*** The moon is in your eleventh house today. Friends play an important role in your day, especially Gemini and Aquarius. You find strength in numbers and meaning through friends and groups, especially a group of like-minded people working for the common good.

***Friday, August 17 (Moon into Virgo, 8:34 p.m.)*** There's a new moon in your eleventh house today. Focus on your wishes and dreams, Libra. Examine your overall goals; make sure they are still an expression of who you are. You have deeper contact with friends now. It's a good day to join a group of like-minded individuals.

***Saturday, August 18 (Moon in Virgo)*** With the moon in your twelfth house, there's a tendency to undo all the positive actions you've taken. Avoid any self-destructive tendencies. Be aware of hidden enemies. Think carefully before you act today. Best to work on your own and behind the scenes. Take time to reflect and meditate. Unconscious attitudes can be difficult.

***Sunday, August 19 (Moon in Virgo)*** Stick close to home; focus on tidying up the house. Attend to details and loose ends. You may exhibit some perfectionist tendencies now. Don't forget to exercise and watch your diet. Stop worrying and fretting. Take time to write in a journal or on a blog.

***Monday, August 20 (Moon into Libra, 12:46 a.m.)*** It's a number 4 day. Your organizational skills are highlighted today. Emphasize quality as you fulfill your obligations. Revise and rewrite. You're building foundations for an outlet for your creativity. However, it's not a day for experimentation or new approaches.

***Tuesday, August 21 (Moon in Libra)*** With the moon on your ascendant today, the way you see yourself is the way others see you. You're feeling physically vital, and your thoughts and emotions are aligned. You're recharged for the month ahead and more appealing to the public. Relations with the opposite sex go well.

***Wednesday, August 22 (Moon into Scorpio, 3:54 a.m.)*** Domestic purchases are highlighted. Focus on making people happy. Do a good deed. It's a service day, so direct your energy toward helping others. Be generous and tolerant; it goes along with your nature, Libra.

***Thursday, August 23 (Moon in Scorpio)*** Mars moves into your second house. That means you put more energy into finances over the next three weeks. You have a strong drive to earn money, but an equal willingness to spend it. You're not afraid to take a chance with finances now. However, look at your priorities in handling your income.

***Friday, August 24 (Moon into Sagittarius, 6:50 a.m.)*** Focus on a power play now. Think big and act big! Open your mind to a new approach that could bring in big bucks. You attract financial success. Business discussions go well.

***Saturday, August 25 (Moon in Sagittarius)*** You're busy keeping your mind occupied with new information. You have a chance to expand whatever you're working on now. You communicate well, but your thinking is unduly influenced by matters from the past. That's especially true in any dealings with siblings, other relatives, or neighbors.

***Sunday, August 26 (Moon into Capricorn, 9:59 a.m.)*** Get out and meet new people, have new experiences, do something you've never done before. Express your opinions dynamically. Explore and discover. Creativity is highlighted. In romance, a flirtation could turn more serious now.

***Monday, August 27 (Moon in Capricorn)*** The moon is in your fourth house today. Try to spend more time at home with loved ones now. Beautify your surroundings with a home-repair or redecoration project. Show that you care. You feel a close tie to your roots. It's a good day to retreat to a private place for meditation and put everything into perspective.

***Tuesday, August 28 (Moon into Aquarius, 1:39 p.m.)*** Take time to relax, enjoy yourself, and recharge your batteries. You can influence people now with your upbeat attitude. Your charm and wit are appreciated. Foster generosity. In romance, you're an ardent and loyal lover.

***Wednesday, August 29 (Moon in Aquarius)*** The moon is in your fifth house today. Be yourself; be emotionally honest. Follow your heart on a creative project. You can tap deeply into the collective unconscious for inspiration. In romance, make an effort to avoid being overly possessive.

***Thursday, August 30 (Moon into Pisces, 6:32 p.m.)*** Variety is the spice of life now. Think outside the box. Take risks, experiment; get a new point of view. Follow your curiosity. However, don't spread yourself too thin.

***Friday, August 31 (Moon in Pisces)*** Mercury moves into your twelfth house today. It's a good time for meditation or therapy or any mind-body discipline. It's also a good time for working behind the scenes, especially on a writing project. You have ready access to your dreams. There's also a full moon in your sixth house, so you can gain a better understanding of a health matter.

## SEPTEMBER 2012

***Saturday, September 1 (Moon in Pisces)*** The moon is in your sixth house today. It's a service day. Others rely on you for help now. You're the one they go to for help, especially family members. You improve, edit, and refine the work of others. Offer help, but don't deny your own needs. Take care of any health-care issues.

***Sunday, September 2 (Moon into Aries, 1:38 a.m.)*** It's a number 5 day. Freedom and change are highlighted now. Variety is the spice of life. Think outside the box. Take risks, experiment. Let go of old structures; get a new point of view, a new perspective on things.

***Monday, September 3 (Moon in Aries)*** The moon is in your seventh house today. Partnerships are highlighted. You get along well with others and feel more secure when everyone is in agreement with you. You can fit in just about anywhere. It's best not to make waves right now.

***Tuesday, September 4 (Moon into Taurus, 11:42 a.m.)*** It's your mystery day, Libra. Best to work on your own. Secrets, intrigue, confidential information play a role. You investigate, analyze, or simply observe what's going on now. You quickly come to a conclusion and wonder why others don't see what you see. You detect deception and recognize insincerity with ease. Maintain your emotional balance.

***Wednesday, September 5 (Moon in Taurus)*** The moon is in your eighth house today. If you are planning on making a major purchase, make sure that you and your partner are in agreement. Otherwise, you could encounter intense emotional resistance. An interest in metaphysics plays a role in your day. You could be dealing with a mystery of the unknown.

***Thursday, September 6 (Moon in Taurus)*** With Venus moving into your eleventh house today, you can gain financially or professionally through the help of friends this month. You work very well with colleagues and friends, especially in a group, and have a knack for putting others at ease. It's also a good time for exploring your artistic talents.

***Friday, September 7 (Moon into Gemini, 12:11 a.m.)*** It's a number 1 day, and you're at the top of your cycle. Trust your hunches; intuition is highlighted. Don't be afraid to turn in a new direction. You're inventive and make connections that others overlook. You're determined and courageous today. In romance, make room for a new love, if that's what you want.

***Saturday, September 8 (Moon in Gemini)*** The moon is in your ninth house today. You yearn for a new experience. Plan a long trip. Sign up for a workshop or seminar. Foreigners or a foreign country plays a role. Your mind is active and you're interested in ideas, mythology, philosophy, or religion. You can create positive change through your ideas.

***Sunday, September 9 (Moon into Cancer, 12:50 p.m.)*** Your attitude determines everything today. You communicate well. You're warm and receptive to what others say. Don't forget to spread your own good news. Your charm and wit are appreciated.

***Monday, September 10 (Moon in Cancer)*** The moon is in your tenth house today. You focus on career or professional matters now. You're dealing with your reputation, your need for recognition. You deal well with the public now and are responsive to the needs of coworkers and the public at large.

***Tuesday, September 11 (Moon into Leo, 11:01 p.m.)*** Promote new ideas; follow your curiosity. Think outside the box today. It's a good day to take a risk or experiment. You're versatile and changeable, Libra. But be careful not to spread out and diversify too much.

***Wednesday, September 12 (Moon in Leo)*** The moon is in your eleventh house today. You have deeper contact with friends now. You find strength in numbers. You find meaning through friends and groups. You work for the common good. Aquarius or Gemini plays a role in your day.

***Thursday, September 13 (Moon in Leo)*** Strut your stuff today, Libra! Be wild and imaginative; be the person you always imagined you might be. Play with different personas. Theatrics and drama are highlighted. You're creative and passionate today, impulsive and honest.

***Friday, September 14 (Moon into Virgo, 5:31 a.m.)*** It's your power day and your day to play it your way. Unexpected money arrives. You pull off a financial coup. Business discussions go well. It's a good day for buying a lottery ticket. Financial gain is at hand.

***Saturday, September 15 (Moon in Virgo)*** There's a new moon in your twelfth house today. It's a good day to stay out of sight and work behind the scenes. You find new opportunities now, but it's best to keep them to yourself for the time being. Take time to reflect and meditate. Pay attention to synchronicities and see where they lead you.

***Sunday, September 16 (Moon into Libra, 8:55 a.m.)*** With Mercury moving into your first house today, you're mentally restless. You enjoy conversing and making connections, not necessary to attract new friends, but to learn something new. You easily adapt to changing situations and express yourself well. You're searching for ways to improve yourself.

***Monday, September 17 (Moon in Libra)*** Pluto goes direct in your fourth house today. Underlying power struggles in your home environment could start to surface, or such struggles could develop. You feel strongly attached to your home or the land you think of as your own. There's a tendency to feel that you need to dominate a domestic situation and make sure others know your position.

***Tuesday, September 18 (Moon into Scorpio, 10:46 a.m.)*** Things take a lighter turn today. Your attitude determines everything. Ease up on routines. Spread your good news, and take time to listen to others. Your charm and wit are appreciated, Libra.

***Wednesday, September 19 (Moon in Scorpio)*** With the moon in your second house, you're feeling a sense of abundance. You expand your horizons with a new purchase, or new money arrives. You're in a fortunate position, but don't overextend yourself. Look at your priorities in handling your income.

***Thursday, September 20 (Moon into Sagittarius, 12:34 p.m.)*** Approach the day with an unconventional mind-set. Promote new ideas; follow your curiosity. Look for adventure. Freedom of thought and action is key. But so is moderation; avoid excess in whatever you're doing. You're courageous and adaptable.

***Friday, September 21 (Moon in Sagittarius)*** With the moon in your third house today, it's a good time for expressing yourself through writing. Take what you know and share it with others. As you go about your everyday life, look to the past for clues about what's coming up in the near future. Expect an invitation to a social event.

***Saturday, September 22 (Moon into Capricorn, 3:21 p.m.)*** It's another mystery day. You launch a journey into the unknown. Secrets, intrigue, confidential information play a role. Make sure that you see things as they are, not as you wish them to be. Express your desires, but avoid self-deception. Maintain your emotional balance, Libra.

***Sunday, September 23 (Moon in Capricorn)*** The moon is in your fourth house today. You're dealing with the foundations of who you are and who you are becoming. A parent plays a role in your day. Retreat to a private place for meditation. It's a good day for dream recall or changing a bad habit.

***Monday, September 24 (Moon into Aquarius, 7:33 p.m.)*** Finish whatever you've been working on. Look for a new approach, a new perspective. The old cycle is ending; a new one about to begin. Visualize the future; set your goals, then make them so.

***Tuesday, September 25 (Moon in Aquarius)*** The moon is in your fifth house today. You can move ahead on any creative project. Meanwhile, you have an opportunity to achieve greater depth in a relationship, but it could take hard work. Be yourself; be emotionally honest.

***Wednesday, September 26 (Moon in Aquarius)*** Groups and social events are highlighted today. You're dealing with new ideas, new options, originality. Bust old paradigms. You get a new perspective. Help others, but dance to your own tune. Your wishes and dreams come true.

***Thursday, September 27 (Moon into Pisces, 1:25 a.m.)*** You're creative and express yourself well today. Your artistic talents and imagination are highlighted. You can tap deeply into the collective unconscious for inspiration. Enjoy the harmony, beauty, and pleasures of life.

***Friday, September 28 (Moon in Pisces)*** The moon is in your sixth house today. Delegate some of your responsibilities; avoid taking on too much work. You help others, but allow them to shoulder some of the burden. Don't become a martyr for someone else's cause. Take care of any health issues.

***Saturday, September 29 (Moon into Aries, 9:15 a.m.)*** There's a full moon in your seventh house today. You gain insight related to a marriage or partnership. A contract could be involved. You reap what you've sown; it's a time of completion.

***Sunday, September 30 (Moon in Aries)*** It's a great time for initiating projects, launching new ideas, brainstorming. You can be very persuasive now. You're passionate, but impatient. It's also a good day to attend a sports event. Wear bright colors. Imprint your style. Look for excitement and adventure.

## OCTOBER 2012

***Monday, October 1 (Moon into Taurus, 7:27 p.m.)*** Travel and variety are highlighted today. You're versatile, changeable. Be careful not to spread out and diversify too much. Freedom of thought and action is key. But so is moderation; avoid excess in whatever you're doing. A change of scenery would work to your advantage.

***Tuesday, October 2 (Moon in Taurus)*** The moon in your eighth house can affect your feelings about your possessions, as well as things that you share with others, such as a spouse. You have a strong sense of duty and feel obligated to fulfill your promises. Security is an important issue with you right now.

***Wednesday, October 3 (Moon in Taurus)*** Venus moves into your twelfth house today. You have a love of solitude. You enjoy working on your own or behind the scenes. You're not telling everyone something that you know. You tend to keep your emotions under control now.

***Thursday, October 4 (Moon into Gemini, 7:47 a.m.)*** It's a number 8 day, your power day. Business discussions go well. You attract financial success. Open your mind to a new approach that could bring in big bucks. You have a chance to expand, to gain recognition, even fame and power.

***Friday, October 5 (Moon in Gemini)*** With Mercury moving into your second house today, you could be dealing with some changes in your finances. There's lots of talk about money issues. Meanwhile, Saturn joins Mercury in your second house, where it will stay for two and a half years. That means you have better structure and stability in your finances over the next couple of years. However, there could be some setbacks and delays, especially if you try a get-rich-quick scheme. Romance now could involve someone who deals with money matters.

***Saturday, October 6 (Moon into Cancer, 8:46 p.m.)*** Mars moves into your third house today. That means there's strong energy for the rest of the month related to whatever you're doing in your everyday world. You're busy keeping your mind occupied with new information, and now you see the big picture. However, try not to get impatient with people who aren't up to your speed and energy level. Keep conscious control of your emotions when communicating, especially with siblings or neighbors.

***Sunday, October 7 (Moon in Cancer)*** It's a good day to stick close to home and spend time with family members. You're intuitive and nurturing, and your home life is important to you. Do something with your children, other loved ones, or sweetheart. It's also a good day to beautify your home or take care of some necessary repairs.

***Monday, October 8 (Moon in Cancer)*** With the moon in your tenth house today, there's lots of activity now in your professional life. You love what you do and communicate well. You feel very emotional about your work or your fellow workers. You're in the public eye and gain a boost in prestige.

***Tuesday, October 9 (Moon into Leo, 7:55 a.m.)*** It's a number 4 day, and it's time to get focused. Persevere to get things done today, and don't get sloppy. Tear down the old in order to rebuild. Be methodical and thorough, and stay on task. Revise and rewrite.

***Wednesday, October 10 (Moon in Leo)*** The moon is in your eleventh house today. Friends play an important role in your day. You find strength in numbers and meaning through friends and groups. Focus on your wishes and dreams. Examine your overall goals. Those goals should be an expression of who you are.

***Thursday, October 11 (Moon into Virgo, 3:24 p.m.)*** A domestic adjustment works out for the best. Don't let it go any longer; it won't get better. You could face emotional outbursts or someone making unfair demands. Be diplomatic and understanding. Service to others is the theme of the day.

***Friday, October 12 (Moon in Virgo)*** The moon is in your twelfth house today. Think carefully before you act. There's a tendency now to undo all the positive actions you've taken. Avoid any self-destructive tendencies. Be aware of hidden enemies. You might feel a need to withdraw and work on your own. Things associated with the past and your childhood play a role.

***Saturday, October 13 (Moon into Libra, 7:02 p.m.)*** It's another power day and your day to play it your way. You can go far with your plans and achieve financial success. You have a chance to expand, to gain recognition, even fame. Business discussions go well. You pull off a financial coup.

***Sunday, October 14 (Moon in Libra)*** With the moon in your first house today, your feelings and thoughts are aligned. It's all about your health and your emotional self: how you feel and how you feel about yourself. You're sensitive and responsive to the needs of others, so you can be easily influenced by those around you.

***Monday, October 15 (Moon into Scorpio, 8:07 p.m.)*** There's a new moon in your first house, Libra. New personal opportunities come your way. It's all about the way you see yourself and how you relate to a romantic partner. Intuition is highlighted. You have an opportunity to expand your life with that special person. Romance is highlighted.

***Tuesday, October 16 (Moon in Scorpio)*** The moon is in your second house today. You tend to react emotionally now to an event in your life related to money or your values. You identify emotionally with your possessions or whatever you value. Look at your priorities in handling your income; watch your spending.

***Wednesday, October 17 (Moon into Sagittarius, 8:26 p.m.)*** It's a number 3 day. That means your imagination is keen now, and you communicate well. You're curious and inventive. You're warm and receptive to what others say. Enjoy the harmony, beauty, and pleasures of life. You have a strong sense of duty and feel obligated to fulfill your promises.

***Thursday, October 18 (Moon in Sagittarius)*** The moon is in your third house today. You tend to move about, going from one place to another or one project to another. You're moving ahead, but your thoughts are focused on a matter from the past. An interest in history or archaeology is highlighted.

***Friday, October 19 (Moon into Capricorn, 9:42 p.m.)*** You're motivated and inspired. It's a good time to pursue self-employment. You're courageous and adaptable. A change of scenery would work to your advantage. You could be moving to a new location.

***Saturday, October 20 (Moon in Capricorn)*** With the moon in your fourth house, you feel a close tie to your roots today. You could be dealing with parents. You're dealing with the foundations of who you are and who you are becoming. It's a good day for dream recall. Retreat to a private place for meditation.

***Sunday, October 21 (Moon in Capricorn)*** Elderly people or authority figures play a role in your day. Maintain emotional balance. Set your goals, then make them so. Be conservative with your money; don't speculate or take any unnecessary risks.

***Monday, October 22 (Moon into Aquarius, 1:03 a.m.)*** It's your power day, your day to play it your way. Business discussions work in your favor now. You could pull a financial coup. Financial gain is at hand. Unexpected money arrives. It's a good day for buying a lottery ticket.

***Tuesday, October 23 (Moon in Aquarius)*** With the moon in your fifth house today, you're feeling a sudden surge of inspiration, a creative urge that helps you break through a block. In romance, there's more depth and understanding in a relationship. Children play an important role in your day.

***Wednesday, October 24 (Moon into Pisces, 7:01 a.m.)*** It's a number 1 day, and you're at the top of your cycle. You take the lead in something new and get a fresh start, a new beginning. Stress originality. You attract creative people and avoid people with closed minds. Trust your hunches.

***Thursday, October 25 (Moon in Pisces)*** The moon is in your sixth house today. Your personal health occupies your attention. Keep your resolutions about exercise, and watch your diet. Attend to details related to your heath. Make a doctor or dentist appointment, if needed. Help others, but don't deny your own needs.

***Friday, October 26 (Moon into Aries, 3:32 p.m.)*** Remain flexible in your schedule today. Make time to listen to others. Your charm and wit are appreciated. Spread your good news; you communicate well. Take time to relax, enjoy yourself, and recharge your batteries.

***Saturday, October 27 (Moon in Aries)*** The moon is in your seventh house today. Loved ones and partners are more important than usual. You get along well with others now. Women play a prominent role. You can fit in just about anywhere. However, you might have trouble getting in touch with your own feelings.

***Sunday, October 28 (Moon in Aries)*** With Venus moving into your first house today, you're more socially outgoing than usual. Others appreciate your personal grace and friendly attitude. Your outlook on life becomes more upbeat over the next three weeks. You develop new friendships. You like the way you look now, but avoid becoming vain about it.

***Monday, October 29 (Moon into Taurus, 2:16 a.m.)*** With Mercury moving into your second house today, Libra, yesterday's energy flows into your Monday. You can come up with some moneymaking ideas over the next three weeks. Your quick-thinking ability is put to use for financial affairs now, and you can easily communicate those ideas so they can be put into place. Your values deal primarily with material success. The full moon in Taurus adds to your sense of abundance. You reap what you have sown.

***Tuesday, October 30 (Moon in Taurus)*** The moon is in your eighth house today. You can expect heightened emotions regarding a troubling matter, especially if it deals with shared belongings. You dig deep, seeking more details. A mortgage, insurance, or investments could play a role. Maintain your emotional and mental balance, and avoid any tendencies toward greed or possessiveness. Meanwhile, you could be looking into a metaphysical subject, such as life after death or astrology.

***Wednesday, October 31 (Moon into Gemini, 2:41 p.m.*** You end the month on another power day, so it's time to make a power play. You have a chance to expand, to gain recognition, even fame and power. You attract financial success. You're being watched by people in power.

## NOVEMBER 2012

***Thursday, November 1 (Moon in Gemini)*** The moon is in your ninth house today. You're a dreamer and a thinker. You may feel a need to get away now, a break from the usual routine. You yearn for a new experience. Plan a long trip. Sign up for a workshop or seminar.

***Friday, November 2 (Moon in Gemini)*** You're feeling restless today and sending text messages to friends and associates to pass the time. Your mind moves quickly from one thought to another. Write, revise, and publicize. You see two sides of an issue, Libra. You're a good mediator now. You keep everyone around you in balance.

***Saturday, November 3 (Moon into Cancer, 3:43 a.m.)*** It's your power day, and you can play it your way. You're in the power seat. You have a chance to expand, to gain recognition, fame, power. You attract financial success, especially if you open your mind to a new approach.

***Sunday, November 4—Daylight Saving Time Ends (Moon in Cancer)*** With the moon in your tenth house today, you're concerned about your career or profession. You're looking for a promotion, a raise, or a boost in prestige. You could be talking with fellow workers, but it's best to keep your professional and private lives separate.

***Monday, November 5 (Moon into Leo, 3:40 p.m.)*** You're at the top of your cycle again. You're inventive and make connections that others overlook. You're determined and courageous today. Stress originality in whatever you're doing, and don't be afraid to turn in a new direction. Express your opinions dynamically.

***Tuesday, November 6 (Moon in Leo)*** Mercury goes retrograde in your third house and stays retrograde until November 26. Watch out for miscommunication or misunderstanding with family members, especially siblings, and neighbors over the next three weeks. Leave enough time for delays in your everyday travel. There could be confusion about matters related to past events.

***Wednesday, November 7 (Moon in Leo)*** The moon is in your eleventh house today, Libra. You work well with others, especially in a group. Friends play a surprisingly important role, especially Gemini and Libra. Focus on your wishes and dreams. Examine your overall goals, and make sure that they're still an expression of who you are.

***Thursday, November 8 (Moon into Virgo, 12:36 a.m.)*** Your organizational skills are highlighted now, but try not to wander off task. Emphasize quality; you're building a creative foundation for your future. Tear down the old in order to rebuild. Be methodical and thorough.

***Friday, November 9 (Moon in Virgo)*** The moon is in your twelfth house today. You might feel a need to withdraw and work on your own. Think carefully before you act. There's a tendency now to undo all the positive actions you've taken. Avoid any self-destructive tendencies. Be aware of hidden enemies.

***Saturday, November 10 (Moon into Libra, 5:36 a.m.)*** Neptune goes direct in your sixth house today. You feel a strong compulsion to help others. Service is a spiritual task for you. You might have glamorous illusions about such work. You also have difficulty concentrating on mundane jobs and attending to details. Routine work can be a continuing problem.

***Sunday, November 11 (Moon in Libra)*** The moon is on your ascendant today. The way you see yourself now is the way others see you. Your appearance and personality shine. You're physically vital, and relations with the opposite sex go well.

***Monday, November 12 (Moon into Scorpio, 7:11 a.m.)*** It's another power day, and you're on top of your game. You can go far with your plans, especially if you open your mind to a new approach. You're being watched by people in power. Be courageous. Be yourself; be honest.

***Tuesday, November 13 (Moon in Scorpio)*** There's a solar eclipse in your second house today. That means new financial opportunities come your way. This is considered a very positive eclipse. Jupiter is also forming a positive angle that should allow you to expand whatever you're doing.

***Wednesday, November 14 (Moon into Sagittarius, 6:53 a.m.)*** Mercury now retrogrades back to Scorpio, your second house, where it will stay until November 26. Watch out for miscommunication or misunderstanding related to money matters. The big opportunities that came your way yesterday might not be understood by someone close to you. You're excited, but the other person is wary, causing confusion. Watch your spending over the next couple of weeks. Put off any major purchases until the end of the month.

***Thursday, November 15 (Moon in Sagittarius)*** The moon is in your third house today. You write from a deep place. It's a good day for journaling. Be aware that your thinking may be unduly influenced by things from the past. You could be visiting with relatives or siblings or spending time in the community with your neighbors. You accept an invitation to a social event.

***Friday, November 16 (Moon into Capricorn, 6:36 a.m.)*** Mars moves into your fourth house today. You put a lot of energy into your home life now. That could mean some major renovations. You could encounter some disagreements and quarreling within the family or a time of activism related to the environment.

***Saturday, November 17 (Moon in Capricorn)*** With the moon in your fourth house today, yesterday's energy flows into your Saturday. You're dealing with the foundations of who you are and who you are becoming. Spend time with your family and loved ones. Stick close to home. A parent plays a role in your day.

***Sunday, November 18 (Moon into Aquarius, 8:11 a.m.)*** You're seeking new horizons. Release old structures; get a new point of view. Think outside the box. Variety is the spice of life. Freedom of thought and action is key. You can easily overcome obstacles today.

***Monday, November 19 (Moon in Aquarius)*** The moon is in your fifth house today, Libra. Be yourself; be emotionally honest. In love, there's greater emotional depth to a relationship now. You might be somewhat possessive of loved ones now, particularly children. But eventually you need to let go.

***Tuesday, November 20 (Moon into Pisces, 12:55 p.m.)*** You launch a journey into the unknown and pursue a mystery. Dig deep and look behind closed doors. Confidential information and secrets are involved. But don't make any final decisions on what you uncover until tomorrow.

***Wednesday, November 21 (Moon in Pisces)*** Venus moves into your second house today. You have a love of personal adornments now, whether that means jewelry, clothing, or even an upgrade in the vehicle you're driving. Wealth, whether you have it or are aspiring to it, makes you feel good. You can make money with your artistic abilities, and that's especially true over the next three weeks.

***Thursday, November 22 (Moon into Aries, 9:12 p.m.)*** It's a number 9 day. That means it's a good time to finish what you started. Visualize the future; set your goals, then make them so. Look beyond the immediate. Get ready for something new. Strive for universal appeal.

***Friday, November 23 (Moon in Aries)*** The moon is in your seventh house today. Loved ones and partners are more important than usual. You get along well with others now. You can fit in just about anywhere. You feel a need to be accepted. You're looking for security, but you have a hard time going with the flow.

***Saturday, November 24 (Moon in Aries)*** Take time to relax, enjoy yourself, recharge your batteries. You can influence people now with your upbeat attitude. Your charm and wit are appreciated. Foster generosity. In romance, you're an ardent and loyal lover.

***Sunday, November 25 (Moon into Taurus, 8:18 a.m.)*** Take time to relax on this Sunday. Enjoy yourself; recharge your batteries. You can influence people now with your upbeat attitude. Your charm and wit are appreciated. Foster generosity. In romance, you're an ardent and loyal lover.

***Monday, November 26 (Moon in Taurus)*** Mercury goes direct in your second house today. Any confusion or miscommunication that you've been experiencing, especially related to finances, recedes into the past. Things move more smoothly now. You get your ideas across. Others understand your values or what you value.

***Tuesday, November 27 (Moon into Gemini, 8:59 p.m.)*** You're versatile and changeable now. However, be careful not to spread out and diversify too much. Get a new point of view; follow your curiosity. Freedom of thought and action is key. But so is moderation; avoid excess in whatever you're doing.

***Wednesday, November 28 (Moon in Gemini)*** There's a lunar eclipse in your ninth house today. You react emotionally to a matter related to long-distance travel or higher education. You could be preparing for a long romantic journey now. You could also develop a strong attachment to a foreign-born person or a foreign land.

***Thursday, November 29 (Moon in Gemini)*** You're restless and busy, getting in touch with friends and associates with phone calls, e-mails, or text messages. You're mentally quick and communicate well. You get your message across. It's a good time to socialize, maybe visit a bookstore with friends or go out to lunch.

***Friday, November 30 (Moon into Cancer, 9:56 a.m.)*** The month ends on a power day. You can go far with your plans and achieve financial success. That's especially true if you act with courage and conviction. Be aware that fear of failure or fear that you won't measure up will attract tangible experiences that reinforce the feeling.

## DECEMBER 2012

***Saturday, December 1 (Moon in Cancer)*** The moon is in your tenth house today. Career matters are on your mind. You're looking for an advancement, a raise, or a boost in prestige. You're more responsive to the needs and moods of a group and of the public in general. You're more open and accessible now, but take care to avoid emotional displays, especially in public.

***Sunday, December 2 (Moon into Leo, 9:58 p.m.)*** It's another power day, Libra; you're in the power seat. Think big and act big! However, be aware that you're playing with power so try not to hurt anyone. Open your mind to a new approach that could bring in big bucks.

***Monday, December 3 (Moon in Leo)*** The moon is in your eleventh house today. Friends play an important role in your day. You find strength in numbers and meaning through friends and groups. Focus on your wishes and dreams. Examine your overall goals. Those goals should be an expression of who you are.

***Tuesday, December 4 (Moon in Leo)*** Drama is highlighted, perhaps involving children. You like to flaunt and celebrate now. Be wild and imaginative, Libra. Bring out your inner child. Be the person you always imagined you might be. Play with different personas. You're creative and passionate today, impulsive and honest.

***Wednesday, December 5 (Moon into Virgo, 7:53 a.m.)*** Use your intuition to get a sense of your day. Don't make waves. Don't rush or show resentment; let things develop. You excel in working with others. You're playing the role of the visionary today.

***Thursday, December 6 (Moon in Virgo)*** The moon is in your twelfth house today. It's best to stay out of public view for now. Difficult issues from your past might surface. Confide your thoughts and feelings to a close friend or confidante. Relations with women can be difficult.

***Friday, December 7 (Moon into Libra, 2:37 p.m.)*** Your organizational skills are highlighted today. Clean out your garage, the attic, or a closet. Organize your files. Get rid of what you no longer need. Tear down the old in order to rebuild. Missing papers are found. Be practical with your money.

***Saturday, December 8 (Moon in Libra)*** You're sensitive to the moods of others now, and you try to keep everyone around you in balance. You're good at developing friendships and making contact with old friends. The way you see yourself is the way others see you. You feel recharged for the month ahead, and this makes you more appealing to the public. Relations with the opposite sex go well.

***Sunday, December 9 (Moon into Scorpio, 5:52 p.m.)*** Service to others is the theme of the day. You offer advice and support. Be sympathetic and kind, generous and tolerant. Focus on making people happy on this Sunday. However, avoid scattering your energies.

***Monday, December 10 (Moon in Scorpio)*** Mercury moves into your third house today. There's a lot to communicate now as the work week begins. You get your ideas across as you go about your business, but it's more of an intellectual pursuit than an emotional one. You're witty, alert, and adaptable. Think of ways to expand whatever you're doing.

***Tuesday, December 11 (Moon into Sagittarius, 6:22 p.m.)*** It's another power day, Libra. That means it's your day to play it your way. Now you can go far with your plans and achieve financial success. Expect a windfall. However, be aware that you're playing with power, so try not to hurt anyone.

***Wednesday, December 12 (Moon in Sagittarius)*** The focus of your activities is more mental than physical now, Libra. You communicate your thoughts and ideas well. You see the big picture, not just the details. But make sure you control your emotions. Avoid arguments, especially with siblings and other relatives. You could receive an invitation to a social event.

***Thursday, December 13 (Moon into Capricorn, 5:43 p.m.)*** There's a new moon in your third house, indicating that you find new opportunities in your everyday life. It's a good day to take a gamble. With Uranus going direct in your seventh house today, you could be involved in a marriage or partnership that is somewhat unconventional. Your ideas about a partnership become more unusual over time. You're looking for more independence, and as a result you tend to behave erratically in a partnership or marriage.

***Friday, December 14 (Moon in Capricorn)*** You're dealing with the foundations of who you are and who you are becoming. Retreat to a private place for meditation. It's a good day for dream recall. It's best to work on your own and stay focused. It's time to eliminate a bad habit.

***Saturday, December 15 (Moon into Aquarius, 5:53 p.m.)*** Venus moves into your third house today. You get along well with family members this month, especially siblings. You could be getting involved with neighbors in a community project that you really enjoy. You're more artistic in your outlook.

***Sunday, December 16 (Moon in Aquarius)*** The moon is in your fifth house today. Your creativity, personal grace and magnetism are highlighted. It's a good day to pursue a creative project. Animals play a larger role. You're also more protective and nurturing toward any children in your life.

***Monday, December 17 (Moon into Pisces, 8:48 p.m.)*** It's a number 5 day. That means travel and variety are highlighted. You're seeking new horizons. Promote new ideas; follow your curiosity. Look for adventure. You're versatile and changeable. Be careful not to spread out and diversify too much.

***Tuesday, December 18 (Moon in Pisces)*** The moon is in your sixth house today. You enjoy your work now and get along with fellow workers. The work environment is harmonious, and you keep everyone in balance, Libra. Be careful not to overlook any seemingly minor matters that could take on importance. Keep up with your exercise plan, and watch your diet.

***Wednesday, December 19 (Moon in Pisces)*** You can tap deeply into the collective unconscious for inspiration. It's a time of deep healing. Watch for psychic events, synchronicities. Keep track of your dreams, including your daydreams. Ideas are ripe. Imagination is highlighted.

***Thursday, December 20 (Moon into Aries, 3:44 a.m.)*** It's your power day, Libra. Time for a power play. Business dealings go well, especially if you open your mind to a new approach. Expect a windfall. You're being watched by people in power. Be courageous. Be yourself; be honest.

***Friday, December 21 (Moon in Aries)*** The moon is in your seventh house today. You communicate well with a spouse or partner. It's all about working together. A contract or a lawsuit could play a role. You get along well with others, but it's a challenge to remain detached and objective.

***Saturday, December 22 (Moon into Taurus, 2:26 p.m.)*** It's a number 1 day, and you're at the top of your cycle on this Saturday. You get a fresh start, a new beginning. Trust your hunches; intuition is highlighted. Get out and meet new people and have new experiences. Do something you've never done before.

***Sunday, December 23 (Moon in Taurus)*** With the moon in your eighth house today, your experiences are more intense than usual. Managing shared resources takes on new importance. It's a good day for dealing with mortgages, insurance, and investments. Other issues of the day could include matters of sex, death, rebirth, rituals, and relationships. An interest in metaphysics plays a role.

***Monday, December 24 (Moon in Taurus)*** It's a good day to use common sense and take a down-to-earth perspective on whatever you're doing. Cultivate new ideas, but try to avoid stubborn behavior when others question your actions. You could be somewhat possessive now.

***Tuesday, December 25 (Moon into Gemini, 3:14 a.m.)*** With Mars moving into your fifth house today, you're energetic and actively pursuing the pleasures and joys of life. Romance is highlighted and so are your creative talents. Avoid any petty jealousies. It's a good day to take a chance. Merry Christmas!

***Wednesday, December 26 (Moon in Gemini)*** The moon is in your ninth house today. If you're feeling somewhat stressed and overworked, relax and take a deep breath. Plans for travel or higher education play a role. Sign up for a seminar or workshop. Study a foreign destination you want to visit or take a lesson in another language. A person of foreign birth could play a role.

***Thursday, December 27 (Moon into Cancer, 4:08 p.m.)*** Diplomacy wins the way. Focus on making people happy. Do a good deed. Be sympathetic and kind, generous and tolerant. But know when enough is enough. Avoid scattering your energies.

***Friday, December 28 (Moon in Cancer)*** There's a full moon in your tenth house today. A new opportunity to move ahead in your career comes your way, possibly an advancement, a raise, or a new project. You get along well with fellow workers, but be careful not to mix your personal and professional lives now.

***Saturday, December 29 (Moon in Cancer)*** Your home and family life are emphasized today. Tend to loved ones; do something with your children or sweetheart. You could be somewhat moody. Best to keep your thoughts to yourself. Don't criticize, condemn, or complain.

***Sunday, December 30 (Moon into Leo, 3:47 a.m.)*** It's a number 9 day and a good day to clear your desk and make room for the new, but don't start anything new until tomorrow. Spend some time in deep thought. Spiritual values arise. Use the day for reflection, expansion, and concluding projects. Strive for universal appeal.

***Monday, December 31 (Moon in Leo)*** With Mercury moving into your fourth house today, you communicate well, especially with family members about domestic matters. You spread your ideas, especially those about a home-repair project. Things move smoothly, and others understand what you want.

HAPPY NEW YEAR!

# Lunar Nodes Ephemeris

Locate your date of birth, find the sign of your North Node, then read the description in chapter 11.

07-04-1930 NN Taurus
12-29-1931 NN Aries
06-25-1933 NN Pisces
03-09-1935 NN Aquarius
09-14-1936 NN Capricorn
03-04-1938 NN Sagittarius
09-11-1939 NN Scorpio
05-23-1941 NN Libra
11-19-1942 NN Virgo
05-13-1944 NN Leo
12-01-1945 NN Cancer
12-10-1945 NN Cancer
12-14-1945 NN Cancer
07-31-1947 NN Gemini
01-22-1949 NN Taurus
07-26-1950 NN Aries
03-29-1952 NN Pisces
10-10-1953 NN Aquarius
04-02-1955 NN Capricorn
10-04-1956 NN Sagittarius
06-16-1958 NN Scorpio
12-15-1959 NN Libra
06-08-1961 NN Virgo
12-21-1962 NN Leo
08-25-1964 NN Cancer

02-18-1966 NN Gemini
08-20-1967 NN Taurus
04-20-1969 NN Aries
11-04-1970 NN Pisces
04-27-1972 NN Aquarius
10-27-1973 NN Capricorn
07-11-1975 NN Sagittarius
01-08-1977 NN Scorpio
07-04-1978 NN Libra
01-11-1980 NN Virgo
09-23-1981 NN Leo
03-16-1983 NN Cancer
09-13-1984 NN Gemini
04-01-1986 NN Taurus
04-14-1986 NN Taurus
04-22-1986 NN Taurus
11-30-1987 NN Aries
05-24-1989 NN Pisces
11-19-1990 NN Aquarius
08-03-1992 NN Capricorn
02-01-1994 NN Sagittarius
08-01-1995 NN Scorpio
01-25-1997 NN Libra
10-19-1998 NN Virgo
04-12-2000 NN Leo
10-11-2001 NN Cancer
04-11-2003 NN Gemini
12-24-2004 NN Taurus
06-19-2006 NN Aries
12-15-2007 NN Pisces
08-22-2009 NN Aquarius
02-28-2011 NN Capricorn

SYDNEY OMARR

Born on August 5, 1926, in Philadelphia, Pennsylvania, **Sydney Omarr** was the only person ever given full-time duty in the U.S. Army as an astrologer. He is regarded as the most erudite astrologer of the twentieth century and the best known, through his syndicated column and his radio and television programs (he was Merv Griffin's "resident astrologer"). Omarr has been called the most "knowledgeable astrologer since Evangeline Adams." His forecasts of Nixon's downfall, the end of World War II in mid-August of 1945, the assassination of John F. Kennedy, Roosevelt's election to a fourth term and his death in office . . . these and many others are on the record and quoted enough to be considered "legendary."

## ABOUT THE SERIES

This is one of a series of twelve *Sydney Omarr® Day-by-Day Astrological Guides* for the signs of 2012. For questions and comments about the book, go to www.tjmacgregor.com.